DATE DUE

DEMCO 38-297

WORKERS' WORLD

STUDIES IN INDUSTRY AND SOCIETY
GLENN PORTER, GENERAL EDITOR

Published with the assistance of
the Eleutherian Mills-Hagley Foundation

1.   Burton W. Folsom, Jr.
*Urban Capitalists: Entrepreneurs and City Growth
in Pennsylvania's Lackawanna and Lehigh Regions,
1800–1920*

2.   John Bodnar
*Workers' World: Kinship, Community, and Protest
in an Industrial Society, 1900–1940*

Workers' World

KINSHIP, COMMUNITY, AND PROTEST IN AN INDUSTRIAL SOCIETY, 1900–1940

JOHN BODNAR

THE JOHNS HOPKINS UNIVERSITY PRESS
BALTIMORE AND LONDON

This book has been brought to publication with the generous assistance of the Eleutherian Mills-Hagley Foundation.

The Johns Hopkins University Press, Baltimore, Maryland 21218
The Johns Hopkins Press Ltd., London

Library of Congress Cataloging in Publication Data

Bodnar, John E., 1944–
  Workers' World.

  (Studies in industry and society; 2)
  Bibliography: pp. 193–94.
  Includes index.
  1. Labor and laboring classes—Pennsylvania—History—20th century. 2. Pennsylvania—Social conditions. 3. Pennsylvania—Emigration and immigration—History—20th century. 4. Trade-unions—Pennsylvania—History—20th century. I. Title. II. Series.
HD8083.P43B6   305.5'62'09748   82-6626
ISBN 0-8018-2785-X   AACR2

*To my mother
and the memory of my father*

CONTENTS

FOREWORD

When I first learned of John Bodnar's work on Pennsylvania industrial workers, the Regional Economic History Research Center happened to be collaborating with the Hagley Museum in the creation of a museum exhibit on a subject very closely related to Bodnar's. Entirely independently, we had chosen highly similar titles for our respective projects. His manuscript was called *Workers' World: Kinship, Community, and Protest in an Industrial Society, 1900–1940*; the museum's exhibit was entitled "The Workers' World: The Industrial Village and the Company Town."

Because of my involvement with the exhibit, I read the Pennsylvania interviews and Bodnar's evaluation of them with special interest. The personal recollections of the workers were fascinating, and Professor Bodnar's deft analysis highlighted patterns in the lives of his subjects and placed them in the context of recent scholarly work on the history of laboring men and women. I was convinced that *Workers' World* was right for the series "Studies in Industry and Society."

Oral history has given students of the relatively recent past the chance to do what historians of more distant days can only dream of doing—to speak directly with the participants. This is especially valuable to those who are trying to understand the lives of everyday people, who seldom leave behind the kinds of detailed written evidence that have enabled historians to portray so well the story of the prominent. Few sources can give such penetrating insights into the attitudes and values of individuals as oral history can. The life stories gathered for *Workers' World* give us a rare and often moving look inside the culture of working-class Pennsylvanians of the early twentieth century. Like so many other powerful devices, however, this kind of interviewing must be used with great care. In this study John Bodnar clearly demonstrates his familiarity with the literature on oral history and his sensitivity and skill in employing the technique.

The people whose words appear on the pages that follow are a highly varied lot. Although they, like the economy of the state they live in, are particularly identified with coal mining and steelmaking, they represent a wide range of occupations and a mix of ethnic and racial origins. Their experiences are especially important because they illuminate a period of working-class history that we still know relatively little about, and many of them were at the heart of the story of the rise of the semiskilled worker in the American labor force. Furthermore, the evidence in Part III sheds new light on the perspectives of the rank and file in the coming of the CIO during the 1930s. Like most recent contributions to labor history, however, this book's main focus is not on public events, formal institutions, unions, or strikes. Rather, it deals with the everyday lives of workers.

Bodnar's major concern is the culture of the workers. *Workers' World* provides strong evidence that there was, in fact, a distinct working-class culture in early twentieth century Pennsylvania. That culture was oriented much more toward "traditional" institutions than toward "modern" ones, toward the ties of kin and ethnicity and religion rather than toward individualism. Even today we are a mix of things traditional and modern, but for the workers covered in this book, the mix was heavily weighted toward the traditional. The working class portrayed here was clearly peopled by persons who were at once constrained and sustained by the roles assigned by their culture. Its outlook was not that of the success-oriented, self-improving middle class, but neither was it radical. Bodnar calls it "realistic" and "pragmatic." It included the expectation that things would probably get slightly better in the future, but would not become dramatically either better or worse. Unlike so many of their historians, the industrial workers in this study seem not to have been vitally concerned with politics or with issues of "worker control" of jobs and the nature of the work itself. Instead, their main concern was with their role in what Bodnar calls "the enclave," the particular working-class social world defined by the obligations and rewards of family, occupation, ethnicity, and religion.

One of the major contributions of this study is that it rescues "the worker" from the two-dimensional world of protest, politics, and constant struggle, a world too often imagined by historians more intent on using the past to affect the present than on understanding the past. *Workers' World* reminds us that the men and women who worked in industrial Pennsylvania were, like ourselves, complex and multifaceted people. They neither struggled ceaselessly against injustice nor adopted the alleged "American Dream" of upward mobility. They usually felt powerless to affect the world outside the enclave, and it is far from clear how they would have wanted to affect it if they had been able to. It was distant people—bosses, politicians, sometimes union officials—who had power, and that power was as immutable a part of the landscape of workers' lives as were the demands of kinship. The workers did the best they could under prevailing conditions, and it was difficult and perhaps somewhat frightening to imagine a very different world, one either vastly improved or vastly worsened. Even unions could be the enemy on occasion, when their leaders aligned themselves with the bosses or when they supplanted the bosses in dispensing favors inequitably and venally. The workers' world depicted here was one in which family and community concerns were paramount, and where it seemed difficult and impractical to consider matters in a long-term perspective. These people lived a highly constrained, pragmatic version of the American Dream, and they did so with a courage and an endurance that were deeply rooted in their complex social roles. It is to Professor Bodnar's credit that he is able to capture that complexity without giving in to the temptation merely to conclude that life is very complicated. He has been faithful to his subject while discharging the historian's task of interpreting his piece of the past in its wider context. That is why *Workers' World* is a significant contribution to our understanding of the social and human meaning of industrialization.

GLENN PORTER
Director, Regional Economic History
Research Center
Eleutherian Mills-Hagley Foundation

ACKNOWLEDGMENTS

The oral interviews presented in this book were drawn from hundreds of recordings made between 1974 and 1981. Various funding agencies and institutions supported the more than thirty separate projects which constituted the bulk of this research endeavor on working-class life in mill towns, mining regions, and factory districts throughout Pennsylvania. Major support emanated at crucial times from The Rockefeller Foundation and the Pennsylvania Committee for the Humanities, and always from the Pennsylvania Historical and Museum Commission (PHMC), which now holds copies of the recordings in its collections.

During the years of this research effort, many individuals provided vital support. Noteworthy were the contributions of Donald Kent, William Wewer, Maxwell Whiteman, Harry Whipkey, Debbie Miller, Joanne Bornman, Dorothy Weiser, Roxanne Kaufman, and Mary Jacobs of the PHMC. At Indiana University I received expert secretarial assistance from Lori Bell, Terri Miller, and Debra Chase as well as a timely grant-in-aid. Although I directed the projects, developed the questionnaires, trained personnel, and conducted most of the interviews that appear in this text myself, several interviews were conducted by highly capable associates. Carl Oblinger interviewed Sarah Greer; Lorraine Matko interviewed Rose Popovich; Peter Gottlieb interviewed Joe Rudiak; Ron Schatz interviewed Thomas Brown; and Angela Staskavage interviewed Helen Mack. In addition, several colleagues informed my thinking on both oral history and working-class life by continually taking the time to give me their ideas and evaluate various aspects of my work. Especially stimulating were the critiques by David Brody, Peter Gottlieb, Matthew Magda, David Montgomery, Carl Oblinger, Daniel Walkowitz, and Michael Weber. The encouragement and advice of Glenn Porter at the Eleutherian Mills-Hagley Foundation and Henry Tom at The Johns Hopkins University Press assisted me tremendously in bringing this project to completion. I would also like to thank Penny Moudrianakis for her editing of the manuscript.

Marley Amstutz of Eleutherian Mills rendered expert cartographic services in preparing a map for the volume. Several residents of the workers' world assisted me in gaining interviews. Indispensable was the cooperation of Stanley Brozek, a retired steelworker; Louis Smolinski, who supplied Thomas Bell with information about Braddock for his novel, *Out of This Furnace*, over thirty years ago; Joseph Molski, a former officer in the United Mine Workers of America; and Rose Popovich, Louis Heim, and Michael Zahorsky. My greatest debt, however, is acknowledged on the dedication page.

WORKERS' WORLD

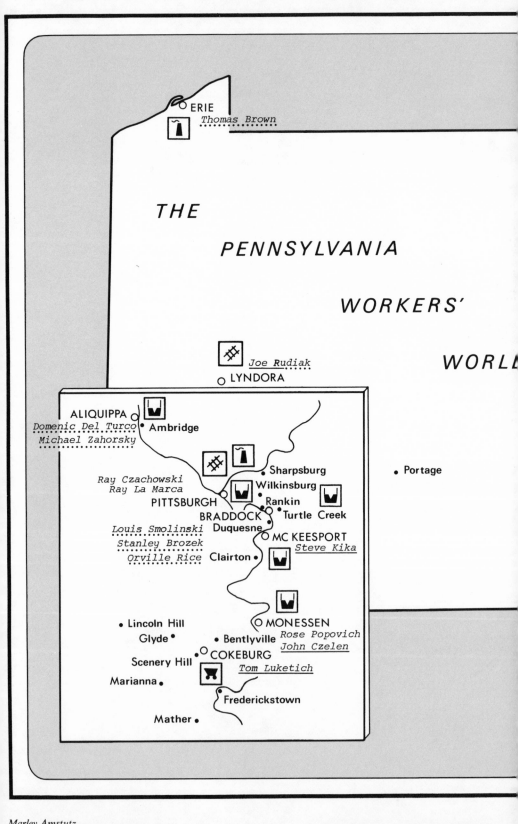

THE

PENNSYLVANIA

WORKERS'

WORL

ERIE
Thomas Brown

Joe Rudiak
LYNDORA

ALIQUIPPA
Domenic Del Turco
Michael Zahorsky
Ambridge

Sharpsburg
Wilkinsburg
Ray Czachowski
Ray La Marca
Rankin
PITTSBURGH
Turtle Creek
BRADDOCK
Duquesne
Louis Smolinski
Stanley Brozek
MC KEESPORT
Steve Kika
Orville Rice
Clairton

Portage

MONESSEN
Lincoln Hill
Rose Popovich
Glyde
Bentlyville
John Czelen
Scenery Hill
COKEBURG
Tom Luketich
Marianna
Frederickstown
Mather

Marley Amstutz

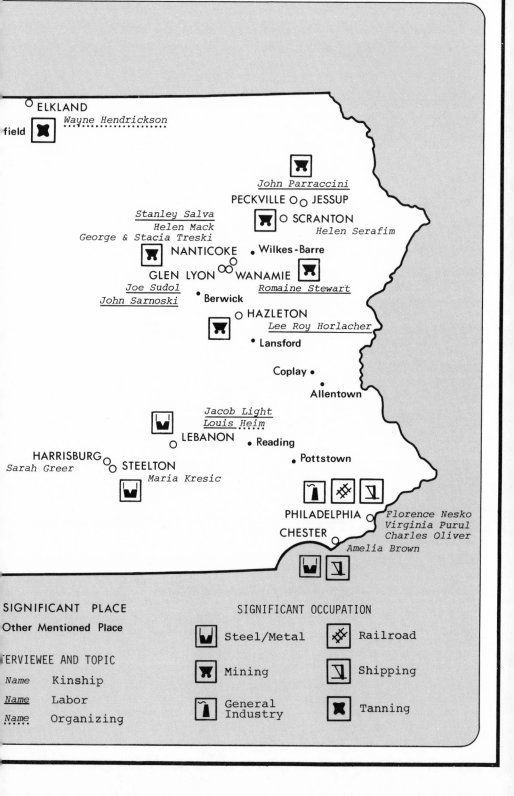

O ELKLAND
field Wayne Hendrickson

John Parraccini
PECKVILLE O O JESSUP
O SCRANTON
Helen Serafim

Stanley Salva
Helen Mack
George & Stacia Treski
NANTICOKE • Wilkes-Barre
GLEN LYON WANAMIE
Joe Sudol *Romaine Stewart*
John Sarnoski • Berwick
O HAZLETON
Lee Roy Horlacher
• Lansford

Coplay •
• Allentown

Jacob Light
Louis Heim
LEBANON
• Reading
HARRISBURG O
Sarah Greer O STEELTON
Maria Kresic • Pottstown

PHILADELPHIA
CHESTER *Florence Nesko*
Virginia Purul
Charles Oliver
Amelia Brown

SIGNIFICANT PLACE

O Significant Place

Other Mentioned Place

INTERVIEWEE AND TOPIC

Name Kinship

Name Labor

Name Organizing

SIGNIFICANT OCCUPATION

Steel/Metal   Railroad

Mining   Shipping

General Industry   Tanning

INTRODUCTION

The recollections presented in this book are those of working people who built a world for themselves in the industrial regions of Pennsylvania prior to World War II. Influenced immensely by the industrial order that surged across America during the late-nineteenth and early twentieth centuries, these ordinary people were forced to adopt new patterns of behavior and cultural values in order to meet the continuing exigencies of a cyclical economy, a circumscribed society dominated by corporate and political power they could not influence, and burdensome work routines. Unable to fall back on government-sponsored security programs and large-scale unions, they sought security and survival through an intricate network of kinship ties, job structures, and community relationships. In relating their impressions of these networks and structures, they have provided threads that collectively begin to suggest the outlines of a rich tapestry of feeling, thought, and behavior. Moreover, it is a tapestry which has largely remained hidden from generations of American labor historians who have been preoccupied with strikes, the rise of trade unionism, and, recently, the struggle for control of the workplace. The world these working people remember, however, was real and was infused with values and patterns that influenced not only their day-to-day existence but the ultimate nature of the protest that found its way into historical accounts of the period.

The expansion of industrial capitalism in America attracted ordinary individuals to states like Pennsylvania, where coal mines, steel mills, textile plants, and countless other opportunities for wage labor existed. Moving steadily into mining patches, mill towns, and urban neighborhoods, these people left behind their farms in the rural South, small towns, and European villages. While the captains of industry sought to streamline their operations and accumulate capital, the ordinary folk modestly sought steady wages, a small piece of property (either in their rural birthplace or their new industrial location), and a continued subsistence for their families. Many, of course, failed to reach even these modest goals and returned to preindustrial homes or moved to other industrial sites. Some, however, persisted tenaciously and survived the rigors of industrial life long enough to record their experiences for contemporary historians.

For much of the half-century after 1880, the working people of America routinely went about the business of making ends meet, raising families, and building separate neighborhoods and communities. This process was frequently punctuated by protests, strikes, and attempts among their own ranks to organize. Until the 1930s, however, the lower, unskilled and semiskilled, sectors of the American industrial work force remained largely disorganized and powerless both in their communities and in their workplaces. The massive unionization drives of the 1930s were in a sense without precedent in preparing the ordinary, nonskilled worker for widespread and sustained protest. Yet historians have failed to penetrate the internal ethos of the workers' world. In fact, they have seldom moved beyond an analysis of skilled craftsmen to view the labor turmoil of the Depression decade as the product of an ongoing effort among ordinary rank-and-filers to obtain what was always preeminent in their lives: family security and stability. Indeed, the very fact that the upheaval of the 1930s assumed the shape of a general drive for institutionalized security in the form of unions not only indicated that hard times had shaken the foundations of the workers' family system but it also hinted at the basic characteristics and values of their world before the thirties. David Brody, a prominent historian of twentieth-century labor, has asked what the rank-and-file militancy in the 1930s was really about. The workers' memories recorded here would answer that the upsurge of the Depression decade cannot be fully understood unless it is linked to the nature of working-class life before the Great Depression.[1]

In an attempt to understand these workers' lives and the nature of their protest during the 1930s, the author conducted oral interviews with textile workers, coal miners, steelworkers, and others in Pennsylvania, a large industrial state. Focusing on the generation that matured just before and during the Depression, the interviewers probed working-class culture by stepping inside the lives of workers and bringing to light their memories of their toil, their kin, and the communities that surrounded them.

Admittedly, oral history has inherent weaknesses and is open to criticism like any other methodology. Michael Frisch has wisely cautioned that oral interviews offer an opportunity for both "more history," in that much additional information can be generated, and "non-history," since a good deal of what is recorded really consists of memories rather than objective facts. For Frisch, as for this author, the only way out of the dilemma was to analyze historical data, the experience of people over time, and to relate it all to historical generalizations. As another scholar has argued, a link must be made between individual lives and a broader historical context if oral history is to be meaningful.[2]

Once the decision was made to place the oral data derived from this study in scholarly perspective, the problem became how to structure the interview situation itself. The authenticity of history secured from an interview continues to be debated. Some observers have concluded that oral history's final product—the transcript—is the "raw material" of history or a "first interpretation." Some have called it history in the form of an "articulating consciousness." Ronald Grele has described the method as a "conversational narrative" that both the interviewer and the respondent help shape. "The recorded conversations of oral history," he concludes, "are joint activities, organized and informed by the historical perspectives of both participants."[3]

The relationship between the interviewer and the respondent is taken further by Peter Friendlander in his work on the emergence of a local auto workers union. Friedlander articulates the need for a "critical dialogue" between the participants in the interview situation. Focusing his interviewing largely on one individual, Edmund Kord, he explains that he is seeking to bring to bear on Kord's experiences a number of theoretical and historical conceptions which he feels bring a "critical focus" to Kord's recollections and enrich his memory.[4]

The interviews presented here were based on a similar concern to establish a dialogue between historian and respondent and on the belief that each could enlighten the other. It soon became clear, however, that meaningful historical data could be generated only if common areas of questioning could be probed systematically. Consequently a questionnaire was developed and modified throughout the subsequent years of interviewing. Such an approach not only provided for the comparison of separate lives but served to strengthen any potential conclusions. Moreover, predetermined areas of questioning "triggered" the memory of the respondents and reduced the likelihood that interviewees would simply drift into meaningless, anecdotal accounts or completely unfocused reminiscences, which can threaten the potential usefulness of any oral-history interview.

Too rigid an imposition of historical models would threaten the potential spontaneity of the respondents, however. Thus, no precise formula was ever devised for the application of such models to the interview situation, and the decision was made to conduct all interviews in a manner which allowed respondents to bring a perspective and "model" of their own. From this dialectic between scholarly constructs and individual memory, a portrait of working-class life emerged.

As questions concerning family and work were asked in the interviews, and as the respondents assisted in the ultimate definition of the material, the fragments of their recollections gradually fused to offer a view of life in the industrial world. Grele has argued in brilliant fashion that if respondents are not seen as bearers of a culture and a world view of their own, the tendency is to impose one's own vision of the past on the data. The present project was conceived with the expectation that intensive life reviews would allow us to move beyond the practice of ascribing historical and sociological models to industrial toilers and to discover—as Grele did —the extent to which our "hegemonic" view of culture functioned in the lives of common people.[5] Thus, the historians brought to the interviews an emphasis on family and work, and indeed, the immigrants and blacks of industrial Pennsylvania told us that they had not blindly followed the dominant pre-World War II ideology of mobility, education, and success, but instead had constantly structured their lives in response to the realities they confronted. Most, in other words, had not accepted or rejected the mythology of mobility, for instance, but had seen it for what it was: an improbable promise that did little to help them make it from paycheck to paycheck.

Beyond the need to reach a common ground that would stimulate an interactional transmission between interviewer and respondent, we felt an acute concern that the lives of the respondents be treated as phenomena that change over time. Thus the decision was made to structure each interview as much as possible on the concept of a gradual review of an individual's life. Clinical psychologists, for instance, have often regarded the life review as the ultimate criterion of truth about a person. In 1949, in his *Criteria for Life History*, John Dollard reasoned that the life history is a crucial part of any attempt to define the growth of a person in a cultural milieu and make theoretical sense of it. Taking Dollard's cue that such reviews might include both biographical and autobiographical material, we sought to explore many of the experiences of working-class parents, now deceased, through the recollections of their children, as well as to gather the details of the lives of the living. Such an approach allowed us to trace the history of the working class at least as far back as the very early experiences of America's industrial workers.[6]

Moreover, it is not accidental that in both the interviewing methodology and the recollections presented in this book, we have attempted to achieve something of a developmental or sequential review of basic family and occupational activities. If workers are to be understood in terms of their past and why they acted or felt as they did at particular times, a longitudinal perspective is needed. Again, the pioneering work of John Dollard proved instructive. Dollard argued that the more complete a life history is, the more adequate any single statement from it will be.[7] His criteria for developing a life history appeared to be crucial to our entire effort. Among other things, he urged that an individual be placed in his or her cultural

perspective, that the role of the family in transmitting culture be acknowledged, and that the "social situation" be evaluated.[8]

Dollard, in effect, offered a prescription for conceptualizing the study
of working-class populations. Unfortunately, most historians have ignored
such criteria and have committed the same mistakes Dollard criticized
sociologists and ethnologists for in 1949. That is to say, they have relied
heavily on abstract social theories and structures and have lost sight of the
"culture-bearing individual."[9]

Even the most cursory survey of interpretations about American industrial workers reveals a tendency to explain behavior and culture in
terms of abstract generalizations and to overlook the reality of individuals
attempting to structure their lives in the face of everyday problems. Certainly this can be said of Selig Perlman's early descriptions of the rank and
file as men and women preoccupied with job consciousness and a desire to
regulate access to employment. With the growth of industry in America,
Perlman argued, workers' concerns shifted from abundance to scarce opportunities. Out of a growing pessimism, he concluded, labor unions such
as the AFL emerged with a pure and simple goal: to preserve the limited
number of employment opportunities that existed. Perlman assumed, in
other words, that union objectives represented the personal aspirations of
the rank and file.[10]

Stressing the central role of national unions and minimizing the impact of individual and local developments, historians were slow to change.
Initial attempts to probe more deeply into the character of the American
working class, a movement which would inevitably generate a more complex view of the worker's frame of mind, reflected a fixation on broad,
national trends. In his study of the impact of industrialization on the
American labor movement between 1865 and 1900, for instance, Gerald
N. Grob shifted the focus away from restricted opportunity and toward
the "dehumanizing" effect mechanization and specialization had on artisans. Grob claimed that the efforts of organizations such as the National
Labor Union and the Knights of Labor to stem the rush of modernization
and retain traditional values were doomed because the traditional status
of artisans had been eroded. He argued that trade unions succeeded in
this period where "reform unionism" had failed because they represented
more than a protest against a system; they actually confronted the reality
of a capitalistic society and worked to achieve a higher standard of living
and security for their members.[11]

Continuing the trend away from Perlman's pure and simple unionism,
historian David Montgomery described labor reforms in the decade after
the Civil War as attempts to impart human and moral values to a society
dominated by commercial ones. Modifying Grob's view that artisans were
trying to recapture a vanishing past, Montgomery argued that labor was

pursuing equality with capital, recognition of the dignity of the working-man, and the imposition of a "moral order on the market economy." Indeed, Montgomery reached a conclusion similar to that of the British scholar E. P. Thompson, who had found a desire among nineteenth-century British workers to "humanize" their environment and temper the drive for production and profit. Both men saw in the behavior of industrial workers a tendency to oppose the drift toward acquisitiveness.[12]

Montgomery attempted an even further refinement of the Perlman thesis by arguing that in the first two decades of the twentieth century the objectives of American trade unions themselves actually changed. Noting the growing militancy of rank-and-file laborers in large-scale modern industries, Montgomery argued that labor's demands transcended simple "bread and butter" issues and moved into areas of work rules, union recognition, discharge of unpopular foremen, and the regulation of layoffs. In other words, workers began to seek greater control of the production process itself. With this bold analysis, Montgomery demonstrated that the ideologies of labor spokesmen and the behavior of the rank and file no longer reflected pure and simple unionism. The concerns of working people were more complex.[13]

Not all lines of scholarly inquiry have reinforced the direction of Montgomery's thought, however. Consider the long-term debate over whether the American industrial worker accepted the prevailing bourgeois notions of the larger society. While Montgomery argued that workers sought to temper the drive toward an individualistic, acquisitive society, other historians described working-class communities as repositories of middle-class values where individuals sought only materialistic goods and higher status for themselves and their children. The attachment of American workers to material values was a view given wide currency by Robert and Helen Lynd. In their monumental study of Middletown, the Lynds found that in the 1920s the community's workers were "running for dear life" in the business of making money in order to gratify more and more of their subjective wants. The Lynds further emphasized that workers pursued education as fervently as a religion in order to obtain upward mobility. It should be noted, however, that here the Lynds conveniently overlooked their own data, which indicated that about one-third of the town's working-class families had no plans for their children's education at all.[14]

Although modified slightly, the Lynds' view was essentially retained in the extensive "Yankee City" series published in the 1940s. W. Lloyd Warner and Leo Srole found that some families encouraged their children to attend college, while others insisted that their progeny find employment as early as possible. Ultimately, however, the authors' adopted an assimilationist viewpoint and argued that American workers and their families acquired middle-class values.[15]

Notions of self-improvement, upward striving, and educational fervor have been discovered among working-class populations elsewhere. E. P. Thompson has shown that in the mid-nineteenth century, England's working class demonstrated a marked desire for self-improvement through literacy; further evidence indicates, however, that this drive had begun to weaken by the end of the century.[16] A proliferation of studies on social mobility has sustained the impression that the desire for individual success was a pervasive notion among foreign-born workers in America. Accounts of immigrants in New York City, South Bend, Boston, Cleveland, and Chicago have all been based on the assumption that workers diligently pursued social advancement.[17]

The strongest support for the embourgeoisment thesis has come from Timothy Smith. Smith's research convinced him that a number of immigrants went into business for themselves and that nearly all possessed a "commitment to the American dream" and an "indigenous thirst for education." He found an even more extensive desire for learning and improvement among black workers in urban areas.[18]

Moreover, Smith's assertions have been vigorously sustained by his students. After examining the backgrounds of Italian immigrants to Kansas City, Utica, and Rochester, John Briggs concluded that they were generally intent on individual advancement and proprietorship in America. He believed that this inclination had emerged in Italy in the late nineteenth century and that the desire for social elevation among immigrants who returned to Italy was just as intense; the only difference was that it was directed toward Italian rather than American society. Briggs's description of Italian attitudes was corroborated by Josef Barton, who depicted Italian immigrants to Cleveland as men ready for improvement and advancement. Barton found that Rumanian immigrants to Cleveland were even more intent on uplift; only his study of Slovaks revealed individuals who diverged from the model of a modern-day achiever. In a recent dissertation on Hungarians, another of Smith's students, Paula Benkart, reported that Hungarians came to America with "rising expectations" and with the intention of returning to Europe to improve their material condition. By way of caveat, it should be stressed that the bulk of the excellent research done by these young scholars has focused on the premigration experience of immigrant groups. The extent to which these aspirations were sustained or altered in the industrial American milieu has not received similar treatment.[19] Suggestive, however, are the conclusions of another of Smith's students, Mark Stolarik, who studied the educational outlooks among Slovak workers in Europe and America and found a diminution in the immigrant's educational expectations after settlement in the industrial confines of the New World.[20]

This departure from the older models of working-class behavior really accelerated, however, when histories of communities and groups of workers in particular localities began to emerge in the 1970s. In his pioneering investigations into late-nineteenth-century American communities, Herbert Gutman found that workers instigated reform and protest movements that transcended "bread and butter" issues and sought to achieve human dignity and racial equality. "Work, Culture, and Society in Industrializing America," the capstone of Gutman's attempt to probe the interior culture of working people, moved beyond economic and political issues to a consideration of cultural background. Correctly observing that an artificial division had for too long separated labor histories from immigration histories, Gutman discovered a subtle interplay between preindustrial folkways and the industrial system in American society. This conceptual framework inevitably led him to a more complex view of the American worker, a view which acknowledged that working-class behavior and attitudes were not merely a reaction to economic conditions but were also influenced by the various subcultures that continually confronted industrial America. Suddenly it was possible to explain why at different times workers could be found protesting, idealizing, submitting, dreaming of lost prestige, or adjusting to economic realities.[21]

In positing an interactional framework between labor economics and culture, Gutman agrued that adaptation to the industrial way of life was a complex process. Montgomery and others, however, feared that Gutman's emphasis on "modernization" theory implied that workers inevitably resigned themselves to the new imperatives of industrial life, and that any appreciation of the cultural complexity and social conflicts of the workers' world would be muted by his work. In fact, the opposite seems to have happened. Gutman actually intensified the thrust toward the complicated interior of the workers' world by demonstrating that lives were shaped out of the interaction of cultural and industrial forces.[22]

Much of the difficulty encountered in expanding the study of working people to include the interior of their world has stemmed not only from the various preoccupations of historians but also from their failure to develop appropriate methodologies. Although the direction of scholarship has moved inexorably toward the examination of individual lives, such history has seldom reflected the perspectives of the common toilers themselves. Certainly the viewpoints of those who lived before the twentieth century are difficult to capture, but the experiences of a substantial portion of industrial workers can still be reached through the reminiscences of the several generations that have labored and lived since the 1880s.

An attempt to capture the interior of the workers' world, to understand "the overall quality of workers' lives," was made by Eli Ginzberg and Hyman Berman in *The American Worker in the Twentieth Century: A History through Autobiographies*, which was published in 1963. In the years since, however, few historians have used personal accounts to probe working-class history. Recent works on the formation of unions in the automobile and steel industries have relied heavily on personal interviews, but have still been grounded in questions raised by the old, institutional labor history. An important new focus—the entire workplace—has been developed through the use of penetrating oral histories of textile workers. Amoskeag, at one time the largest textile mill in the world, has been vividly brought to light in all its complexity. That narrative, however, depicts such an aura of cross-currents in the work and family associations of the people involved that an attempt has not been made to place the study in an overriding framework.[23]

After several decades of scholarship, then, it is clear that much of the world of the common worker in industrial America has yet to be delineated. Characterizations of workers have for the most part been based on economic pragmatism, social idealism, middle-class aspirations, or the worker's attempt to control production, and thus have uncritically reflected the perspective that ordinary lives were being acted upon solely by larger societal forces. Montgomery would suggest that worker protest is shaped solely by the dynamics of the workplace. Workers are seldom thought of as culture-bearing individuals whose complex world contains enduring values they want to preserve. Historians have readily portrayed them as victims whose behavior and thought are shaped by external forces such as technological determinism, management initiatives, or even political and state action. Montgomery, for instance, argued that the New Deal co-opted the worker movement of the 1930s.[24] In truth, the working people who speak here interacted with the society around them and helped shape a world of their own, a world which had considerable influence on the ultimate nature of the working-class protest during the 1930s. Only by reconstructing the realities of these peoples' lives over time and thereby uncovering their internally established goals can we obtain an accurate picture of their consciousness and understand the ultimate thrust of their behavior.

NOTES

1. David Brody, *Workers in Industrial America: Essays on the Twentieth-Century Struggle* (New York: Oxford University Press, 1980), p. 152.

2. Michael Frisch, "Oral History and Hard Times: A Review Essay," *Red Buffalo: A Journal of American Studies* 1 (1972): 226–30; Tamara K. Hareven, "The Search for Generation Memory: Tribal Rites in Industrial Society," *Daedalus* 107 (Fall 1978): 143.

10   Workers' World

3. Ronald J. Grele, *Envelopes of Sound* (Chicago: Precedent Publishing, 1975), pp. 131, 135; William W. Cutler III, "Accuracy in Oral Interviewing," *Historical Methods Newsletter*, June 1970, pp. 1–7; Saul Benison, "Oral History: A Personal View," in *Modern Methods in the History of Medicine*, ed. Edwin Clark (New York: McGraw-Hill, 1971), p. 291.

4. Peter Friedlander, *The Emergence of a UAW Local, 1936–1939: A Study in Class and Culture* (Pittsburgh: University of Pittsburgh Press, 1975), pp. xi–xii.

5. Grele, *Envelopes of Sound*, p. 4.

6. See Glen Elder, "Family History and the Life Course," *Journal of Family History* 2 (Winter 1977): 281–82; John Dollard, *Criteria for Life History* (New York: Peter Smith, 1949).

7. Dollard, *Criteria for Life History*, p. 142.

8. Ibid., p. 8.

9. Ibid., p. 271.

10. Selig Perlman, *A Theory of the Labor Movement* (New York: Macmillan, 1928), *passim*.

11. Gerald N. Grob, *Workers and Utopia: A Study of Ideological Conflict in the American Labor Movement, 1865–1900* (Evanston, Ill.: Northwestern University Press, 1961), pp. 187–89.

12. David Montgomery, *Beyond Equality: Labor and the Radical Republicans, 1862–1872* (New York: Knopf, 1967), pp. 445–47; and E. P. Thompson, *The Making of the English Working Class* (New York: Vintage Books, 1963), pp. 830–32. See also Alan Dawley, *Class and Community: The Industrial Revolution in Lynn* (Cambridge, Mass.: Harvard University Press, 1976), *passim*.

13. David Montgomery, "The New Unionism and the Transformation of Workers' Consciousness in America, 1909–1922," *Journal of Social History* 7 (Summer 1974): 509–23; idem, *Worker's Control in America: Studies in the History of Work, Technology, and Labor Struggles* (Cambridge: At the University Press, 1979).

14. Robert S. Lynd and Helen M. Lynd, *Middletown: A Study in American Culture* (New York: Harcourt, Brace, 1929), pp. 80, 87, 186–87.

15. W. Lloyd Warner and Leo Srole, *The Social System of American Ethnic Groups* (New Haven: Yale University Press, 1945), pp. 79 ff.

16. Thompson, *The Making of the English Working Class*, pp. 719, 728; Gareth Steadman-Jones, "Working-Class Culture and Working-Class Politics in London, 1870–1900: Notes on the Remaking of a Working Class," *Journal of Social History* 7 (Summer 1974): 464–67; Stanley Aronowitz, *False Promises: The Shaping of American Working-Class Consciousness* (New York: McGraw-Hill, 1973), p. 400.

17. Dean R. Esslinger, *Immigrants and the City: Ethnicity and Mobility in a Nineteenth-Century Midwestern Community* (Port Washington, N.Y.: Kennikat Press, 1975); Stephan Thernstrom, *The Other Bostonians: Poverty and Progress in the American Metropolis, 1880–1970* (Cambridge, Mass.: Harvard University Press, 1973); Josef John Barton, *Peasants and Strangers: Italians, Rumanians, and Slovaks in an American City, 1890–1950* (Cambridge, Mass.: Harvard University Press, 1975); Thomas Kessner, *The Golden Door: Italians and Jewish Immigrant Mobility in New York City, 1880–1915* (New York: Oxford University Press, 1977); Humbert S. Nelli, *Italians in Chicago, 1880–1930: A Study in Ethnic Mobility* (New York: Oxford University Press, 1970).

18. T. L. Smith, "Immigrant Social Aspirations and American Education, 1880–1930," *American Quarterly* 21 (Fall 1969): 522–25; idem, "Native Blacks and Foreign Whites: Varying Responses to Educational Opportunity in America, 1880–1950," *Perspectives in American History* 6 (1972): 311–13.

Examples of working-class women seeking a higher status and seeking a divorce to get it are found in Elaine Tyler May, "The Pressure to Provide: Class, Consumerism, and Divorce in Urban America, 1880–1920," *Journal of Social History* 12 (Winter 1978): 191.

19. John W. Briggs, *An Italian Passage: Immigrants to Three American Cities, 1890–1930* (New Haven: Yale University Press, 1978), pp. 7–10, 68; Barton, *Peasants and Strangers, passim*; Paula Kaye Benkart, "Religion Family, and Continuity among Hungarians Migrating to American Cities" (Ph.D. diss., Johns Hopkins University, 1975).

20. M. Mark Stokarik, "Immigration, Education, and the Social Mobility of Slovaks, 1870–1930," in *Immigrants and Religion in Urban America*, ed. Randall M. Miller and Thomas D. Marzik (Philadelphia: Temple University Press, 1977), pp. 103–16.

21. Herbert Gutman's work is conveniently collected in *Work, Culture, and Society in Industrializing America* (New York: Vintage Books, 1977). See also Robert H. Zieger, "Workers and Scholars: Recent Trends in American Labor Historiography," *Labor History* 13 (Spring 1972): 252–66, for an excellent overview of the development of labor historiography in this area.

22. David Montgomery, "Gutman's Nineteenth-Century America," *Labor History* 19 (Summer 1978): 416–17, 425; Daniel T. Rodgers, "Tradition, Modernity, and the American Industrial Worker," *Journal of Interdisciplinary History* 7 (Spring 1977): 655–67.

23. The author assumes that the WPA interviewing effort of the 1930s was not primarily an attempt at analytical history. See Eli Ginzberg and Hyman Berman, *The American Worker in the Twentieth Century: A History through Autobiographies* (Glencoe, Ill.: The Free Press, 1963), pp. 5–24; Friedlander, *The Emergence of a UAW Local*; Sidney Fine, *Sit-Down: The General Motors Strike of 1936–1937* (Ann Arbor: University of Michigan Press, 1969); Alice Lynd and Staughton Lynd, eds., *Rank and File: Personal Histories by Working-Class Organizers* (Boston: Beacon Press, 1973); Tamara K. Hareven and Randolph Langenbach, *Amoskeag: Life and Work in an American Factory City* (New York: Pantheon Books, 1978), pp. 1–31.

24. Melvyn Dubofsky, "Hold the Fort: The Dynamics of Twentieth-Century American Working-Class History," *Review in American History* 9 (June 1981): 244–51; Montgomery, *Worker's Control in America*, chap. 7. Montgomery's view of the New Deal is shared somewhat by James R. Green, *The World of the Worker: Labor in Twentieth-Century America* (New York: Hill & Wang, 1980), p. 178.

THE LIVING ROOM OF A COAL MINER'S HOUSE IN PENNSYLVANIA

Part I
KINSHIP:
THE TIES THAT BIND

Maybe we look at it different now,
but family life was instilled with you,
and I tried to do everything for my
family.

Ray Czachowski, Pittsburgh

Running through the fabric of American working-class life in the early decades of this century were intricately woven kinship associations. At every turn in the life course of common people in industrial society, relatives stood ready to assist. Whether one needed a place to reside, a contact through which to acquire a job, or financial and emotional support, a relative was invariably involved. More than an important source of aid, however, kinship also implied a sense of responsibility, an on-going commitment that was rewarding when fulfilled, but that could be burdensome if too demanding. Either way, the system—which was virtually an economy—was based primarily on a shared sense of responsibility and a degree of reciprocity between parents and children and between other members of the family as well.

The interviews with Ray Czachowski, Maria Kresic, and Rose Popovich in particular illustrate the profound sense of loyalty and attachment individuals felt toward their family base even when inevitable tensions emerged in such relationships. Czachowski reluctantly eschewed opportunities to leave Pittsburgh in order to remain at home and support his kin. He not only felt strongly about his family responsibility but knew that a good family reputation was indispensible for getting a job in his Pittsburgh neighborhood. Maria Kresic and Rose Popovich both sacrificed individual pursuits to the claims of their fathers, who insisted they work at home. All three disliked such obligations and—especially in the case of Popovich—

13

came into conflict with their parents, but they remained tied to family responsibilities throughout their lives. The persistence of family control was recalled vividly by Virginia Purul and Charles Oliver, who lived out their lives in the Pennsport section of Philadelphia continually rendering support to their families of procreation and to their parents as well. Purul cared for her parents in their old age and lived with them for several years after her own marriage. Oliver eventually bought his parents the only home they ever owned.

Families were important not only for the extent to which they shaped individual lives with their collective needs but also because they managed to assume crucial functions in an industrial society. After moving to industrial regions, immigrants and migrants invariably relied on kin for knowledge of work opportunities and available lodging. When families were splintered due to marital discord or death, workers took in cousins, grandparents, and other relatives. Sarah Greer depicts a pattern of constant assistance within her extended family. At different times Greer's nephews and sister-in-law lived in her girlhood home.

No function was more crucial in the context of family life or more widespread than job procurement. Kin determined not only when people would start work and for what purpose but also where. Florence Nesko, for instance, tells us that her father and other relatives were always passing on jobs to kin on the Philadelphia waterfront. Nesko's brother, in fact, secured positions on the docks for four of his brothers.

Historians who have recently investigated the movement of working people from preindustrial regions to the factories, mines, and mills of modern America have emphasized that family considerations were the product of premigration cultural patterns. Although this view corrects the older model that depicted industrialization as a destroyer of family life, it implies a somewhat rigid view of culture and the adaptive process and neglects the pragmatic, interactional adjustments made by newly arrived industrial workers.

Industrial capitalism's demand that workers seek assistance on their own wherever they could find it combined with traditional patterns of kinship associations to infuse working-class families with important and necessary functions. In addition to serving as sources of occupational and housing information for workers in transit between various locales and workplaces, families proved to be surprisingly effective support systems during periods of emotional stress, sickness, old age, strikes, and racial crisis. Parents became architects of the lives and careers of their progeny; children became essential generators of income during hard times and whenever household heads were injured or died prematurely (a pervasive phenomenon in industrial society). Leaving school early to assist the parental household, and extending lifelong assistance both to one's family

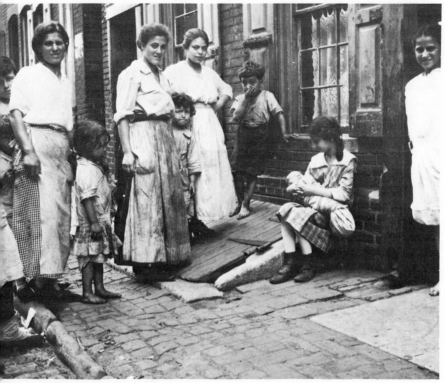

Urban Archives, Temple University

A WORKING-CLASS NEIGHBORHOOD OF PHILADELPHIA

of orientation and to one's family of procreation, were the dominant patterns in these people's lives.

VIRGINIA PURUL AND CHARLES OLIVER

Virginia Purul was the daughter of Polish-born parents and was born in 1920 in the Pennsport section of Philadelphia. Her mother had joined an aunt in the Port Richmond section of the city because of a deteriorating relationship with her stepmother in Poland. Virginia's father, Stanley Olszewski, had left a farm in Poland at the age of twenty-six and followed a brother to Wisconsin and later another brother to Philadelphia, where he found employment sorting scrap and metal at the Ajax Metal Company.

The family initiated by these two Polish newcomers would make substantial claims on Virginia's life.

Charles Oliver was originally named Charles Olszewski and was the brother of Virginia Purul. As indicated in the following recollections, Charles lived in the home of his parents throughout his life and actually bought the home for them when he reached adulthood. A sense of family responsibility determined the life course of this second-generation Polish American.

Virginia: "My mother worked in a factory where they made men's clothing. She worked until she began having children. She had met my father through her brother. In fact, her aunt, with whom she was boarding, felt it would be more economical if she moved out on her own and more or less arranged for her to meet my father. So my mother was lonely and decided to marry him. There must have been some love for they were married fifty-four years. She was about seventeen or eighteen when she married; my father was ten years older.

"They first lived on East Cambria Street but moved shortly to the Pennsport area because my father had friends down here. It was farther to work, but my father was a very active man. He walked from home to Port Richmond and back every day. Everybody along the river front knew him, especially the brakemen. But he would walk every day, even if it snowed.

"My parents rented a home until we were raised. All those years we stayed in the home on Ellsworth Street, until my brother bought the home much later. There were eight children. When the owner died, his wife was going to sell the property and my brother, who was a bachelor, actually purchased it for my parents. He was working as a clerk at the First Pennsylvania Bank.

"My oldest brother was working as a checker on the Pennsylvania Railroad. They would check out the merchandise as they loaded and unloaded boxcars. It was right across the street from here and he just went down himself and got the job and stayed there. Another sister of mine, Olympia, married at an early age—sixteen—and never worked. Another younger sister, Wanda, got a job through my brother at the bank.

"I graduated from grade school but left high school in my third year. This was about 1936, and my dad was sick. I worked making cigars. I did not want to leave school, because I loved school. But I had no choice. Things were rough at home so I decided to leave myself. Well, it was a let down to me because I always liked school, but I thought I should help out. My mom and dad wanted us to have an education.

"I entered a cigar factory and worked eight hours a day. You had to feed the tobacco into a machine. There were three girls together. One would put on the top wrapper; another would put on the last wrapper, and one would examine it. So I was called a feeder and a binder putting the last wrapper on.

"I finally stopped working because although I was married I was still at home. And when my three brothers and my husband entered the war [World War II] they all agreed that I should stay home and take care of Mom and Pop. My older sisters were married, but they had moved from the area, so I was chosen to stay at home. I'm telling you, it wasn't easy. I went through hell worrying about my husband and brothers in the service. Whenever the man came down the street with a telegram you would bless yourself and hope to God he wasn't coming here and that you had the strength to face it.

"After my husband returned from the service I moved out of my parents' home to a home next-door. We bought it. My husband, Frank, worked for Centennial Cleaners & Dryers. He worked for the company and he got so much commission. They gave him a route among different tailors and he would get thirty percent commission plus a salary on all the business he would bring in. They arranged a route for him. He had the job before he went into the service and returned to it when he came back.

"I still lived next to my parents and would do anything I could for them if they needed it. When they were sick I paid for their doctor bill. My husband idolized my parents because his parents had died when he was eleven. He took it very bad when they died. My brother Charles actually lived with them and kept house for them."

Charles: "When I went to work as an office boy for the Clark family in 1919 the boss said to me that my name would be Oliver not Olszewski. I didn't understand it, but it became established.

"I left school when I was fifteen. I think it was a mistake now. But then I didn't. We still have the trend in this neighborhood. My nephew just quit in his last year in high school. When I was young you just had the feeling that you had to leave. And I guess because there was a big family the parents didn't object too much because there was all those mouths to feed. The girls got some high school, but none of the boys did. The oldest brother started out as a photographer's assistant up in town. In 1929 when things slowed down he went over and got hired unloading wagons for railroad freight.

"In the old days, to get a job on the docks men would line up each day. The bosses would hand out numbers and give you slots. That's why a lot of kids still drop out of school around here. The pay was good on the docks, and [there] you'll find a lot of family relatives from fathers to sons and cousins to cousins. Even the clerks on the pier made good pay. But it helped to know the boss too. They lived around the neighborhood and they were tough and loud.

"After I worked in Clark's law office, I delivered newspapers and would run errands for Clark. I worked there three years. And then they called me in and asked me what I was going to do with my future and that kind of baloney. I asked them to get me a job next-door at the bank. They did. Everything seemed contented. The income was regular and they treated you pretty nice. Before you know it a lifetime went by. At the First National Bank I sorted checks manually. Later I wound up in the collections department. As I was working there, part of my wages went to the family fund. My wages were twelve dollars a week, but I could keep enough for lunch and transportation. Mom ran the rest of the family finances. Mom and Pop were not too tough once you started to work, but before that my father would be tough and get out the strap if you stepped out of line. But after you worked you were on a par. My pop figured you were a wage earner and he was a wage earner and he left you alone.

"I finally bought the house for my parents in 1949 and I lived in it [with them]. I wanted to buy it for my parents, but they insisted that the deed be in my name. They lived there, though, and they both died there.

"As a young man I didn't have any initiative to plug out for anything special. I liked to spend time at the men's club at Southwark House. I thought about leaving a few times, but you think about the 'old folks' and you didn't leave. You get in that kind of routine. You start working and you're in your thirties and your forties and after work each day you go to the pub and 'bum' around there until seven o'clock. By the time you get done there you get a couple more on Second Street. By the time you get home it's time to go to bed. Then, you know, you have one of them wasted lifetimes, you might call it. You get in that rut and time went by."

FLORENCE NESKO

Born in 1916, Florence Nesko lived her entire life in the waterfront area of Philadelphia. Her memories include not only experiences from her own life but also the work and kinship associations of the Pennsport neighborhood in which she lived. They also show how deeply those associations and a sense of family responsibility pervaded her father's feelings.

"My father started early at about age fifteen as a teamster; then he became a stevedore and worked there until he died.

"My mother never worked as a young girl because she married very young. I think she was seventeen and my father was nineteen. They lived in the Queens Village area and raised a family of eleven children.

"My brother Michael was the oldest child, and I was the oldest girl. We all went to St. Philip's Church and school, but I had to leave [school] after the eighth grade. I then went to work in a factory, and Michael became a water boy on the waterfront. You usually had to work as a water boy before you became a stevedore. The water boys would carry buckets of water to the dock workers. They were usually very young.

"It seemed like you had to have relatives on the docks to become a stevedore. It was always fathers passing jobs on or getting jobs for younger generations. In fact, I had four brothers who all became stevedores along the waterfront. My father's name really helped them get a job because he had the reputation of being a good worker and was known for always being for the workingman. After my father died it was my oldest brother, Michael, who got jobs for my younger brothers.

"I was born in 1916 and left school in 1929. I helped myself get a job by applying to a newspaper ad. I just went to a very small factory packing baseball caps but only stayed one week because the hours were so long and the pay was small—about four dollars a week. I thought I could do better so I went down to Mifflin Avenue. I remember my brother Michael went with me to each place I looked for work to make sure I would be secure there and [to] look the place over. Finally, I was hired to pack metal polish bottles. My job was to label the bottles. You would be paid twelve dollars a week no matter how many labels you would put on. That line just kept coming. I worked at a whiskey place and a paper-box factory. Then I went to work at Whitman's chocolate factory at Fourth and Race. I usually changed jobs because they were seasonal, but I liked the jobs. I was not unsatisfied.

"At Whitman's I was a packer putting chocolates in the box at fifty-one cents an hour. There were lines of four or five women. The box would come down a conveyor belt and you would put a particular piece of candy in the box. You would roll the candy in a cap first and then place it in the box. I worked there eight hours a day with a ten-minute break in the morning and ten minutes in the afternoon. There was a supervisor on each belt. It really wasn't tough, but you had to abide by certain rules and regulations. For example, you could only eat at certain times. You couldn't smoke in the building. I know you felt like you were in a reform school because you had a uniform to wear and there were too many restrictions, although most women seemed to accept it. But I was also complaining that you couldn't eat when you were hungry and you couldn't even smoke in the bathroom. But I think people were so afraid of losing their jobs they were afraid to complain. They had a union, but it was always a company union. After five years at Whitman I stopped working when I had children.

"I was glad to get out of school. I didn't like school. Some of the nuns were very good to me. But I wanted to grow up to be out of school because it meant you were grown up. My parents didn't ask me to leave. My parents stressed that I should go to school even if it was only elementary. Also, if Michael could go to work, and I could go to work, that would help out at home with the other children growing up. That's why I gave my wages to my mother. What else? My mother controlled all the family wages. I gave her my wages until I was married, as did my brother Michael.

"My younger sister Anna never really worked much. We used to call Anna 'Greta Garbo' because she was always in the mirror looking at herself. My younger brother Jack did go into the service during the Second World War, but then when they returned they went to the waterfront, although they were waterboys before they entered the service.

"In 1933 I married Lawrence Nesko. He was born in Carteret, New Jersey, and his parents were born in Poland. His father was a carpenter and came to Philadelphia from Allentown, where he was out of work. Larry was only about twelve and was in school. When he became older he became a paperhanger and that was his trade all his life. He never had his own business because he could never be a businessman. He would do the work in the neighborhood for the people, and he would never be paid for it. But he felt sorry for the people. Most of the time he worked for a contractor and often traveled over a wide area. He had to be away quite a bit.

"We were renting an apartment for two years. Then we rented a house. We purchased a home in the late 1940s. We always wanted to own our home. My husband was a handyman and always fixed up the places we lived. But we thought if we could own our home and fix it, then it would be ours and nobody could put you out. We only had a couple of hundred dollars when we bought the home, but we only needed five hundred dollars down. It was tough to save money, especially when the children were sick. But my husband always said that you live for today and the hell with tomorrow. That's contrary to what they say 'Polacks' believe. They say they are tight, but he wasn't, and I went right along with him.

"He always worked because he could do carpentry and electrical work as well as paperhanging. He was the type who could make a dollar. It wasn't big money, but it was an income. When I returned to work at least I could buy the kids clothes they needed.

"As a young girl I had no aspirations; neither did my husband. We were churchgoers when we were young. We went to a primarily Irish church, even though a Polish church was nearby. It didn't matter to him [Florence's husband] where we went. He stopped going because you just get so much of it. You went to a Catholic elementary school and all the religious holidays, and you just get to a point where you get too much of it. My oldest son also enlightened me when he was sixteen and gradually we stopped going altogether.

"We lived in Pennsport. The men were truck drivers, stevedores, firemen. After my mother died I also raised three of my younger brothers, and my brother Michael raised the others. I took in Frank, Eddie, and Jack, and Michael took in three girls. My father lived by himself and came to eat with us. We couldn't leave the children with him because he started to drink heavily. That is the only reason we broke up the home.

"He had started to drink before my mother died, and I think it was because of his job. He was a boss along the waterfront and had many friends. But some of his friends were killed and injured [on the job]. My father had testified on their behalf and when he returned to work, the company told him that he was really not a company man. That was a blow to his pride. He had testified that the company was at fault in the death and injuries of his friends, who had also been his neighbors for years.

"Sometimes I would be coming from work, and I would see my father standing on the corner and I would ask him if he was all right. Once and a while I would give him money and he would just throw it in the street. He never took anything from the kids. I knew his corner where he would be with his friends..."

GEORGE AND STACIA TRESKI

George and Stacia Treski were both raised by parents who had immigrated from Poland in the 1890s. Ironically, both of their fathers had worked first in Pittsburgh mills before deciding to locate friends from their respective Polish villages then living in Nanticoke and obtain employment in the mines. Reaching adolescence around 1930, George and Stacia knew full well how economic difficulties would translate into family difficulties before and after their marriage. In this selection they relate the mechanics of family survival through the first half of their lives.

George: "I grew up in Slocum Township on a farm with four brothers and four sisters. First, I started to work for the Lehigh & Wilkes-Barre Coal Company, but they closed down. I was only sixteen and my brother Stanley already worked there on consideration. That meant that you were not on piecework but worked for the company and got paid by the hour. Under consideration you might make as much as a contract miner who loaded a lot, but usually you made more than a laborer.

"I went underground at age sixteen and the section foreman saw me and asked how old I was. I said, 'Eighteen.' He said, 'You are a liar.' But I stayed and gave my wages to my mother. I gave them to her until I was twenty-eight. I felt like turning it over and so did two of my brothers who still worked on the farm."

Stacia: "When my father worked in the mines he decided to build another home himself, even though they already had one. My parents figured that the extra home would get a little more income. They also thought that they had two children, so one home would eventually be for one girl and the other home for the second girl.

"At that time, however, my father had an accident in the mines. The coal came down and knocked over a prop on my father's hand and took off four fingers. He could never go back to work any more. And by 1931 he had black lung, although there was no compensation for that. He had black lung so bad he would only walk up the stairs once a day to go to bed.

"I was going to school then and my sister was fourteen years old. She got a job in a silk mill where they paid ten cents an hour for ten hours a day, six days a week. So there was a little money. But after working one year she had a nervous breakdown and I had to put her in a mental hospital. I then went to look for a job. I was about fourteen or fifteen, and nobody in the family was working. This was around 1932, and you had to wait in long lines to find a job.

"But we raised our own food, had our own chickens and ducks. We even tried to make moonshine. We sold a couple of quarts and got a little money that way. My mother was also the midwife for the area. She got paid in food—chickens, ducks.

"We had three silk mills in town, a cigar factory, and a sewing mill. Every morning you would make the rounds from one to another. You just stood there and maybe they would hire someone. If you knew someone maybe you got a job. The same as it is today. Maybe you had an aunt working there and they would talk to you.

"I never did get a job, so I finished high school. That's the only reason I stayed in school. After I graduated I stayed home over the summer and then in September I went to New York [City] to do housework for twenty-five dollars a month. The lady would even hold back five dollars a month to make sure you didn't quit.

"A lot of girls from this area went to New York to work for Jewish families. One summer we even cleaned houses at the ocean. And my parents wanted fifteen dollars a month from me, so what could I buy myself? They wanted it every month when you came home. When we were in New York we didn't do much except visit free museums, eat hot dogs, and drink orange juice.

"When I was a teenager I always wanted to be a nurse. But how could you get to be a nurse? I mean you just couldn't. If you didn't have money you just didn't go to school. We really didn't have any money. My father wasn't working; my sister had a nervous breakdown. We finally went on relief. Everybody needed it. My parents didn't realize, though, that when they took it you had to have a lien on your house. First they gave us seven dollars and fifty cents per week, but then an investigator would come along and practically tell you how to live. And if you had anyone staying in

Library of Congress

A POLISH FAMILY IN THE ANTHRACITE REGION OF PENNSYLVANIA, 1940

the house like a married daughter or a married son, you had to hide them when the investigator came along because they would want to know if there was any extra money coming in. In fact, when my father died, my mother had an insurance policy, and we had to pay all the expenses of his funeral, like a new suit. We didn't really buy him a suit. We went to a place where they sell suits and had them give us a bill. We needed to keep a little bit of that money from the insurance.

"We never did lose our home. After I married I lived there with my mother. My husband was going to a school to be a mechanic. Even when he was going to school I went back to New York and did some more housework.

"My sister then returned from the state hospital and we took her in. She always had illusions that someone was chasing her, but someone had to care for her.

"I'll tell you that when we were small we didn't get a lot of good food to eat. If you got sick and had a fever, they gave you oranges because they thought they had to. I was so darn skinny all the years I went to school I had 'malnutrition' on my card. The people at school who examined you would stamp your card. They would look at you and say you had malnutrition and that your mother should take you to the doctor. He would say you needed milk. Well, my mother would go out and buy one quart of milk and that's the last quart of milk you would see for months. We had chickens and ducks but never any red meat. And we only had vegetables in the summer. We got some fruit from the hucksters that would come around. It was the same old diet all the time, with chicken soup on Sunday and cabbage and potatoes. Everyone had a cabbage barrel and lots of potato pancakes."

George: "By the early 1930s you was only getting a few days [of work] a week. Usually your pay would run out pretty fast. You'd only get two or three days' pay for two weeks.

"We would then work on the family farm to get more food. You had to depend on the farm to get food. We would kill hogs, calves. You raised your own potatoes and cabbage. So we at least had food.

"This was still my parents' farm. I stayed there until I was twenty-eight and got married."

Stacia: "There really wasn't any money. During a strike in 1935* there was a young man that went to work and his wife was expecting a baby. He was from this area and had to work because he had two children and a wife who was expecting another. He went to work—crossing the pickets—and was killed in an accident in the mines. The people were so mad that he went to work they wanted to dig him out. They had to get the police to keep him in his grave. But the strikers didn't like the idea that he went to work.

"There was another man who went to work, and not only the men got after him but the women got after him too. They stripped him of his clothes and he had to go home without any clothes on. Because he worked and they called him a scab. Everyone else's husband was sitting at home and he went to work.

"After marriage my husband wasn't working steady so he went to Patterson, New Jersey. I stayed here, but I didn't like the idea. He had a sister in Patterson so I moved out there and we had a baby. We lived in New

---

*This was the strike of insurgent mine workers in the anthracite area against the United Mine Workers.

Jersey for four years; this was during the war [1941-1945]. But the first day the war was over the factory closed down. There was no more job. We were in New Jersey for four years and saved five thousand dollars, so when we came back to Nanticoke we bought a tire business and lived with my mother again. We had two children by now. But my husband was so soft-hearted he would fix tires for his friends, do them favors, and never charge them. Sometimes we didn't have money for milk. So George went into the mines for two more years. But he would come home so wet, so black, coughing and everything, we looked for something else [he could do] with machines."

RAY LA MARCA

Ray La Marca, the son of a small industrialist, was raised in the Sicilian town of Villa Rosa. Ray remembers his father operating a sulfur mine near his village. When the mine became flooded and could no longer be operated, La Marca's father moved to Pittsburgh to find work. Nearly a decade passed before Ray and his mother were able to join him in America.

"Things were very hard in Palermo. They used to get boys twelve and thirteen years old to work in the mines. And the reason they used to work in the mine was that their daddy maybe needed the money. And they used to come to the 'straw boss' and say they had a boy about twelve or thirteen years old and needed a thousand lire, two thousand lire. And then this boss examined the kid to see if he was healthy. They had fifteen or twenty kids in every mine. And this 'straw boss' used to go to the house every morning, get them all up, and walk them two or three miles to the sulfur mine.

"In the mine they took their clothes off because it was so hot in there. You couldn't stand it down in the mine. And they had three-foot sacks, and they used to fill up these sacks with sulfur. Then these kids had to carry this sulfur two or three hundred steps out of the mine. And then moaning could be heard going up the steps and singing going down, all day long. After the day was done, about four o'clock in the afternoon, they had another three-mile walk home.

"I remember very well the people used to come to our home and complain, 'Where's the "straw boss"? Where's the "straw boss"?' I saw many spaghetti pots boiling and no spaghetti to put in. So they were looking for the 'straw boss' to give them a little advance in money. That's how bad things were. They wanted advance money so they could eat. My dad was half-owner of that mine.

"But my dad came to Pittsburgh in 1909 when the sulfur mine was full of water and they shut it down. He left us over there [in Sicily]. In Pittsburgh my father had a barbershop on the North Side. Then every month he used to send so much money for us to survive. He had learned to become a barber in Rome and pull teeth. The barber was a dentist then. He also learned to cure people. If you had pneumonia, they would lay you down on your stomach. They used to get a quarter and dip it in oil and light the quarter. Then they would put a glass on the top of the quarter to get all the bad blood in one place. You had to do this two or three times in back of your spine. And then my dad used to make slices in the skin and the suction of the glass would draw out the blood. The blood was as black as anything, you know. Even in the United States my dad couldn't sleep at night for all the people wanted him to do that for them. He wasn't a doctor so he only done it for a few who wouldn't say anything.

"Soon after we joined my father on the North Side, where the Lithuanian section used to be, my brother got killed on a bicycle. My dad and mother couldn't take it. They said, 'Oh my God, why didn't we stay wherever we was.' And so we went back to Italy. This was after the war, about 1921.

"After a few years we come back to Rochester, New York, because my mother had a sister over there. And her husband say to my dad, 'Why don't you come into partnership with me?' He had a barbershop, but it didn't work. So we came to Pittsburgh again and things started to pick up. We had another cousin over here. We was broke, but we got a little money when my brother was killed. My cousin had a barbershop in Portage, Pennsylvania, and he was a good man. He loaned my father seven hundred dollars to buy a barbershop on the North Side on Beaver Avenue. My father stayed with that barbershop until he died. My brother Joe opened a shop later in Penn Township.

"When we got over here, we rented a little house on Rebecca Street because everybody used to live there, mostly Sicilians. And that's how we started living. Then my dad had a godfather in the Homewood section [of Pittsburgh] and we moved there. We lived there until the neighborhood started changing. My dad died while we were living in Homewood.

"In a sense my mother was more educated than my father because she used to take care of the mine business and everything. She used to take all of my father's income. She had a high-school education. They were in favor of education a little, but the people used to be different than [they are] today. On Saturday I used to see that wagon come around full of beer. And they would drop half a keg of beer or a quarter at every other door. And the people used to get together and be more sociable. Not like today, when you don't know your own neighbor. The people was more close together than they are now. In the backyard on Sunday they played the guitar and mandolin and cards. It wasn't like today.

"Over here I started work at the Fort Pitt Spring Company at age sixteen. My parents didn't like the idea, but between the rent and the loan on the barbershop they liked the help. See, my dad had the barbershop, and one of the fellas was an Italian fella named Silvestri. He was a very good friend and he helped me. I get a job over there. My mother wasn't sure, but my dad said, 'Let him go,' and that was it.

"The first job at the spring company he got for me. It was on the North Side. They used to make hinges over there. They used to use these brass hinges on windows on a boat's portholes. First they give me a job as a laborer. Then they give me a job on the machine. The machine used to put a notch in the spring, in a wire. And then these wires were passed through a frame and used to make box springs for beds. I stayed over there for a long time. Then we returned to Europe.

"When I came back I was making twenty-one dollars a week as the head counter man at 'Dutch' Henry's restaurant. I stayed there for a while until I got a job at the Union Switch & Signal, and I stayed there for many years. I was always looking around for work, you know, and everything like that. Oh, Christ, in them days there used to be one of these Thompson restaurants. If I didn't have nothing to do, the man said, 'Well, you want to work tonight?' And you know what job you get? I would mop the floor, clean up, and things like that. I done several jobs like that. They used to pay you, but not that much.

"This was during the Depression. It was hard to get a job. When I got a job at Union Switch & Signal, they didn't hire me right away, because they didn't know if I was sure of working with a press. Then I put my application in an office in Wilkensburg. I didn't know that I had to pay for the job. They sent me down to McKeesport in the tin mill. I worked three days. I couldn't take those big tongs. The tong was bigger than me. You had to put the steel [ingot] on the roller and roll them out, thin out the steel. I couldn't do that. I couldn't take it. So that's when I paid twenty-five or thirty dollars to this agency, and they get me a job down at Union Switch & Signal.

"When work was slow a lot they put me on the night turn for three or four days. I used to sweep up. Little by little I learned how to put electric plugs together. They put me in the electric shop to become a maintenance man and I stayed there. I liked it very much. All the people treat me very good. Between the company and the people, we used to have picnics and things like that. Union Switch & Signal was a very nice place to work. And when I could I would even work in my dad's barbershop. I would make suds and put lather on a customer's face before my dad would shave them.

Library of Congress

A STEELWORKER'S HOME IN ALIQUIPPA, 1943

And that's the way life was. When you work, you understand, you used to bring your pay home and give it to your parents. And whatever they feel they want to give you, they decide. There was no disagreement. That was their style. And don't you dare talk about paying board, especially in my dad's house. If you want to pay board you have to go somewhere else. We never thought of that. We never had it in our mind. There was no such thing. The minute you wanted to pay board they would throw you out. 'There's no board here,' my father would say. 'This is no boardinghouse. This is a family.' He said to us to bring our pay home and whatever it was, we would make do.

"You know, I didn't have it as nice as my dad. All his life he had a very nice job. The money was easy when he first started work. I had it more tough than him in the way of living. He had it nice because money was left to him and the mine. He was better off.

"I barbered for a little while too. My dad sent me to the barber school on Third Avenue. All them goddamned drunks used to come in over there.

If you turned around, they used to drink the bay rum we used on their face. I worked for a barber for a while. But not that much; I didn't care about it.

"When I was young I always liked music. I was musically inclined all my life. I used to sing. In Europe my friend and I used to sing outside school. If my brother wasn't killed, I would have studied to be a musician. That ruined everything. That's the reason I can't stand a bicycle. He was hit by a Rick's Ice Cream truck. They gave my dad three thousand dollars. They said he was already twenty-one and would not have turned wages over to my father much longer. What a dumb way to figure. They took advantage of Dad. That was the most disgusting thing that ever happened in our family."

SARAH GREER*

Sarah Greer was born in Anderson, South Carolina, in 1896. She lived with seven brothers, a sister, and her parents on a two-hundred-acre farm her father owned before moving the family north to Harrisburg, Pennsylvania. Admittedly, serious differences characterized black and immigrant families in Harrisburg; immigrants, for instance, were allowed to use kinship ties in gaining jobs more frequently than blacks were. Both groups, however, relied heavily on family connections.

"When I started to school in a small log house on my dad's place, there was no school for ten miles in no direction. When the house could not hold them all, they built a larger building. There was so many black children in that community growing up, and no school to go to. My father and mother could not read or write, and my father said he wanted every one of his children to learn to be able to read and write.

"In order to get to school, we had to cross a creek. My dad made a footbridge by placing two logs together and nailing planks on top of them. And he made hand poles to hold on to on each side. Do you know, I was the first child to fall off of the bridge in the creek. They had to carry me back home.

"Boy, I remember the first doll I ever had. My grandmother made it out of old flour sacks, stuffed it with cotton, cut up one of her old dresses, and made it up. I was the happiest child in school. After Christmas they let me carry it to school one day; because I talked about it so much, the girls that did not get a doll said I was telling a story. Children were not allowed to call each other a liar as they do now. So to prove that I got a

*Name changed at the request of the respondent.

doll for Christmas, the teacher said it was all right to bring it to school. And what a day that was! I was seven years old.

"And my oldest brother was working at that time at a saw mill. He lifted a log, and the other man took advantage of him and let the log fall on him. The weight pulled his spine cord in his back, and he was paralyzed the rest of his life. There he was. I was given the responsibility. I would give him water and anything through the day, while the rest of the family worked in the field, in the summer.

"I went to school three months in the winter. Then my dad put four small wheels on a chair so that I could push my brother around the house and out on the porch. There he could get out of the chair and slide down the steps with my help, and get into his chair. And I would gather apples and peaches, and he could peel and cut them to be dried in the summer, and also get in the buggy to go for a ride in the fields. And I would carry gourds of water, fresh water, for them to drink and get blackberries and plums. I could put the bridle on the mule, but I was too little to put the harness on. Then I would lead the mule to the porch, where my brother would help me to place the harness on the mule's back. And I could fasten it and hitch [the mule] to the buggy. [My brother] was plenty strong from the wrists, but could not use his legs very well.

"Oh, I didn't tell you that my father, mother, and grandmother was slaves. My grandmother was put on the slave block to be sold by her master. But his wife would bring her home. My grandmother was only thirteen years old when my mother was born. Of course, my grandmother was quite a dancer and used to entertain her mistress. But she had to sleep on a trundle bed by the side of her mistress's baby—after my mother was born. My grandmother's baby was two months older. My grandmother nursed Miss Deal's baby, and my great-grandmother had to feed my mother on what was known as a sugar-teat made of bread, butter, and sugar. That is how my mother was raised. [Her mother] could not nurse her because in the day she saved her milk for her master, little Emmett. So Grandmother raised my mother that way.

"But my 'grannie' was a lively old soul. She used to tell us all kinds of things about what her life had been like in slavery. She was a wonderful dancer. She would entertain her mistress and her guests so many times. And it was quite common that she could dance very well. My grandmother could dance with a cup of water on her head and never spill a drop. She tap-danced and taught us how. It was a great pleasure to see my grandmother dance and hear her talk about slavery times.

"There was a time when we used to go out to the neighbors' homes and my grandmother would take us along. We would all have a good time dancing in the yards, in the summertime. And she taught us to use our heels and our toes to dance.

"I could name and bless my grandmother for the work in the garden. She had something all the year round—greens in the winter, vegetables all summer. Then, as I grew, I was a real farm hand. All of the others were grown except one brother, who was sickly all his life. I plowed a mule all day like a man; cut wood and hauled it on the wagon with two mules; cut grain with a five-finger cradle; bound wheat, oats, behind my father. I remember one time the bucket fell in the well, and they let me down in the well to get the bucket. I was not afraid until I looked up at the top of the well and it seemed to be closing.

"My education was only to the sixth grade, which I regret now. I was brought up in the church. We would go to the church in the wagon, and drove five miles every fourth Sunday in the month, as our church is in the country. We had to go only one Sunday a month. And my father decided that we should go to Sunday School. So he asked the teachers to teach Sunday School in our schoolhouse. And we could go there. When I was fifteen years old, I was singing in the choir and taught Sunday School. My second brother was married and had three children. His wife passed away. And the two boys and I grew up [together], my mother taking these two boys to raise. And we grew up more like brothers and sisters. They stayed with us until their father was married the second time, and then they went home to their stepmother. My mother raised their three children. Their father died in his twenties. My sister couldn't get a farm to work on, so I raised three of her children that was left to her after her husband passed— two girls and one boy—one was five, [the others] seven and nine.

"Often time my sister-in-law's son would stay with us, and there was at least thirteen in the house at times. For over two years there was thirteen in one house. I cooked and cared for them, raised them as best I could. I think I had a very hard life, but I loved what I had done, and I was brought up the way I was brought up.

"I had seven boys and one girl, and four sons were in World War II, which I didn't have here. They all came back safe and sound. I have three sons dead now. I have four sons living. At the present, one is married and my daughter is married. I have two sons with me. Both were veterans and they are both sick. One has had TB and one lung is gone. And one has arthritis of the spine. And if I live to see the fourteenth day of next month, I'll be eighty years old and still working five days a week.

"When I was older, my mother was living here in Harrisburg, with my brother. When he passed away, I came to see about my mother. She would not go back with me to the country, so I decided I was coming to Harrisburg to live with her because she was living with her grandchildren, and I didn't know how they would treat my mother. And she was old, so I decided I was coming to Pennsylvania, and I came here in 1941. It was the second Sunday in October. I got here with my husband and my youngest child.

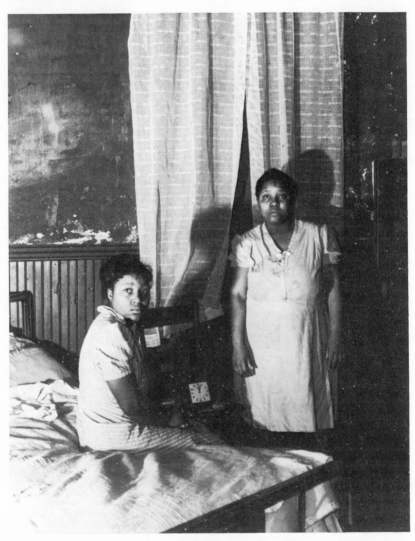

INSIDE A BLACK STEELWORKER'S HOME IN ALIQUIPPA, 1943

"My husband got contract work. He taught my boys plastering and cementing. One learned to plaster, one tried [to be a] carpenter, one became a plumber, and one was trying electrician's work until he electrocuted himself with a cord and was killed. My husband quit trying then. He couldn't take it any longer.

"My husband went to the state hospital in nineteen and forty-three. And the year he went I lost my mother and my last son out of the four sons that went in the service. I had two sons to go in the service in 1943. That was a trying year with me. And I suppose that's why my hair turned so white.

"In Harrisburg I rented until my boys came out of the service. They come out of the service and they bought it. My husband was ill in the state hospital. I had rented from a widow lady. I don't remember her name now. And after the boys came home and bought the house, they deeded it over to me. They deeded it over to me and said, 'Now Mom, all you gotta do is keep that and you got a house.' And, of course, it had an outside toilet and dirt floors and a basement. So my son was working with a plasterer, and he used to give him a lot of the waste left over. And he'd come home and plaster it from top to bottom. And it's three stories. The one son that was working with a plumber put in a bathroom and that didn't cost me anything. And we double-floored the kitchen and the front room. And we was heating it with coal and oil. Then we put an oil heater in the basement, and my son cemented the basement. It was wonderful! Of course, we had a big grate in the middle of the floor and that let the heat come up. We had it almost near the steps so the heat would go on up the steps and heat all over. I had just put in a new tank when they took our home down there to rebuild that part of Harrisburg. [Because of urban renewal] you had to buy or else get out of town because nothing went up. You couldn't rent nothing. Everybody put up everything for sale.

"I looked at another house and I called [the realtor] 'cause I seen it in the paper. He said, 'Now someone will come to carry you up to look the house over.' He said, 'Now what is your address?' When I told him that, he said, 'Oh, I'm sorry.' I said. 'Yes, I'm black, if that's what you want to know.' He said, 'Well that's a restricted area.' I said, 'What do you mean restricted? My money's just like anyone's money.' So I began to look elsewhere and found a house. They were taking my house and I didn't have the money I needed. I could not borrow a thousand dollars in Harrisburg nowhere. So I was working with a man from New Cumberland, and he finally helped me get a loan."

AMELIA BROWN*

> *Working-class families were subjected to numerous strains, but most continued to exhibit resiliency in one form or another. Amelia Brown was born in Waycross, Georgia, in 1898, but her parents separated when she was four and her father took her to Jacksonville, Florida, to live with a woman named Margaret. She remained with this woman for a considerable period before eventually returning to her mother in Georgia.*

*Name changed at the request of the respondent.

"We attended a church in Jacksonville. I think the church is still there. It was a Baptist church. I had three books that I read all the time: *Pilgrim's Progress, Uncle Tom's Cabin*, and the Bible. I used to read the Bible to her [the woman named Margaret] each night until she fell asleep. That was my job. And she was nice to everyone, I mean, but me. She was the meanest person I ever saw because she was just severe in her treatment of me.

"Well, my mother had friends living in Jacksonville, and they found out that I was there. My mother came and got me at eight years old and brought me to Waycross to my family. Well, of course I never heard of my father anymore. But my mother brought me back with my sister. Then I went to school the first time, at eight years of age. And I was always kind of in a different category because I could read. I knew all about reading, but I couldn't write. I never remember learning the 'ABC's,' but I knew how to read. I could read those three books.

"Now, my mother was a domestic. I guess they call it that now, but she was known as a chambermaid. Everyone thinks when you say Georgia that it means you lived on a plantation and that you picked cotton. But Waycross was a railroad center. The Atlantic Coast Line shop was there and people would come there from far and near to work in the shop. My father was a railroad man. He did something along the pumps—a pump inspector. They used to have pumps along different places that you would put water in. The train engine used to run like that and he worked on that. And my mother worked with different white people.

"After she brought me back to Waycross then I went to school. And Waycross only had one high school and that was Reidsville High School. And I went through that school. Only blacks were in that school. In fact, in all of Georgia then it was white and colored. And I went as far as that school went, and it went to the eleventh grade. There were too few students to have a twelfth grade.

"Well, in the meantime the professor of my school in Waycross—we didn't call them principals—had gotten my mother to see if I could go to Tuskegee, Morris Brown, or Florida A & M College. He was going to get me a job teaching summer school to make my tuition. But I didn't take this job, because I was afraid. I was so small. I was always small for my age, and when these people came in the church for school with all these great big boys, it frightened me. Well, of course I didn't take that job, so I couldn't say that I taught because I didn't. My mother was afraid to leave me out there with them. So I got a job in Waycross with a white family by the name of Stovall, and I worked for them all summer. They were the nicest people. And I was supposed to go to school and start the school in October. Meantime I met a man and instead of me going to college I got married. This was in 1915, I believe. It was in August, and I'd be seventeen in October. And a year later the influx had started coming into Chester, Pennsylvania. Well, in 1916 the people had started coming up North. They heard about how much money the people were making and they started the influx up here. And my husband was working at the railroad shop in Waycross. Down there my husband was supposed to be a man making a lot of money. He was making a dollar a day. One dollar a day! He got paid on the eighth of each month. And he decided to come here because they were making two-and-a-half, three, and four dollars a day, and they thought that was something, of course.

"Some of our friends came up here from Waycross. That's how we found out. They wrote back and told us what was going on. But they had settled in Philadelphia, not Chester, and some had gone to Detroit and just all parts up here. So we decided to come too. Then we had some friends here that came in 1916. They had the Penn Steel, the Atlantic Steel, the General Steel, the Eddystone plant, and the Chester shipyard. So people just came up here, and in April 1917 he [Amelia's husband] sent for me. I was eighteen, and the war was going on. That was the first time the women would start working that way, out in the public works. Up here they were working doing daywork, but they were only giving two dollars and fifty cents a day plus carfare. My husband got a job working with Sun Ship. He worked the boiler room and I got a job working at the Sun Ship as a 'water boy,' carrying water to all the men that were working. And well, I just thought that was something 'cause I was getting four dollars a day and we women had never made that much before. I worked there for a while, and then I went to work at the Remington Arms because they were making gunstocks. They were made of white pine, and we would have to paint them. There was a lot of overtime work. We'd have to do piecework and I was making all kind of money so I stayed there until the war ended. And when the places closed down, a lot of us went to Eddystone. I'll tell you this because this will go down in history. We went to Eddystone to get a job and they wasn't hiring. They wasn't saying 'blacks' then. They wasn't hiring any 'colored.' They were paying more money there, but they wouldn't hire us. And then about a month later someone made the mistake of lighting a cigarette and the place blew up and hundreds of people were killed. I know they hardly had any place to bury them all. Well, we were just fortunate because they didn't hire us.

"I lived on Edward Street with a couple by the name of Dutton. We roomed there and then my husband, who was a man that always liked to do things himself, started buying a place on Third Street. I would say that I was the first black down here with apartments because in the back of this twelve-room place downstairs and upstairs was apartments. We rented them out. But this place was too large for us anyway, and it was more than I could take care of. I had two children by that time. And so my husband sold the house.

"We then moved to West Third Street, right next to a white family. One of the little boys used to play with my boys and now he is the principal at one of the schools here. When we lived on Edward Street it was all black and, of course, we couldn't move where we would like to live. That's why my husband had to buy a place, because we'd either have to do that or just stay all cluttered up with blacks. [The whites] wouldn't rent to us. We wouldn't even walk down this way, let alone try to get a place to live [here]. This was up North too. But that was it. This was Pennsylvania. You didn't know about the race riot they had here in 1918.* Yes, they had a race riot, and it started right down this part of town, and this girl and her boyfriend was coming from the movies. I think this happened on Jeffrey Street, about two streets away. These white boys accosted her. They said something to her and of course her boyfriend resented it, and they started to fight. Just from that it was a race riot. Nobody never knew why these boys did this at this particular time, and some people tried to say that the girl had been familiar with these boys, these white boys. But if she had been, she had to keep it a secret.

"During the riot we couldn't come out on the street after six o'clock in the evening because all up and down the street they were just shooting at people. Oh, several people were killed. The whites started to attack the blacks, and the blacks started to defend themselves. But the people from the South were up here then, and people in the South believed in guns, not so much knives and bricks. They were throwing bricks and that wasn't doing any good. Southern blacks had guns and that's what stopped them. They had to call out the mounted police. They were just up and down there at nights on their horses. I know it lasted maybe a week. It took at least a couple of weeks to get that quieted down because my husband was working at Penn Steel at the time. This is what they used to do. They would search you as you were going in if you were black. And he used to carry a lunch kettle, and he had a gun in the bottom. They had to. They were afraid, you know. They didn't know whether they were going to let them in or not. So his lunch was packed on top of his gun.

"There was a lot of black men working at night. Whites could come in the black neighborhood and be throwing stones, just making a nuisance. And we were afraid to even look outside. And you didn't know whether they were going to break in the house or what they were going to do. And the women would all go in one room of a home and would have a gun or something. And someone would try and stop 'em. They were afraid. Everybody was just scared to death. Some people died. I just can't remember now how it ended, but I know my husband had to work through it at night.

"They had discrimination on the job. My husband worked at Penn Steel during the riot before he went to Sun Ship. Then [after Penn Steel]

*The riot started on July 31, 1917.

he went to Baldwin's [railroad shop]. At Baldwin's (he had learned the work at the Atlantic Coast Line shop in Waycross) he was making more money than anybody in that department. They hadn't been used to a black man doing that kind of work. And that's why he was able to start buying his home I was telling you about. He didn't pay any attention to the mortgage. He just paid any money because at that time he was making good money. Then they brought a white man into this department and wanted him to learn the job from my husband because they didn't like all the money he was making. He's up North too, right in Chester. And before he would teach this man how to do what he was doing and give him his job, he quit. That's the type of man he was. He quit. He said that no one was going to take his job and pay him to teach somebody to do what he was doing. Then he went to Sun Ship and he had this good job there, and that's where he was working when he took sick and died in 1948.

"This [the North] is supposed to be the land of the free because you didn't have to sit on the back of the bus and things like that. But you didn't have anybody to speak for you. The blacks that were in power, it looked like, were just kind of all for themselves and were afraid. They didn't do anything. They didn't go any further. I guess whoever they were working for told them to stop. That was the situation.

"We had a man here by the name of Burt Reading. Oh my, everybody who wanted anything went to Burt Reading to see what he could do. He was big in the Elks and in politics. You know, if they have somebody locked and you wanted some leniency or something like that, you'd go to see him. Then he knew who to see.

"I also managed the cafeteria at the Douglass Junior High School for about seventeen years. When I went there for a job, I went there to work in someone's place. The person didn't come back, so I continued to work. And nobody said anything to me, but I had a job. And I registered Republican and most everybody down here did. So after I'd been working down there about ten years, they gave me notice to come to the eighth floor of the Crozer Building. I met this man. And I think he was the main employer and he wanted to know who I was. They told him, 'Well, she works at the cafeteria at the Douglass Junior High School. She's been working there for seven some years.' I found out my hands were gonna be tied [she was going to be dismissed from her job]. I figured I'd get out of this because my husband never believed in getting into things like that. But before I had a chance to do that they closed the cafeteria down at Douglass and decided they weren't going to have it any more. So they opened up a new school and I was expecting to get a job there, but I didn't because they didn't call me. So the NAACP and one of its members, George Raymond, wanted to know why wasn't I working. I told him that I didn't know. 'Well, we're going to look into it and see why you're not working,' he said. So he wrote to Harrisburg. So the man came from Harrisburg and

I explained to him the situation. He said, 'Now we're gonna meet with all the board of directors.' So they did, and I got the job back. I know the NAACP put me back.

"I first voted in 1924. Women were allowed to vote here then. Coming from the South we were Democratic, you know. And this woman came to my sister and myself and told us if we would vote for her she would give us ten dollars a piece. And she did. She gave us ten dollars and went with us. And she voted Republican. She was black and worked for the organization. Anybody will tell you that Delaware County has always been Republican. So that's what we got the first time. Well, it got less and less then. It got down to a dollar. But after we knew what it was all about we didn't want anybody. We had to say we couldn't read. You had to lie and say you couldn't read in order for somebody to go in with you. It was a long time before we even knew what it was all about. It made a lot of difference around here when people stopped voting for a dollar or for a drink. If they drank, you know, they'd go and get a drink or something. It was one of the political bosses down here who was an undertaker for whites. You'd always go to his place. We'd always have to go to get our money there after we voted. We'd line up and go and he'd give us a dollar apiece. It went on year after year. My husband would tell me not to do that, and then I found out later nobody could tell me how to vote. I wouldn't take a dollar then.

"During the Depression my husband was laid off. We were living on West Third Street and we did own a rooming house. There was only one person in the house working. He was working at the Sinclair Oil Refinery. This man and his wife lived there. And it was pretty bad times. I had three children at the time and my little girl died. We didn't have any insurance, and we didn't have anything to bury her with. So an undertaker buried her, put her away for us, and gave us time to pay later. He was the one I was telling you about before, and he was very political minded. In fact, I call him one of the political bosses down here. And it was kind of a terrible time. The only job that my husband had was at Commission Row, where they sold chicken and everything. It was opened on weekends. It was something like the Farmers Market, but they just sold chickens. He worked there on Saturdays and helped kill the chickens and clean the chickens. He'd bring chicken feet home and we'd have all kinds of fixings. We'd make a meal out of that for a couple of days. He finally went back to the Sun Ship where he was laid off from."

HELEN MACK

Helen Mack grew up in the coal town of Nanticoke, Pennsylvania. Here she relates what happened to her family after her father was

killed in the mines in 1884, five years after his arrival from Poland.
It is a graphic description of how powerfully immigrant women
were tied down by family obligations.

"My dad was born in Lithuania and my mother was born in Poland,
near Warsaw. My dad came in 1880. His uncle came in 1865. He landed
in New York when President Lincoln was shot. There was a lot of confu-
sion, a lot of running around, and a lot of excitement. They got excited
too. Then they came here; they landed in Alden, a little town near here,
with a few people who were friends. My mother came in 1885. She came
from a village near Warsaw. My mother's name was Bardusky. It's hard
to pronounce [so] they went by the name of Smith because it was very hard
to pronounce their name. They were in business and pretty well off here.

"My mother's mother died when she was eleven, and her father died
when she was fourteen. They had a business place, grocery and butcher
shop. When they died, everything went. There was quite a few children.
One relative took one, and older children took the other. When my oldest
sister got married she couldn't take all of them so my mother's brother
came here to Nanticoke from Poland. Then he got my mother and her other
sisters and brother to live with him.

"It was different in them days. She [Helen's mother] had to go and
work as a maid. She was about fifteen, sixteen years old. In Poland she
had learned to cook in Warsaw. And my father was a cabinetmaker. He
made cupboards. His father was, I can't tell you in English, like an overseer over several manors or places. He would get on the horse. They
wouldn't see him for a month or two. That was the only way they traveled
at that time. He was from a well-to-do family, but Russia took their land
and took everything away from them during the 1863 uprising. My dad
had a tutor until he was fourteen, but when he couldn't go to school, he
had to take up a trade. That was what he was doing. He came here in 1880.
His uncle wanted him in Chicago because he was a good cabinetmaker.
He wanted to stay with his uncle, but since he couldn't talk English, he
was afraid to venture out. When they came here [Nanticoke] they did go in
business, but a strike broke them. They had to give it up. He went to work
here in the Susquehanna [Coal Company] as a maintenance man. He was
a carpenter and was one of the men hurt when twenty-nine men were
buried here under this dirt bank in 1885. They thought more of a mule
than they did of a human being. So he was trying to save them from a
landslide which blocked them from going out. They're still there. Never
got out. When he was trying to save them, he was hurt and was put in
what they called a city hospital for six weeks. After he came out, then he
went back to work at the Susquehanna.

"They went to Polish or Russian school, but not too long. When the parents died, they didn't watch those things. When my mother came here, she came to her brother. He had a butcher shop. She stayed with him until she met father, and then they got married in 1887.

"I was born on March 2, 1891, in Nanticoke. I went to school to the sixth grade. But I went two years to Polish school. So I can talk good Polish. My parents talked only Polish. They couldn't talk English. The kids would understand, but they said everything in English. My first job was clerking in a dry-goods department store and then in a shoe store. I worked at the shoe store because it was good; so I just worked two or three days a week. When my aunt went into the shoe business, I went to work for her. I was about twenty or twenty-two, but I stayed home most of the time because there was a lot of work. In fact, I never left Nanticoke.

"The coal companies at that time ran Nanticoke. Johnson's shoe factories wanted to come here in an old brewery. There was an old brewery and they gave it up. Johnson's wanted to take that up and have a shoe factory. The Republicans stopped it, because they didn't want people breaking away from coal companies and working there. They didn't want the coal companies to have competition. They [the Republicans] were of English nationality. The mayor was English. The head of the coal company was English. After a while the coal company closed down anyway. We would of had a factory then.

"My parents felt that work was important to achieve something. They wanted their children to be educated, but we older ones couldn't be educated because there was no money coming in. But Mamie was born in 1905 and she went and graduated high school. And Ted was born in 1907 and graduated from Pittsburgh University. I helped him. He appreciates that. The older ones got married, but I was home and inherited some money from my aunt because I used to help her out.

"I always liked bookkeeping and numbers. I liked to figure, but I never could because I had to stay home and help raise the other children. The older ones like Bill, I, Stanley, Henry, Johnny, were the oldest and worked early. Henry got married when he was eighteen. Johnny got married at seventeen. When he was eighteen, he was a father. I sacrificed. But I'm not sorry, because I helped them. I helped Stanley. Stanley went to school till he was sixteen. Then he went and worked in men's furnishings and went into business on his own. And I helped him. Then Leonard took it over after him. That was the oldest one. All had to give their pay to my parents.

"In 1930 I bought a half of a house and always cooked for the whole family. They all claim I'm a pretty good cook. I don't cook now, but I used too. When the holidays, came, like Christmas, birthdays, or Easter, they'd all come home, and I made sure they had plenty to eat. I'd always have a big ham, a whole ham. At Thanksgiving Day we'd have a turkey. And if

Library of Congress

CHILDREN IN A COMPANY TOWN OF PENNSYLVANIA, 1937

we were going to have company I'd make sure we had a ham or sausage because they'd come in with their family. There were a lot of big eaters. And for Easter we always had a ham. But Christmas or Thanksgiving we always had a turkey.

"Sometimes I wanted to get married and at times I didn't want to get married. Certain things were private, so I wouldn't say anything about them. I didn't have a chance to think about any other person because that's more or less on the outskirts, since we all lived together. Never got in anybody's way. Even the next-door neighbors would bake for each other.

"We don't get together on holidays like we used to. They are all dying out. Out of nine there is three left. There is a brother and sister besides me and that's all. When they were living we would all get together for holidays and for many Sundays. Many Sundays they would come home and eat with their families. There's enough food. We used to sing Polish songs and verses. My sister would understand; she could talk Polish. Stanley could too. Henry did, but he married an English woman and never talked Polish. So he forgot. Jack was the same way. Little by little they left the home."

HELEN SERAFIM

Helen Serafim's father came from Poland to Scranton, Pennsylvania, in 1901 when a brother-in-law sent him passage. Unfortunately he was killed in the mines when he was thirty-eight, and Helen's mother was left with the task of rearing six children. Helen, the oldest, recalls that when her father died, only four hundred dollars in insurance money from his fraternal lodge was left for the family to live on after the priest and undertaker had been paid.

"My mother did not have boarders, because her children came rather fast and there were only two little rooms. And then we had three rooms later. The house I was born in did not have a stove. My parents didn't have the money. There was a company store. It was very important to us. You had to buy there once a month if you worked for a particular coal company or they would say something to you about it.

"We had quite a few Welsh people move into the mines. They had a fabulous knowledge of mines. Because of the mines in Wales, they were good miners. I think they became the bosses right away because they didn't have the language barrier and they were so good with the mines. This was how my father was killed, drilling a hole by hand. They had these drills that you had to turn into the rock to drill. They had very, very crude methods of drilling. And as he drilled he disturbed the coal; both he and his laborer were killed because of the falling of the roof. It was terrible! They brought him home in a black buggy with two black mules. They just brought the body in and put it down. When my father was killed they brought him into the front room that also served as a bedroom. They brought him in the buggy that we called the 'Black Mariah.' They were really black. And they just brought his body on a stretcher and put him on the floor and they left. And we had very good neighbors, and they all helped. It was awful that these people had to face this in their lives.

"[We had a] four-hundred-dollar [insurance] policy, [and] my mother said to my oldest brother, 'I want you to go looking for a house.' And my mother said to be sure that it had a garden. He hunted and he found a house that had eight rooms. Imagine six children moving into an eight-room house from a three-room house. And I remember going to the first mass after we were there, and I wanted everybody to know that we lived in an eight-room house. We had a bedroom of our own, imagine! So I thought she did very well for an illiterate woman, and my father was proud he could sign his name. We lived there until the family grew up and moved away.

"I went to Polish school from September to December, and that was the end of my Polish learning. Then I went to Suffix Street School after that and it was nice. It was a public school.

"There were a lot of different people. Everyone had their own churches. And you went and sang in the choir, and there again you needed choir practices, and that was another social event, getting together and practicing. But then you had to be in the mines by six, and you worked ten hours.

"My two older brothers didn't go to high school. My father's death greatly affected our lives. And the oldest brother got a job, but I don't remember where. And the next brother worked in the mines, and he did until he went to the war. My younger brother always liked watches, and he makes lovely watches.

"I knew my husband just about all our lives. We went to the same parish, and we were from the same neighborhood. He was an organist in our church. He was an adult when I was just a child, but later it was a different story. I'm only sorry that I only had him for twenty-five years, because he died in 1949, at age fifty-two. We were poor but never hungry. Everybody took in boarders, because they needed the money. These men had separate books [at the store] and if they bought a pound of meat and didn't eat it all, then your family got the rest of it. My mother didn't [take in boarders] because we didn't have the space, and there were a lot of children."

ROSE POPOVICH

As a young girl growing up in the mill town of Monessen, Pennsylvania, Rose Popovich labored to assist her Croatian immigrant parents. She reflects upon her youth with some bitterness over the extent to which she was tied to her family of origin, and she describes how family ties were transferred through marriage.

"My parents were raised in Croatia cultivating their own land and raising vineyards. They raised their own grain and eggs. That's something we didn't trade back and forth. They would use their corn to make corn bread and would go to the mill and grind their corn. They traveled a mile to the grist mill where they would grind their grain. They would use the money they would get from selling things in town to pay for getting the grain ground. You didn't do it for nothing. You had to pay. They had very little money as far as money goes. It was mostly like a trade back and forth. One grew whatever another didn't have.

"They had this land that was given to my father by his father. They built a little house, but it wasn't called a house. They called it a *coliba*. That's a little like a shanty. You built that yourself. You didn't have no beds. They slept right on the ground, but they had feathers. They had it well padded underneath with straw and everything that kept it dry. We didn't have no rain come in to get it wet. If you did have a bed, you would just bring in a few logs from the woods and build something crude. They didn't have no gas or electricity; they used mostly kerosene. They would burn these lanterns to light up the place. They had different types of stoves. They didn't know what coal was. You went out in the woods and got some logs for firewood to keep yourself warm.

"My father came to America in 1910. He got a job here and then sent for my mother and me. I had an older sister who died right after being born. You needed a passport but you didn't need reservations. You could go any time as long as you came to the boat and the boat was leaving for America. You could get on if it wasn't full. People went before and never had nothing but a passport.

"Everybody that went here before him [Rose's father] wrote back and said that jobs were easy to get and you made yourself a little bit of money, which in those days meant you worked for about twenty-five cents an hour. They thought that they could work ten hours a day. When they made two dollars and fifty cents they thought it was great because in Europe if they got that much they almost had to do little things for somebody else the whole month. Then in 1912 my father sent for my mother and me.

"He came to America and there were people living here in Monessen already. There were the Matkos. He boarded with them. You just looked around to see who came. Like some of the people who came to Europe said that they are living in Monessen, and there is a lot of our people there. When my father came here, they called it Wireton; now that's part of Monessen. That is like a Croatian village. There would be three, four rows of houses and they were all Croatian people. We had three Polish families among us, and we had two colored. All Croatian; the rest were Serbian and 'Krannish,' [Slovenes]. And a lot of other nationalities couldn't find no place to board. So they asked my mother for board, although we were Croatian. But you couldn't find a boardinghouse, and they didn't want to go and live in hotels of any kind. Hotels weren't as big as they are now.

"I know my mother, when she came here, right away started a boardinghouse. She would try to get two to a bed, but they were so in need of housing that they were willing to sleep even three on one bed, just to take them all in. Of course, then you have no single beds. They were all these

Author's personal collection

ROSE POPOVICH

big beds. Three people could sleep on them. Maybe if you turned around you would knock one off. I know at one time she had twelve boarders.

"She did their clothes, and they paid five dollars for their room and to do their clothes. And whatever the store bill would be, it would be divided by how many boarders. But the only thing is, she made sure that she didn't have to pay, or my father or me either. That went just among them. They paid whatever it was. So that's all she got out of it, just to feed me and themselves. In those days everything was cheap. Outside of her five dollars, that's all she got. That was five dollars a month for doing their clothes and giving them a bed to sleep on. I remember those things. Everybody paid board by the month. Extra would be after she had the store bill all figured out; that would be divided among the twelve boarders. There were twelve. Each one gave her five dollars. That was sixty dollars from the twelve. That was all she got for doing the clothes. We didn't have no washing machines. We did it by hand. I used to stand on a box to reach the washboard so that I could do some socks. I was only six years old. But my mother had so many clothes to do. A woman in those days never thought of having laundry done and not boiling it. You had these stoves with four plates on them and you burned wood and coal here. Then you heated your boiler up on top of the stove and you boiled those clothes. That was the hard way of doing [it]. But there were no washing machines. We had gas for light. If a train went by, it shook the house.

"My father worked in Pittsburgh Steel. He stayed there until he retired. In 1912 he sent for us. He didn't like to work, but you have to. Sometimes it was hard. It was no piecework. He always worked daywork. He never worked piecework. But he said some days they had it pretty rough; then other days it would be a little easier.

"You needed boarders. That was the only way you could get yourself a little bit on your feet. You got so little bit of pay by the time you paid your gas and food bill and paid your rent. We lived in company houses which Pittsburgh Steel owned.

"We lived down in Wireton a good many years. We moved up on Walnut Street in 1919 when there was a steel strike. We had to move because they tore down the houses and built barracks for scabs.

"They [Pittsburgh Steel] brought in Mexicans and Spaniards by the truckloads. They had these mounted police.* If anybody got in their way, they trampled them if they didn't get out of the way. They were really rough on the people. They built these barracks and they brought in food for these people so that they didn't have to go out and do their own shopping and the police escorted them to the mill. Some of them stayed in the mill, but those that wanted to go home, they wanted to go out of the mill,

*Pennsylvania State Police.

[so] the police escorted them back into the barracks that they built and they stood guard so nobody got through. Of course, some of them found out what it was like, and some of them just refused to work. They refused to work and they stayed here. Some of them went back where they came from, but we have a few families left here that quit their job when they found out what was going on. But they were taking bread and butter away from someone else, because [people here] were fighting then for a union to organize.

"Before the war we found out that there was a house for sale that was reasonable, and my father thought that as long as he could get a mortgage, he would. At that time he was working, although whenever they went on strike, naturally he wasn't working. They went up on the hill with what my mother accumulated. In those days the people in homes would even let a card game go on. They weren't so strict about it. They played cards in the house. They didn't stay up all night for nothing. Whatever went into the pot was for the woman of the house. My mother would get sometimes twenty dollars, or thirty dollars, for a couple of nights. You tried to make money any way you could in those days because otherwise there wouldn't be enough. You had to eat, but you need clothing. If you got one pair of shoes a year you were lucky. When the war broke out they were buying Liberty bonds. When men weren't working, the store would take the Liberty bonds for payment of your groceries. In that way my father had a little bit of money saved up, and he would pay the grocery bill with the Liberty bonds. Any little bit of money that they had saved they put on the house.

"The way our house was built we had a bedroom for my mother and father but none for me. I was right in the bedroom where they had to sleep. We had a kitchen and cellar underneath the length of the bedroom and the kitchen. On the opposite side of the kitchen was a room just for boarders. There were four beds and six boarders. As years went by they paid a little more. It came to where they would pay ten dollars just to have their clothes washed and for their rooms. And if they wanted some favors done, I used to shine shoes for them. They would give me a quarter. That all went to my mother because I thought I was helping. I felt proud. I shined the shoes on Saturday so that [they] would be all shined up for Sunday. If there was six boarders, I made myself one dollar and fifty cents. They would say, "Shine them up good and I will give you a quarter.' My mother's boarders always treated me nice. On holidays they would ask me what I needed. Some would give me enough to buy a dress. I always look forward to Christmas and Easter.

"There was six in our family, but three died. In those days children weren't treated like they are today. Children today don't appreciate their parents. I had an awful rough home life. I never could go out and play with other children. It was always work, work, work of some kind for me as a youngster. They always found something for me to do. I missed a lot in life. I never had any fun. My father especially didn't believe that a child should just go out there and play and do nothing. He thought that that wasn't amounting to anything. If you were doing something that wouldn't benefit you in any way, he didn't think you should do it.

"I quit school when I went into the seventh grade. I went out and I just said I was sixteen and I got a job. I wasn't born in this country, and I couldn't produce my birth certificate right away. So I worked in the tin mill for nine months. I had started school down in Wireton when I was six. When I come up to this school on Ninth Street they said I wasn't learning too much down there so they put me a grade back. But I was only there three months and they put me back where I belonged. One year I skipped a grade. By the time I was thirteen I was done with six grades. I quit in the seventh grade mostly because I didn't have the proper clothes to wear. I got a coat and it was too long for me. But my parents said, 'You will grow.' They said they can't afford another one. So I was so embarrassed and ashamed and quit. I said I would rather go out and work and make money and dress myself properly. I went to the mill. I was making bigger money than my father for two weeks. It made him think that he is a man, and I am making more than he is.

"I would sort sheets. They had sheets of tin about two feet wide by two feet high. Some would be smaller. You would have a pair of gloves and keep separating the sheets and put them on the roller. They used to roll and oil them. You would give them to the roller, and the more you worked, the more money the roller would make. Then when payday came they made the money, but we didn't. If we hurried up and worked fast the roller would make thirty dollars a day. He was working piecework but we weren't. Then I quit there. That's because I didn't have my birth certificate. I didn't see any sense in sending to Europe for it because if I gave it to them they would kick me out anyway. I was big for my age so I got away with it for a while. After I quit I got myself a job in a meat market. I worked there for Joe Chick for about a year and then got married. I was fifteen when I married in 1924.

"Until I married I lived with my parents and gave them my wages. You know what I got out of it? I got one dollar in spending money. It was ridiculous, and I thought, 'When I go to work I will have a little more clothes.' I found out if I got one dress I was supposed to go and wear that dress week after week after week. [It] just got to the point [where] I felt when I had the chance to get married I would. I would have married a fellow I didn't care for and that was it. I saw that my life wasn't too pleasant the way it was going. I might have a nicer life so I was just going to go ahead and get married. I would go with the next one that asks me.

"I said before that when my father was working my mother would let me go out and play. She made sure I got back in the house before my father came home. That's why I favored my mother, because she was more lenient with me. I know a lot of times I did things that I should not have done. She was the kind that would maybe smack me, and I would forgive her because I knew I was wrong. My father had a habit that if my mother mentioned something to him, why he made such an issue out of it that he just about half-killed me when he started beating me. I never took to my father too much. He always thought my place was at home learning how to do things. Some day I was going to have to do things myself, and I was not going to learn them by playing out on the street. That's the way he figured.

"When I see children play now, as old as I am it hurts me to think I never got to play with other children like that. Then, when I did get out, it was just like letting an animal out of a cage. I really went wild the few hours that I had. It was a wonder I didn't break my neck the way I was running, hide-and-seek and all. Innocent games. I remember one time I went clear from my home on Walnut Street all the way over the hill behind where Francy Yackovack lived. Now who was going to find me that far? There was no fear in those days. You didn't have to fear.

"I learned at an early age to crochet and knit. I had to do those kinds of things and any kind of sewing. I was taught that. Not to sew anything on a machine, because I don't even remember my mother having a machine. It was by hand. My mother was always this way. If something tore, you made sure you fixed it before it tore more. I had to keep every stitch the way it was supposed to be because if anything was ripped I had to go and fix it and then do dishes and scrubbing. I scrubbed floors and different things.

"My family also butchered pigs. We would have to do it out here in the wintertime, even out in the yard, because you have to singe it over a fire and scrape it. Then you know you are cold. You washed it with cold water. I think a lot of times maybe my arthritis stemmed from all of that, just freezing out there. My mother, she had a habit, whenever she would have to cook beans she would forget about them and the pot would burn. I would come home from school and her pot was all black. My father used to [say,] 'You clean that pot before you go to sleep.' I used to have night work to do. He said: 'I sent you to school to learn. You don't bring that work home.' Now that's another thing. He never believed in those kind of things that had to be done. How many times I didn't get my night work done. In the morning before I would go to school I got a beating with a 'dumb hose' because I didn't have my night work done. It wasn't my fault. The way my childhood life was I could make a book. I don't know if anybody had such a hard life.

"My mother had a midwife for the third child that was born. That child was born stillborn. At that time my father always claimed that the midwife didn't take proper care of that child. While this one was a midwife, she liked her booze. She was drunk at the time. There weren't too many doctors about 1914 when the little boy was born dead. I assisted my sister when she had her baby. I did when little Albert was born over at my mother's house. She lived there with my mother.

"After marriage my husband never discussed too much about his own work.* Just some days the machines didn't work, and he would hardly make anything because he was on piecework. The machine used to break down for him. They would have these adjusters for the machines, and if they were busy on another machine my husband had to wait and lose time. So some days he would be working for ten or twelve dollars, where he could of made sixteen or eighteen dollars. That was the only thing he complained about. He would be tired because naturally, once the machine was fixed again, you would have to oil it and everything, because you know that barbwire is greasy. It has to be. The machines are awfully oily. I know when I bought him a pair of shoes he was lucky if he could work in them for three months. They would be soaked in oil. The oil splattered from those machines.

"My husband left the finances up to me from the day I got married. The better you are going to manage with money, the better off you will be. He said: 'I feel this way, I earn it. It's up to you to see what has to be done.'

"You couldn't save very much because my husband was more out of work than working. At the beginning there was a job that was seasonal. While the farmers were using the barbwire they would have good business. He would be working steady. When the war was on they needed barbwire [and] then he worked. The first year that I was married, 1924, things were kind of slowing down. It wasn't quite what you would call a depression, but it was on the verge of coming. So I bought the house. I didn't have much to put down on it. I tried to fix different things because it needed fixing badly. Once I got them fixed my husband stopped working. By the time he started back to work I owed so much. By the time I paid what I owed, he stopped work again. The only time that he worked good was during the war. He worked steady for two years without stopping. There were times when he worked just one day a month. It was just awful. You couldn't get a job anywhere because everybody was being laid off. You couldn't say 'Well, I'm going to look for another job somewhere,' because, he always said, 'I don't know how to do anything else.' When he didn't have work maybe he would just go and sweep or something like that. A few times he got in the bundling room and would bundle wire. Anything with wire he would know. He just couldn't do another job that he didn't

*Rose Popovich's husband worked for the Pittsburgh Steel Company in Monessen, which manufactured a good deal of barbed wire.

know anything about. Sometimes he would work where they had all their supplies. He would clean the storeroom or something like that and stack everything up nice. But they wouldn't even put him someplace where there was a job he had to know something about.

"During the Depression it was worse. You didn't have any money and the stores didn't trust you. Not only me, but others, because everybody was the same way. If you owed them fifty or sixty dollars, then you were out. They couldn't carry you anymore; you must pay what you owe. We had to go on relief. That's all. I know it was terrible because I remember paying interest. I know I paid [for] my house over three times the amount of the mortgage. I just paid interests; I couldn't pay on the principal. My debt was one thousand eight hundred dollars. My husband had one or two days' work a week, and we had two children to support. It wasn't easy. When I paid the interest I could get no relief. They asked me why I didn't keep the money to eat on. Then my husband would walk from one person to another trying to borrow ten or fifteen dollars so we would have money to eat. Everybody was down and out. Nobody could give you money like that. We had one special friend that we asked, and he gave my husband fifty dollars. He said, 'I know you are going to pay it when you are able.' I know his own sister had the money and she wouldn't help us. I went down on my knees and begged her. You wouldn't believe me, but I said that it was not for my sake but for the children. You never go through anything like I have. I had a life that makes me wonder how I kept my faculties together.

"I even give the Red Cross a nickel today. I used to stand out on that sidewalk where we had our old police station before. They had a storeroom, and the Red Cross was giving out material. I would sew my Joey's shirts or dress material if I got it for Kathy. And there would be lines clear down to the corner. We weren't allowed to block the sidewalk. Policemen would come and tell us to move over. Raining, snowing, you were out there. When it would come to about two before me, they would say, 'No more today.' You would stand there from morning to night, hungry. And you are begging, you are actually begging, and you don't get it. We used to go down there for weeks like that. Then I hear of a person that was giving; if they gave you a ticket, you could get it. And I heard that he was giving tickets, but the person that told me didn't tell me that if you would give him a little bit of money he would give [you] a ticket. 'Well,' I said, 'if I had that money I would buy my material. I wouldn't have to go down there and beg.' And I wasn't going to give him no money. So you think people are crooked today? They were crooked years ago.

"The only thing was that I had a good husband. We would try to pull together, and whatever. He said that after we lived through all that, there is nothing that could bother us any more. We survived. How many times I would fix something up and maybe there was just enough to feed the kids. We could just taste it. But when you are hungry, who wants to just taste it? That's worse than not eating at all. I would say we were not hungry so the kids would have it.

"Right after the Depression started, our road was built by the WPA. That was a good thing because it took a lot of people off the relief rolls. They worked for the WPA. They were paid because that was a thing when Roosevelt was in. He thought of all these things that would somehow bring prosperity back. They built a lot of it. My husband worked three days a week under the street in the big sewers, cleaning out those sewers for our money. He worked for that. It was a relief, but you worked for it. I really can't be ashamed that I was on relief, because my husband worked for it. He didn't expect anything for nothing. He said he was willing to work to make a living."

RAY CZACHOWSKI

The Lawrenceville section of Pittsburgh was home to thousands of young Poles for whom life in America was filtered through the eyes of immigrant parents. Ray Czachowski, who was born in 1918, talks of his experiences in a family initiated by an immigrant father from Łodz, Poland. Czachowski reveals that family concerns were important, but that some workers clung to notions of individual success as well.

"When my father came over, he got work in the spring works on Twenty-eighth Street, and he worked there till he saved enough money and went into business for himself. He opened a hotel on Twenty-seventh Street. And he was with that until Prohibition came in, and then he went into the real estate business. He 'lost his shirt' in 1928 and started all over again. Then he died a young man in the 1930s.

"At home we had my father and mother, myself, my brother, and my sister—just the family. We all had our chores around the house—sweeping, scrubbing, washing dishes. My parents were both Roman Catholics, very staunch Catholics, very strict Catholics. Church was almost a second home to us. I mean we never missed a novena or any service at all. That was it. There were no questions asked. You just went. I'm pretty grateful for that start, I think. It helped me, and it helped me later on with my family.

"Outside of our formal education in school, we did a lot of reading, getting books from the library. And they supervised us and they watched over us, although my mother had more education than our dad; he sort of

Pennsylvania Historical and Museum Commission

A POLISH FAMILY OF PITTSBURGH, C. 1918

partook in it with me. She had an eighth-grade education, which at that time was a lot. My dad had a fourth-grade education in Poland.

"When I got out of high school I was offered scholarships to colleges for both swimming and football, but we were in pretty dire need in 1936; we couldn't even raise money for clothes. Let's put it that way. I remember once going for a job at Pittsburgh Railways. I went down there and put in an application, but as soon as they looked at the 'ski' on the back, they tore it up right in front of me and said, 'We'll call you if we need you.' And that sort of stuck with me all my life. It seemed that being a Pole and a Catholic hurt you in some places. That stuck with me. I eventually got a job, but I think you really had to prove yourself. They really give you the 'dirt,' so to speak.

"As I said, my father's business went bankrupt, and we lived very meagerly. But we lived. To this day I don't eat potatoes, because we ate them in every way, shape, and form—bread and everything else—just to keep us going. But we never took nothing from anybody and we managed. We managed. When I tell my kids today about eating meat maybe once a week or once a month, they laugh. But that was the case. But we pulled through it.

"As a youngster here I worked at the Boys' Club in the bowling alley. It wasn't much; it was something. It was enough to keep you in lunches at school. That was in 1928. Here at the Boys' Club I was setting pins downstairs. Then later on, through athletics in high school, I got a job with the meat-packing company, Armour's, who wanted coaches in swimming for the summer. I turned it [earnings] all over to my parents. Then when I needed money I got some back.

"This Boys' Club was more or less the home. I mean, it may sound odd now, in these days, but we did our homework here in the library because it had heat. We took our showers here because we didn't have hot water at home. And from being around the club here—of course I'm a member of this club now, since 1928—they asked if I would like to make a few extra dollars a week. And the man who is now dead—he's been dead for quite a long time—he had given me a job down in the bowling alley.

"I started working regularly for a real estate company in town, and I was clearing titles there before I went into the army. I did that and then I lifeguarded in the summer.

"For a while I wanted to go and have a military career. I had contacted a congressman about an appointment for the military academy. But I never took the test. Things were so bad at home—that was in 1936—that I couldn't leave. My dad had died by then and my mother was alone. Both my sister and my brother were younger. Maybe we look at it different now, but family life was instilled with you, and I tried to do something for my family.

"After I come out of the service back in 1946, I aimed for my own business, like my dad's. I think back in my mind then that I made up my mind that the way things were, the only way you were going to get anywhere [was to] do it yourself. I thought my quickest way to achieve anything was just going out and do it yourself. Picking yourself up by your bootstraps, and maybe failing once or twice, but going ahead and doing it.

"I never thought of leaving my neighborhood. I never gave it a thought because I figured I had obligations. Things were tough. They were very different then. They were tough. And I figured that was my obligation. They had helped me, and I was going to return it.

"I was raised in the Depression and any sensible person could see you had just so much, and that was it. There was nothing you could do about it. You had to make do. You couldn't go out and rob somebody, or something like that. You did with what you had, and I think even though we didn't have much, we had ties that kept us together. I consider we had a good life, a close-knit life.

"I wasn't urged to work so much. I did that on my own. In fact, they [Ray's parents] worried a little bit when I worked so late here. They thought that maybe my studies were being neglected, but they weren't. And they didn't want me to do that.

"I remember when the [college] recruiter come to the house. I mean I know [it] really broke my parents' heart that I couldn't go. But I think I'm the only kid from Schenley [High School] that graduated with a different suit. I mean I had to borrow pants and a coat to graduate. And I mean I just couldn't leave 'em. In fact, when I was gonna go away to school, you still needed money, and that was a commodity we didn't have. That hurt them quite a bit: that they couldn't supply me with money to go away to college.

"Then when I went back to work for Armour's I was making good money, I was making twenty-five dollars a week. But I turned it all over. They would give me some to spend if I needed it. I mean we didn't spend it foolishly, you know. You went to a show once in a while, or something. Of course, shows were cheap. And maybe get a milkshake after the show. That was the extent of it. My brother and sister started working when they were fifteen. My sister went to work at the hospital as a candystriper. My brother worked with a man that was a gardener. When I come back from the service I began keeping a portion of my wages and started saving to get married.

"My dad lost his house in 1929 and that had put me in debt. He lost everything in the 'Crash.' He couldn't make the payments and was quite in debt to the Polish Falcons on the South Side. They had helped him get started in business and, of course, after he died we had to pay that. It's taken a number of years till we paid them all off. We've paid our debt completely to them, which to me is a rarity because once somebody's died the debt's gone. But my mother would have nothing of it. She just scrimped and saved and paid them off. That was for his business, not for the home he had lost in the 'Crash' of 1929. We didn't pay that off, I guess, until after I come back from the service. We paid that debt off. We used to pay so much a month to the Polish Falcons.

"My dad brought me up to the Boys' Club and started me. The dues at that time were a quarter a year. And it may sound silly, but we had to pay in installments. I became very active here—swimming, basketball, and at that time we played mushball. The fellas, they drew their people from as far as the bridge—Sixty-first Street and as far as around Twenty-second Street. And it was a mixture of ethnic groups—Slavic, Polish, predominantly Polish. They probably came here for the same reason I did. I mean we had heat and light here. We did our homework here. This library was well staffed; they had a librarian that'd help us with our homework. And, of course, we had the opportunity to take showers. They had very dedicated people. The people back in those days didn't make money in the way of salary the way these fellas are making [it] today, but they were very dedicated. They tried to do things for you. They tried to get you jobs. I made a remark earlier, 'I guess I was the only one who graduated in 1936 with a different coat and a different pair of pants.' Well, I had the pants, but here at the Boys' Club Mr. Baughman got the coat for me from a relative so I could graduate in style. But they did things like that. And at Heppenstalls and McCormick [local factories], they went out of their way to try to help these people. They worked with the churches; they worked with the schools. There was a different atmosphere. Now they call it professionalism. Back then it was just dedication. People didn't make money, they didn't make much money, but they did an awful good job.

"The club even had a band in 1932. They took us to Camp Trees, and we worked at the camp. I came here faithfully until the war, and then, of course, I was gone for four years. When I came back I went back to the club, and after I got married and started raising a family I brought my children here.

"The club started in 1923 down at Twenty-eighth Street. They had their regular program of athletics and the pool and different games upstairs for the small ones. They started Christmas programs back in the Depression when you didn't get much for Christmas. They received a lot of apples and little gifts from merchants. Now, of course, the kids just look at an apple or an orange, but back then that was a big thing to us. And when they had a lot of athletic events it was their way of keeping us clothed. Instead of giving trophies out they would give us merchandise certificates for a pair of pants or shoes, which meant more than a trophy. I also played water polo there and for the first time could really travel. If I went on a streetcar to McKees Rocks it was a big deal. Through water polo

I went to New Haven; Fort Worth, Texas; and Florida. Without that, I know I wouldn't have got around. Most of us never were out of Lawrenceville. But the club scrounged around for some money. People like Heppenstalls and McCormick and other industrialists footed the bill for us.

"This Boys' Club—it's a little different now—took an awful lot of interest in you. They tried to do many things. A lot of people that work in these mills today, like Heppenstalls and National Valve, all got jobs coming out of the Boys' Club. The club would send them down to the plants. Those that are working now or in retirement got their jobs through Frank Baughman, who was the athletic director and who had contact with these companies. I don't think it was cut out to be an employment service, but that's what it turned out to be because a lot of people through his efforts got jobs. He hac the contact with the company directors and other people who had money. .\e'd say to them, 'Oh, I got a boy that needs a job.' They would tell him to send them down. They usually got a job. Even when girls wanted a job in the area, a local merchant might call up the club and ask what kind of brother she had. The would ask about the family she came from; that was the main recommendation."

MARIA KRESIC*

In the immigrant household of Maria Kresic, personal enterprise coexisted with family dominance over individual pursuits. Maria's brother became a physician. Maria labored throughout her life among Slovenes in Steelton, Pennsylvania—not for herself, but for the benefit of her kin.

"My father couldn't read or write, but you couldn't fool him on anything. We had a butcher business in Steelton. We had a wagon that used to go around loaded with meat, and the ladies would come and get their meat. They would tell him what they wanted the next day. They wanted rice or beans or macaroni. He would come home and tell my mother everything. He could figure out interest faster than I could. He couldn't read or write anything, but he had a head for business. He owned seven houses at one time in Steelton.

"There are ten of us in our family, five boys and five girls. My brother will be eighty-five in December. He went to grade school and then he went to high school, one of the first boys of the foreigners to go through high school. Then he went to medical college. And I had a sister who was a nurse. He [Maria's brother] went to college in Philadelphia, and he finished at the University of Maryland. It was unusual at that time for a young boy

*Name changed at the request of the respondent.

growing up in a mill town of immigrant parents to think that early about going to medical college.

"[It] was unusual [for him] to go to high school. My dad was made a fool of when he sent that boy through high school. They [the Slovenian people] thought he was crazy. 'He should have gone to the mill to work,' they said. [They said my dad] was crazy for sending him to school. 'Why didn't he send him to get some money, go to the steelworks,' they said. I guess [my dad] thought, 'I didn't go to school, [but] this guy is going to go.' My sister was a registered nurse. She was the first nurse of foreign people. She died of a heart attack.

"The next older brother, he lives out on the farm, Frank Kresic. He has got a big farm out there. He never worked in the mill. He was too young. We went out on the farm.

"We lived in Steelton and then sold that butcher business on the West Side and went to Reading. My dad found all kinds of business opportunities. Somebody told him about this hotel in Reading, and we moved out there. My brother, this one on the farm, was just a little kid. He was beginning to crawl. We lived there a short time. Then [my dad] came back to a farm near Steelton.

"My father thought he would like the farm better than anything else. My mother was very happy there too. My father had it [the farm] for a long time. Then, when he had a stroke, my brother bought it from him. He took over. It's still there. It's terribly old, [a] terrible-looking place. My dad used to keep that place spic and span. Us girls had to work out in the field. I worked out in the field just like a man. But he don't care. He don't give a darn. I guess it's pretty well fixed by this time. He could sell it for a fortune.

"I went to St. Mary's Croatian School. But my father told me to get married. 'You don't need no schooling,' [he said,] which was a big mistake because I loved school. I was crazy about school. So he took me out when I was twelve years old and I never went to school after that. None of my sisters finished high school. The one was a nurse, but she didn't finish high school. She got into nursing school in Philadelphia—St. Joseph's Hospital.

"There was a friend of my mother's. She had six boarders, five children, and was expecting another baby. She had a running sore on her leg. So my mother and father pitied her. So I got out of school to help her. They had a grocery store, too and a boardinghouse. The man had a horse and he used to haul wood and sell wood. You did anything to make a living in those days. It wasn't easy. So I worked there and helped her peel potatoes for sixteen boarders. I was paid a dollar a week, but gave it to my mother.

"My daddy didn't even want me to marry my husband. My dad said, 'You marry that Croatian guy, I won't give you a penny,' [and] he didn't give me a penny. But I didn't care because I got along anyhow. He had a

Slovenian picked out for me. You know how in Europe they pick your husband and your wife. So he had a guy picked out for me, and this guy [after he married] lived up here with his wife and used to make moonshine. And if she didn't make enough moonshine until he got home from the steel plant during the night, he beat her. She's up in the state hospital. He is dead.

"I told him if he don't let me marry him, I was going to run away and marry him. I said, 'My boyfriend has a priest that's a friend in Cleveland, and we are getting married there.' My son-in-law's father is Croatian and his mother is Slovenian. His mother was the first girl that married a Croatian, and man what a mess that was! They eloped.

"After that I was married, but my husband couldn't work. There was a strike and my husband worked at the furnaces in the steelworks. He didn't want to strike [in 1919]. My husband just stayed out, I think, for two days and then he went back to work. He didn't care about the strike. He wasn't interested in no strike. When promotions came around they kept him back a little bit, but he came to be a foreman before he died.

"When I was young I just wanted to go to school. I cried when my daddy took me out of school. I was good in mathematics. I still have a prayer book that I got for having the highest average in school. I still have that prayer book, which is about I guess 1911 or something like that, maybe before that. I liked school, I wanted to go to school. But Pop was the boss. But my mother collected all the money. He [Maria's father] gave it to her. She took care of it because she was good with figures. My mother could run a business good.

"My husband came here when he was sixteen, from Croatia. He was four years older than me. I was born in 1896. So he was born in 1892. That means he would have come here about 1909, approximately. He came from Karlovac.* Lots of Croatians came from that Karlovac area. He came to make a living because he couldn't get along with his half-brothers. They couldn't stand him because he was a half-brother. Later his half-brother came to Steelton and boarded there. It was hard to get a job right then, but he got a job. I think for a while he worked somewhere in the open hearth. Then he got a job in the steel foundry, where he stayed till he died, about twenty-four years.

"When my husband did work he never wanted to leave the mill. It was a good job as far as he was concerned. He was a 'first helper.' Just before he died they made him a foreman, and then he didn't work for several years. It was hard to buy coal, you know, and everything else. So he would take walks over on some wooded land owned by the steel company and collect firewood. But the people got greedy and even took planks from a bridge on the property. People still needed wood, but the company said no more wood could be taken.

*Karlovac is a region of Yugoslavia.

Eleutherian Mills Historical Library

A STEELTON PLANT, C. 1910

"We bought our house in September and our child was born in November of 1922. There was no place to rent. My husband had lived with
them before we were married. My husband and I lived with that family—
it was only a husband and wife—until after my first baby was born. My
first baby was premature and the doctor advised us to move out to the
country to raise her. I lived out there until we found a house to rent across
the street here. Then we rented somewhere else, but it had no electric
lights. We finally bought the home because I was tired of moving and carrying oil lamps up and down steps.

"I also spent a lot of time working for the Croatian church. I would
sell tickets and collect money from house to house. Sometimes I would
work a week or two preparing for bazaars and banquets. To get food for

our banquets the milkman would give us a truck and we would go from house to house and collect potatoes and cabbage. One entire day would be spent scouring knives and forks. Then we would carry baskets of dishes from other churches. After the banquets we would spend several days cleaning up the place. I know how I worked.

"My husband was a guy who never stopped for a drink after work. During a flu epidemic all the saloons were closed. If you drank whiskey and tea you weren't supposed to get the flu. I was expecting my second baby and my husband went to get me a bottle of whiskey. But you needed a prescription. So this neighbor of ours—he was an 'American'—gave my husband a sheet of paper and told him to go to this distillery and shove the paper in a window. I know it was no prescription, but we got two quarts of whiskey. It helped to know someone like him; everybody knew this man. You should have seen how big his funeral was! In fact, so many died from the flu that they just rang the church bells; they didn't dare take him into the church.

"I don't know which department my husband worked in first. Then he went to the steel foundry. Somebody knew the foreman. He was working around the furnaces. They got an electric furnace. That was the first one in Steelton, and my husband was taught to run that furnace. And they wanted to send him to Chile, in South America, to run the furnaces there. He wanted to go. Why? Because he would get three hundred dollars a month if he went there, and here he wasn't making nothing. So I said, 'All right, you go. But I go along with you.' 'Oh you can't,' he said, 'because they live in terrible places.' So then he told his boss that I said no. That I won't let him go unless he takes us all along. And heck, I have three kids by that time. So they sent me a book. And these guys were living on stilts; the houses were up on stilts, you know. I don't know if it was on account of snakes or what. I don't know why. It was a terrible-looking place. They didn't have planes in those days. It [would have] took him three months to get there from here. He did not go. He said, 'Mary, we could get ourselves out of debt and everything.' It [their house] didn't look like it does now. It was always painted white. It was a beautiful little house. He said, 'We can get out of debt and all.' 'I don't care about the debt,' I said. If you go, then we all go.' Then he said, 'No, I don't go. Suppose one of the kids get sick and dies.'

"He was forty years old when he died. He had ulcers and he had a bum heart. The doctor said he had rheumatic fever. How should I know what they had in Europe? They didn't go to a doctor for everything. They were so far from doctors they almost died. They later told me he had a leaking valve in his heart; then he got ulcers and died on May 5, 1933.

"I had four kids in school. The youngest was in the first grade and one girl was a sophomore in high school when he died in May. They took me on public assistance at forty dollars a month for all five of us. Then I got a letter that I had to pay that all back—four hundred twenty-eight dollars. What was I going to pay it back with? So I got a job the year my girl graduated in 1935. I got a WPA job sewing for the people who were on assistance and welfare. Since there were only two of us who knew how to cut patterns, I had to do that, even though it meant standing on my feet all day long. I was cutting and cutting all day for the rest of the girls to sew. They were sitting at the sewing machines.

"My daughter graduated in June and in November got a job at a program for the unemployed, like mine. But one of my neighbors reported that one of us already had a job and that there was enough income coming into our house. I remember my forelady walking past me with this pink slip in her hand. I said, 'Miss Gaffney, I know you have bad news. You might as well just tell me.' 'Mary, I don't want to get you out of here,' she said. 'What am I going to do if you leave?' She knew that I was back in my taxes and said, 'I don't know how you are going to make out.' When my daughter came to work the boss asked her why she didn't look happy. She said, 'My mother had to quit; they fired my mother because I'm working.' Her boss then found out that one of our neighbors reported that we were both working. That was that. We lived awhile on what she made.

"I finally got a job working for the state as a dishwasher in a cafeteria. If you think that was easy, I cried for two weeks. Every night [when] I went to bed my shoulders ached. They didn't have aluminum things to put the dishes on like they have now. They were wood. When they were soaked with steam and water and you pulled them out they were so hot you thought your insides were coming out. One day there was a colored man sitting nearby fixing a fan. He said, 'Lady, I want to ask you something if you don't mind?' He asked me if I had a political job and I told him that I did. 'That's a job for a nigger,' he said, 'not for a white woman.' It was so hot in that job that by eight o'clock in the morning my girdle was wet. I was wet all day, summer or winter. My doctor finally told me to get out of there; so I had to quit. After that my son-in-law, God bless him, got me a job at the courthouse as a cleaning woman from four to ten at night. I worked there for ten years.

"Before my husband died I did work for a little while in a coat factory in Harrisburg for four dollars a week. There were so many women working that you had to stand in line to get a piece to sew on. Sure as there is a God in heaven, I'll never forget the time two women (one was Italian and the other was Jewish) were grabbing and fighting for the same coat. My husband was out of work for three years at that time. We got into a hole so bad we couldn't pay our taxes. We did have a big garden and raised most of our food. I canned all my stuff. Sometimes there was as high as nine hundred jars in the cellar. We even had peach trees and I canned my own fruit. That's how we got along."

Part II
THE ENCLAVE:
A WORLD WITHIN A WORLD

*There was no such thing as public
assistance, no such thing as welfare.
You were on your own. [But] you
had [the help of] other people. You
sort of worked in a cooperative
thing.*

Joe Rudiak, Lyndora

As seen in Part I, the workers' world was built on two pillars: the family and the workplace. But work and family were not distinct categories or mutually exclusive spheres of activity. Rather, they gave rise to a complex phenomenon known as the enclave, a "community" born of the shared experiences of family life and toil. The ultimate objectives of workers were not determined by any one variable alone, such as power in the workplace. On the contrary, life goals were shaped by the subtle and intricate influences of the enclave.

Enclaves emerged wherever industrial workers and their kin congregated. It is important to remember, however, that these communities were not identical in nature. They grew up around such bases as race, ethnicity, skill, or shared economic status. The one characteristic they did share was their tendency to be circumscribed, cut off from social and political influences, from those of higher social rank and even from other workers. American historians have long recognized the fissures and factionalism of the industrial working class, but few have acknowledged the existence of the enclave; few have seen it as a common experience that fostered community- rather than class-based behavior, or as a kind of loyalty based on the knowledge that limitations existed on what was obtainable from the larger society.

In the recollections that follow we find numerous illustrations of the intimate link between family and work. Many children learned skills from their parents and other relatives. Lee Roy Hohrlacher's father introduced him to carpentry on the job at a coffin factory. Stanley Salva acted as a laborer for his father, a contract miner; when his father became too old to mine, Salva changed places with him. John Parraccini, a newcomer from Italy, found a job with the help of friends of his father who were already in America. Moreover, entrance into the workplace conferred an important status at home. Tom Luketich's father allowed him to smoke only after he "came of age" by securing regular employment. And Louis Heim's words convey the loss of self-esteem he felt when he was prevented from supporting his family: "I think Roosevelt's program saved the self-respect and the sanity of a lot of men."

It should not surprise us to learn that many workers measured the value of their lives in terms of their families and kin more than on the basis of their daily toil. Industrial work was generally routine and menial; it was seldom self-satisfying. Most of the workers whose thoughts are presented here were pulled into the unskilled jobs that were multiplying rapidly as corporate managers sought to exert their control over the workplace

Library of Congress

"Two Women," Shenandoah, Pennsylvania, 1938

by diffusing skilled tasks and breaking up the production process into simple but separate tasks. Joe Rudiak points out that some of the immigrants who worked around him were skilled violin- and furniture-makers who had no choice but to work on a production line building boxcars. This trivialization of skills forced laborers to find satisfaction outside their work—in their families and communities—and, along with an erratic economy, contributed considerably to the continual transiency so many workers experienced. Rudiak began working on flat railroad cars, moved to boxcars, and later joined a labor gang. Tom Luketich hand-loaded coal, worked on track, ran a mine locomotive, and became a fire boss during a career that never took him from the mines.

Moving within the intricate confines of occupation, family, and community, workers were understandably preoccupied with the immediate concerns of day-to-day living. The larger society that surrounded them seemed beyond their influence. Every time they moved beyond the invisible boundaries of their world they were reminded that invisible boundaries were nevertheless real, that their ability to influence and penetrate the world outside the enclave was severely limited.

The limitations of the workers' world were felt most keenly, though not exclusively, in the workplace, where workers continuously faced arbitrary authority. Jacob Light relates how a "corrupt pusher boss" tried to exploit him at a Lebanon steel plant, and John Sarnoski explains that it was necessary to maintain a favorable relationship with the foreman if a miner hoped to work where coal was most accessible. Some men actually paid for better jobs. Joe Sudol lost his job for nine months when he refused assignment to a location that was so filled with dust that it threatened further damage to his lungs. Treatment at the workplace was often so unfair that it became an issue that not only threatened worker security but obscured the formulation of larger social and economic goals. Several of our respondents recalled the vigorous attempt of anthracite miners in 1935 to end the blatant collusion between local union officials and mine operators, a relationship that rested on rigged elections, undisguised favoritism, and a splintered work force. Such internal strife underscored not only the workers' intense desire for secure, steady work but the ability of managers to exploit elements of the workers' culture. It also suggests that although some workers agitated for fair treatment and greater control over the operations of the workplace, many attempted to ensure their security by cooperating with those who were more powerful. Contrary to the arguments of many labor historians, workers' control of the workplace did not mean the same thing to all workers. In Glen Lyon, Joe Sudol reveals, miners obtained a production limit for years, not in order to challenge owner authority at the workplace but ultimately to make their jobs last longer.

In industrial towns and neighborhoods, however, the pattern of limited power and halting gains for workers and their kin persisted. Joe Rudiak claims that during the 1930s many of his friends did not even have sufficient connections to get WPA jobs. Many were simply blackballed from a town or plant if they spoke out on behalf of controversial subjects such as unions. According to Steve Kika, it was so difficult for steelworkers to organize in McKeesport in 1919 that "Jesus Christ wouldn't be able to come down here and let you have a meeting."

Forced to rely on their own resources, workers built complex enclaves that revolved around community as well as family and occupational networks. John Czelen remembers well the support rendered by working-class shopkeepers during difficult times in Monessen. Others recall groups of families banding together to build homes, distribute food, and, as in Glen Lyon, attempt to keep workers from other towns from gaining employment in their locale. Community weddings and picnics further strengthened the sense of group attachments. Weddings were not only times for celebration but were the rare occasions when food and drink were plentiful. Miners relished picnics and games where men competed to see who could drill through rocks the fastest. Not surprisingly, workers who were forced to leave the enclave during particularly hard times often came back as soon as they could. Tom Luketich, Joe Sudol, Stanley Salva, and John Sarnoski all relate instances of returning to the coal mines as quickly as they could after being forced to work elsewhere.

JOE RUDIAK

Industrial workers were forced by numerous factors continually to relocate in order to obtain work and make ends meet. Joe Rudiak, who grew up in a Polish family, here documents the transiency of working-class life and the realities of living in a company town such as Lyndora, Pennsylvania.

"My father came from Poland in 1900 and began working as a miner near Berwick, Pennsylvania. Then we moved to Lyndora, near Butler, where he worked for Standard Steel Car Company. He did physical labor, very hard work. It was building freight cars, fabricating freight cars. He worked in the paint shop. He painted cars, and did odd jobs, mostly in the paint department.

"We lived in company houses owned by the Standard Steel Company, and each one of these—we'll say it was six apartments—were all frame and painted red. And at that time there was a shortage of housing because there was a need for labor, hard physical labor, and there was [many laborers,] all mostly from the Eastern part of Europe—the Poles, Slovaks, Yugoslavs, the Serbian people. [This labor force] even touched the Middle

East. It was a ghetto. They had, lined up for let's say about half a mile and about five hundred feet deep, rows of these shanties. We called it shanties. As high as five, six, seven boarders would come in. They had to find places for 'em. So here they'd come in from their hometown; one pulled the other in, for instance, to house him until they'd be able to find something. And you take in our family—let's see, the last boy, Stanley, was born possibly in this shanty. There was nine [of us] and as high as four boarders. Mostly it was all relatives and folks from home [Poland].

"It was sort of a stopover point. They would work in the car shop; some of 'em could take it; some of 'em couldn't take it. And they were seeking other accommodations as far as rooms and better working conditions [were concerned]. And they would scatter some. This was more of a stopover point for 'em. They didn't know it, but the first thing you know, the man would leave, and he would be in Chicago or working in a steel mill in Cleveland or Detroit. Detroit was [getting] active then as far as the automobile industry was concerned. And they were mostly moving from one city to the next, more or less like migrant labor. And that was it. So then another one would move in until finally the Depression came along. And there was no such thing as boaders at that time.

"They had a public school. The Standard Steel people that lived in these particular shanties went to the Butler public schools. And the people that lived across the street that belonged to the township, they went to the township schools. And there was no such thing as parochial schools. They did not provide much as far as schooling was concerned.

"I would say the population living in Lyndora and the shanties right across the street—made up of all the ethnics, a few Germans, a few Italians, no Irish, and no English—was about three thousand including the children.

"It was very rare that anybody from that section of Butler, or that suburb of Butler, up to 1925, would graduate from high school. I would say in that period of time up to about 1929 that about eighth grade, elementary school, was normal for a person to stop going to school.

"The children would work or they would be unemployed and leave town to seek other employment, such as [in] Detroit, which was becoming very popular with the automobile industry.

"I quit high school because I became sick and [then I] went to work. My oldest brother was sort of crippled. I don't think he went to work till he was about seventeen or eighteen years of age, that's the oldest brother. The next-to-the-oldest brother went to work about nine years of age, in the glassworks. There was also glass plants where they employed child labor and all that. So my brother was about nine years old, and it was quite common.

"My brother John worked before he was sixteen years of age. He worked in the coal mines, in the hard-coal region. See, now we're going into the

period before we reached Butler. The family [consisted of] four brothers
and my mother and father in the hard-coal region. At that time we were
living compactly, with boarders, working twelve hours or fourteen hours a
day. As far as communication [was concerned,] it was almost impossible
for the parents to talk to the children. As far as the parents' backgrounds
were concerned, you had to get it from somebody else, particularly the
boarders. Maybe when he was sick, and stayed home from work, he would
say, 'Well, your dad was here.' And I'm picking up his background today,
what type of a fella he was in Poland, and the mother's background, which
they didn't communicate with us because they were very, very busy, you
know. But most parents didn't have the time to communicate with their
children. It was 'Go to work, whatever it is,' and 'You're a tough guy. You'd
made a good man in the steel mill. You'd make a good provider.'

"And of the things my mother insisted on, education (as far as elementary school was concerned or high school) was one of them. Mother insisted, with a few other families, at least to educate us [in] our own native
tongue and [in] writing [at the] language schools. They formed language
schools through the churches. And that was a must with most families.
That was a must. I don't know why they did it. I guess it was on account of
their background, [their] loneliness and everything for their own countries.
And my mother insisted that we all become musicians. And that's what
happened; seven of us became musicians and played instruments. Every
day—about two hours every day—there was catechism. And during the
summer months we had to attend school. During school vacation we had
to attend the language schools. The Polish church was a good distance
away. There was the problem of shoes, clothing, and weather conditions
and all that. And sure we were down a good distance away also from the
public school. Mother insisted that we go to the Greek [Orthodox] church;
they had the language school. When they had a problem of not having any
money, we joined the Ukrainian Orthodox. So I've learned how to speak
Ukrainian, but it wasn't my mother's tongue. It meant another language,
which came in very handy.

"We celebrated various holidays together. We did it as musicians, you
see, in our family. And different churches went out caroling, and they
gathered money for support of the band and their cultural activities. And
this was done during Christmas. We each had costumes of our own native
lands. You know, the Slovaks had [boys dressed as] sheep herders going
from house to house singing. The women would have embroideries of different colors. It was beautiful, beautiful, made out of linen. It was all hand
made and they're still in existence, and they're still carried on in many,
many places.

"Since we went to the Ukrainian school, [we kids spoke Ukrainian.
And] my mother spoke very good Ukrainian and my father spoke good

Ukrainian because he spoke it in Europe. So there was no problem as far as learning the language [was concerned,] because you got to repeat [it] at home after you came from elementary school. But when the Polish friends would come in, then it was Polish language. It just happened that most of them lived around their own churches, tried to get as close as possible to their social activities. And the church was part of their social activity.

"We didn't join American organizations though. There was no drive on among the nationality people, no drive on by the politicians. You've got to understand that they didn't want these people to vote in the first place. The companies controlled the towns. They controlled the courthouse. They controlled the police. They controlled the state police, the coal mine police. There was no encouragement for people to vote up until the Depression. I would say [that] even then, among the immigrants, every one of them that came into this country had the feeling that they were going back. And once they would take their citizenship here, they were breaking up their ties with their home countries. That was a cruel thing, that they were never able to get enough money to do it. And they were still communicating with many people in their home country. You know, they'd have people coming in a year later, two years later, and they'd say, 'Well, how's things there? Are they better? Nothing new? No? Well, that's the reason I'm here.' So about 1934 was when people would start to talk about voting. 'Let's change the system. Let's change...' It was always strictly Republican. Still, people were beginning to see it, and it was still dangerous then, so they were not encouraged.

"Things were real bad in 1919. Well, my father was blacklisted in 1919. There were at least six of us at that time, six children. He was blacklisted on account of he was a stool pigeon. I was telling you that he was a very frank person. He couldn't read or write. And with his background that he had in Europe, he worked in the coal industry and the toughest jobs. And when he came into this country, he didn't know the danger of saying the word 'union.' So these steel companies, we found out they supported taverns, beer gardens. And there was conversation of different things going on. My father, I guess, was asked, 'How do you feel about the union and all that?' And he stood up and he says, 'I'm one hundred percent for it!' And then he was blacklisted.

"After the steel strike came along, we were thrown out of the company house. And with the help of his friends that were union-minded and all that, they built us a house. They built us a house—well, while the strike was on, it didn't take too long—they built this thing and about five families lived in about five rooms.

"All these families were blacklisted. And so Father was out of a job and you could say the entire family was blacklisted. Well he was blacklisted in 1919, and we just couldn't make it any more. We moved from

Lyndora to Coplay, Pennsylvania. There was a car shop there. I don't know whether it was a pressed-steel car works. The entire family moved there. We moved into a company house there also. I was about ten years old; I was in the third grade of school. And there was four of 'em working. And these jobs were gotten by friends from his home town. And they settled there. He worked there for about six months, and he was blacklisted there, the entire family [was]. So we came back home to the old homestead in Lyndora, about 1922. And Father had to go out, and he went to the coal mines to work in Butler. He'd get up about four o'clock in the morning with his two sons, John and Charlie, and load coal knee deep. [He would get] back about eight, nine. No transportation of any kind. And [they were] nonunion mines because the mines had lost their strike. And through the help of other people, Father was able to at least feed us. Mother had a garden. And this was up until 1929. There was a real demand for labor and all that. By that time three or four of us brothers became musicians, and we became popular in the community. And we were able to slip back into the stream, the mainstream. Wally got into the American Rolling Mill as a laborer, very hard work. My brothers were able to get into the wheel works, two of them. I got into Standard Steel, [but] just about that time things closed up and the Depression began.

"And as far as the Depression was concerned, everybody was unemployed, particularly in this community. The children and all, they were disappearing, going [to] seek work in [other] places. Whole entire families disappeared. They either went to Pittsburgh or Detroit, and then Chicago, and just drifted.

"It was very tough. You got to remember the war ended in 1919 or 1918. And in those communities—I guess it was all over the same—there was maybe four or five shoemaker shops. They bought army surplus shoes and sold 'em for a quarter or fifty cents. And this was the type of shoes that I had, no dress shoes of any kind. There was no such thing as a suit of clothes. There was patch-up things. And as far as food was concerned, there was what we were able to get out of the garden in the summer months. And we raised a few hogs and a couple of cows. And pasture was three dollars a year. You know, we watched the cows during the summer months. We had our milk, and we had our cream. And we had our hog for Christmas, and what little money that came in from Father working. There was no such thing as public assistance, no such thing as welfare. You were on your own. [But] you had [the help of] other people. You sort of worked in a cooperative thing. You didn't know it, you didn't realize it, but there was a lot of malnutrition, a lot of it. And every time I go back and hear [of] my buddies that were athletically inclined ballplayers, basketball players for their churches and fraternal societies [who] died at age thirty-two, thirty-five, of heart attacks, [I feel] that was due to malnutrition.

"You take influenza. Let's see, there was a flu that killed quite a few people in there in 1918–1919. And sanitary conditions weren't proper. The shanties were filled with cockroaches—nothing unusual. So as far as we managed, we were very fortunate because we were musicians, four or five of us at that time. We were able to go to weddings. Now, when you go to a wedding, there's got to be food. That was one of the compensations you got because you drank and had food. If you had one good meal a month, maybe that held you up. And this is how we existed.

"I don't know how we stuck it out. But I give credit to my mother, you know. We didn't leave town. We only made an attempt to leave that town for six months, and then we were thrown out of Coplay, Pennsylvania. But we decided to stick it out because I guess my father [was] not the type of fellow that [said], 'Well, look, I'm going to go to Chicago,' [or] 'I'm going to go to Detroit,' and different things. He was just not that type, and my mother was not that type. She figured her base was there; why should she move into another community? I don't know why they stayed there. And we were blacklisted up till the period of 1929, and then there was a short period of maybe five or six months' work and then finally the bottom dropped out. And then we went through a period of the Depression. And even the weddings had slowed up. The churches were falling apart, the social activities and everything. So we went hungry with the rest of them.

"One thing about government relief. It wasn't publicized among the ethnic community. We had no connections of any kind with the county courthouse. We had no connections at all with the politicians. They were all Anglo-Saxons out of this district, and the one that did represent the district was more or less in favor of the company and the Republican stronghold. Of a population of three or four thousand, only about three hundred voted. The ethnic people, up till today, you know, they don't want no welfare of any kind. And so they didn't go to the courthouse. They had to go to the courthouse to get county relief. It was the time Roosevelt got elected and then things started moving and there became public assistance. And this was the time that some of the people applied for public assistance, but they were very much in shame.

"Not too many worked in the WPA from this community. That was again controlled by the Anglo-Saxons. That was controlled, and the jobs went to people who were known and politically did the things that could help. But there was quite a few from the community with an ethnic background who went to the CCC [Civilian Conservation Corps] camps, quite a few of 'em.

"In 1929, I was hired at Standard Steel Company. I worked for a period of about two months. My job was on flat freight cars—[building them]. And you were practically on your back. It was a very easy job. We made six of those a day or four a day, and I made four dollars and twenty cents for a ten-hour day. And if you worked Saturday, it was straight time, but very seldom did you work on a Saturday. Finally this job was completed. The foreman sort of liked me, and he took me [aside] and said, 'Look, I have a job here where you could make eight dollars a day, now that this job is completed.'

"And I worked on a line where they were building twenty-seven box-cars a day. And all I had to do was put up two, three, four signboards, small signboards. [But] I didn't start on the line from the beginning, so I wasn't used to it. And I went over and finished about three cars, and I went over to the water fountain, got a cold drink of water, and I was passing out. And I told the foreman, 'I'm not coming back anymore.' And as I walked out—I was walking out of the plant—a labor foreman says, 'No, how about the labor gang?' I said, 'Sure!'

"So I worked in the labor gang. I was tamping ties, railroad ties, cement work, general labor which took me all over the plant into every de-

Eleutherian Mills Historical Library

A PENNSYLVANIA STEEL MILL, C. 1935

partment. So I worked there for about three or four months all over the plant. I was able to size up each department; I was curious and everything. And one day we were working at the erection department, where they're putting the car together, fabricating it together, and another day at the paint department.

"It lasted about—let's say the stock market crash came around 1929, I guess in November or somewhere in October, and about two, three weeks after that the place closed down. Everybody lost their jobs. So there was no work. I didn't get back to work at the plant again up till about 1936–'35 maybe.

"Well I always looked back to it. There were many 'hot jobs.' In this particular plant, that's putting steel into freight-car steel sheets. That had to be heated and from there, once it's practically white hot or cherry red, you know, above cherry red, then it's put into a press. And it's got to be hot; then it's put into the press. Mostly the Russians, people from Russia, worked there. And you had to be tough. You had to be tough. Then if you go into other departments, mostly it was broken down into nationalities almost. You take in the erection department—it was the hardest and noisiest and everything—it was mostly all Slavs. It was Polish and there was Slovaks and Lithuanians, not too many Lithuanians.

"And in order to get into this country—I'm not speaking about the women or anything—they were brought here according to their strength and bigness. I've seen men that were such giants that they picked up a freight-car wheel. And I've seen one person, 'Dulia,' that picked up a coupler of a freight car which weighed about four or five hundred pounds. These are the types of people they brought in. And the company employment agent's job was finding where he could fit this person. If there was a small person, he found a job for this small person. And you had to take a physical examination.

"Now you take if a Russian got his job in the shear department, and he's looking for a buddy, a Russian buddy. He's not going to look for a Croatian buddy and all that. And if he sees the boss looking for a man he says, 'Look, I have a good man.' And he's picking out his friends. In the erection department he's picking the fella he'd like to have. It wouldn't be a Ukrainian fella. And this is the way it was worked. The Russians would be in the Russian department probably. And it was a beautiful thing in a way.

"We only had a few blacks. They gave them the worst jobs, which paid little money and all that. It was sandblasting. If they sandblasted for six months, you had silicosis for the rest of your life. I didn't mention this: they had Greeks there too. Greeks, and also in the community of Shantytown there was quite a few families of Hungarian Gypsies. And they were musicians.

Author's personal collection

THE POLISH WOMEN'S FRATERNAL GROUP OF NANTICOKE, C. 1912

"Slavs did not become foremen, but they became pushers for a few cents more an hour. They were useful to the company because they were able to speak some of the languages. And they used them more or less to communicate. Some of the pushers couldn't even read or write, but they were able to communicate with the foreman. They were pushers and very useful to the community. And also, as far as craftsmen were concerned, they had the good jobs, we'll say in the pattern shop, or the carpenter shop; it was very, very quiet and cool working with wood. There was no ethnic people working in these places, although they were craftsmen too. These people were even able to build violins and build furniture. And they built their own violins and built their own guitars. Many who came into this country were craftsmen, but they were not put on [those] jobs. Some of them who were craftsmen lost their hand maybe, or lost their eye and lost their craft forever: painters, singers, beautiful craftsmen.

"As I explained, I was a musician during the Depression months. I became very popular. All of us brothers became popular, and we entertained anywhere they needed entertainment, like the Veterans of Foreign Wars, because during the Depression there still had to be entertainment. There was social activity; regardless of whether you were hungry, people still had to get together. That was a part of it. You still got to have, as I said, social activities. So we entertained the American Legion, Veterans of Foreign Wars, Knights of Columbus, and at high schools and dances and different things."

JOE SUDOL, JOHN SARNOSKI, AND ROMAINE STEWART

In the anthracite mines of Pennsylvania, men continually confronted the power not only of mine operators but of officials of the United Mine Workers of America as well. The reactions of rank-and-file miners to the various forms of authority they faced and to the demands of the workplace are delineated clearly here by three of those miners. Joe Sudol, born in 1905 to immigrant parents from Poland, became a miner like his father and brothers and eventually found his way to the mining community of Glen Lyon. John Sarnoski came to America at the age of nineteen and secured a job laboring for his brother-in-law, who was a contract miner. Romaine Stewart, born in 1912 to a Dutch father and a Scotch-Irish mother, began working at a breaker in Wanamie at the age of sixteen. Unknowingly, these three men all worked toward a common future in the Glen Lyon–Wanamie area.

Sudol: "My father had five sons and I was the second oldest. We all had to go to work in the breaker picking slate. Well, there was rock and coal coming down the chute. You had to pick the rock from the coal. There would be a fellow who would let so much coal come down in this section and then send it to another section where a group of boys would keep picking.

"There was a breaker boss and assistant foreman. They would watch you. If you let some rock go through [one] would poke you in the back with a stick and tell you what you missed. 'Get it all out,' [he'd holler]. Up on top someone would pick and cut big rocks before it went into the rollers. My older brother, Adam, was already in the breaker. After the breaker we both went to the mines to be 'nippers,' that is, to sprag cars. You put a stick of wood in the wheels to stop cars of wood coming from the mines. You couldn't let cars fall back down a grade into the mines. It would knock the timber down and you would have a mess. After three or four years of being a nipper you would become a motorman. Well, the motormen would supply the empty cars back to the miners to load again. But you had to work at least five years there as a laborer before you would become a miner. I labored longer than that though.

"When the West End [Coal Company] gave out I came to Glen Lyon and that's where I became a miner. I was doing mostly motorman work in Mocanaqua, but when I came to Glen Lyon I landed a job laboring for a while before I became a miner.

"It was not hard to get a job in either place. There was always an opening for work because they were always digging more [mine] openings. If one area caved in they would start a hole in a different section. Here in Glen Lyon they were digging into at least six different veins. We never ever took out the coal [that was hard to get], only what we could get the easiest.

"When I was a youngster a union organizer met my dad in Mocanaqua and asked him to go to West Virginia to organize the union down there. The organizer felt the best way to organize a union was to get a job and work in the mine so you could talk with the men. So he took my dad with him. We first moved into Glen White, [West Virginia]; they we moved to McCaulpin and then to Eccles and finally to Tams. At Tams the superintendent was the mine foreman and everything. He told my father to load his furniture and move out because he didn't want no union in there. My dad said, 'We'll organize the union whether you like it or not.' So he went over the hill to Eccles and organized the union over there.

Author's personal collection

WORK GANG AT A GLEN LYON BREAKER, C. 1930

"In Glen White the superintendent didn't want my father to leave, though, because he knew his timber work. That's what they liked. When he put up a set of timber it was done right.

"My father understood four languages and spoke Polish. That's the real reason they wanted him to work as an organizer. He understood Polish, Slavish [Slovak], Hungarian, and English. And there were a lot of Hungarians down there. When he spoke to the men he was welcomed in the homes.

"He came back to Pennsylvania because he didn't like working in soft coal. He felt there was more dust and [therefore] more explosions in the soft coal [mines]. We lived in one town and there was an explosion in the next one. I remember walking over the hill and [seeing] all those people who were killed laid out. What a smell from the explosion that burned them people. My father seen that and he figured, 'This is not for me. I'm going back to hard coal.'

"I then went into West End Coal Company and every one of my brothers followed me. Frank, George, and Mike came after me. Adam later left the mines and landed a job in a foundry in Berwick. My younger brothers went into trades. One became a cabinetmaker and another a plumber. My father was a carpenter before he came to America. Same with me. Before I came to Glen Lyon I was a carpenter around the mines. My father taught us carpentry. Even my grandfather was a carpenter, near the Russian border. But my father never forced me to go into the mines. I wanted to go. It was better than picking potatoes on the farms.

"We lived like one family. We turned our wages over and Mother took care of the money. She gave us our spending money or a dollar if we were broke.

"In Glen Lyon my father-in-law gave me a job as his laborer. We were working three-handed. You would have a miner and he would have two laborers. I labored with him for a while; then I had a chance to get with a miner and a single laborer—two-handed [work]. So I left my father-in-law. You could make a lot more money. But not that much because in Glen Lyon they had a car limit so you could only make so much. Where you would make your extra money is if you put up timber, props and stuff like that. In Mocanaqua you could make money because they would let you load as many cars as you want.

"They had a limit in Glen Lyon because the men wanted the mines to last longer. Susquehanna Coal Company ran it, but it was the union that wanted the car limit. It was not the coal company. They [the company] tried to break the limit but never really did before World War II.

"I was out of work for a while—the 1925 strike. I went to New Jersey and landed a job in a car shop. My godmother lived in Clifton and said, "If you want a job, Joe, come up here. I have a place where you can sleep and go look for a job.' The first job I landed was in a printer works. I went there and there were about thirty people waiting for jobs. When the boss arrived I asked him if he needed help. He asked if I had experience and I said I did. I had heard an 'old Polack' mention the word 'plinka machine' [meaning print machine]. So I said I had worked on a 'plinka machine' and he gave me a job turning the crank for a roller which rolled the paper after it went through water. After the strike I came back, though, because I didn't like the wages there. You were making more money in the mines.

"When I returned to Glen Lyon I never cared to become a section foreman. I was always contract mining, driving airways, proven holes. If they wanted to prove a vein they would send me in there to prove it. You take once we went out with the vein and we would find out how far it went and how thick it was. The engineer would send you up and tell you where to set your gangway. They'd give you a line, the laborer would mark it with chalk, and I knew then where to drill my holes. We never had any trouble with the fire bosses either. He would just tell you where he wanted a prop or a timber and you would just put it there. Section foremen would come in to see that the work was done. When a boss told you to do something you did it. As long as you did what you were told, there was never any trouble.

"I remember once when they had me proving veins. Well, there was an old slope they called the No. 24 slope. That vein was very loose and shell-like. You didn't know where the bottom or the top was, there was so much coal there. I had to drive an airway and put props all around it. Then they wanted to drive breasts in there. They sent a man in there to work with me but he didn't know anything. So I went to see a man in Glen Lyon they called 'the drunk.' He drank a lot but he knew more about that vein than anyone else around, to tell the truth. He told me, 'Joe, be careful. Don't put too many [drill] holes in it because it will run away on you.' I knew then what I had to do. So then the company sent another man in, and he began to fire many holes. I told them not to keep firing or the vein would run away. About four days later the vein really caved in. So we had to start from the bottom and dig it all out; it all caved in ninety feet below. You just couldn't use as much powder on this one.

"I was mining in No. 6 shaft in Glen Lyon and they wanted me to go move a new vein—to see which direction [the vein] went and drive an airway. The general mine foreman told me, 'Joe, if you do that for me I won't forget you.' So he gave me a good job putting up headings. You could make more money.

"But then Red Harvey comes in and he needs another drill hole. He comes to me and [says] he needs me, that he heard about my work and [he] needs another hole down at No. 5 tunnel. I said, 'Mr. Harvey, I did that already here. Give somebody else a chance to do that. I've only got one pair of lungs and that kind of work is awfully dusty; it's pretty bad.' But because I didn't go he kept me out of work for seven months. This was around 1930. Then again I got a job back, but when it finished [after] nine months I was again out of work. He did that because I wouldn't go down to No. 5 tunnel. Well, my goodness, he was the big boss."

Sarnoski: "For four years I worked as a laborer. In 1924 I started with my brother-in-law in Glen Lyon, No. 6 colliery. But my brother-in-law was a big boozer; he would get the pay, drink, and not come home for two days. Then he said to me if I [didn't] go drinking with him I [wouldn't] have a job. He was making nice money, one hundred fifty dollars for two weeks. But he wouldn't keep me working steady. Sometimes I wouldn't get a shift when I came to work. The boss asked me, 'What the matter you no working steady?' I said, 'My brother-in-law fire me.' So boss said, 'Get your papers and I give you job as miner.' That's a miracle. I went to court-house on April 1, [1928]. It was a holiday,* [but I] got my papers. Solet-sky, the mine foreman at No. 6, went with me. He was European too, a good man. Some of the men were complaining though. One said, 'How come Sarnoski get a job mining? I've been here from Europe fifteen years and I still a laborer.' Soletsky said, 'I put him there, he gonna stay there.' Seniority didn't really matter then. You just had to know [the] foreman well or be a very good worker. I was a hard worker, even though I just came [from] Europe.

"I got married in 1937 and I thought it was good then to bring home a twenty-dollar pay for two weeks. The collieries weren't working all the time. You tried to get on any shift to load your cars. Some miners went home with little on their paychecks after expenses were deducted for powders and laborers.

"If you were out of work you'd go to a priest in Plymouth and you'd get a job. Even if you were in Glen Lyon he could help you because he was with the companies. He was a stockholder, I think. Some felt Father Lypinsky in Glen Lyon even kept the breaker open in Glen Lyon. It was a holy breaker because it was working six days a week and nobody in the country was working that much in the 1930s. 'That's gonna change some day,' people said, and the year after he died [1936] they shut the breaker down for remodeling. We were off for six months. In fact, I went back to Europe for four months. Most of the people thought that it was Lypinsky [who] kept it open because he had shares in it, especially when it closed for a while the year after he died. Lypinsky was pastor with St. Albert's, [the] Polish church.

"There used to be a lot of payoffs to foremen for jobs. Some men wanted to get a decent chamber [with easily accessible coal] on a good gangway. They would meet foremen in beer gardens on payday and pay them, buy them drinks. If you got a better place in the mines you could

*Miners were celebrating the anniversary of the establishment of the eight-hour day.

make more money. But you couldn't do nothing about it. If a boss didn't like you, you could lose your job. And the union leaders didn't fight it, because they were friendly with the company. Union leaders and local officials would be given the best jobs in them days. If you [were] a miner, president of a local and have two laborers, you could put your bedroom slippers on in the morning and just go and see how your laborers work. And you'd just give them orders what they gonna do and you came home. And you would get more pay than two miners did. This was true at Glen Lyon.

"The Glen Alden Coal Company had the most collieries in the valley. And in 1935 when the insurgent miners were active, they had a meeting at Glen Lyon. Frank Shifko of the UMW told the men to stay with the union and not go with Maloney.* Shifko said we would lose our jobs if Maloney would win. I said to myself, 'I might as well stick with my union.' The United Mine Workers was big at that time.

"What hurt is that the insurgents couldn't really succeed in Glen Lyon. The union had the iron hand on you. Even when the insurgents had meetings they found out if you attended. I remember one meeting at the Roosevelt School. One UMW official went through and [said] anybody attending that meeting would have no job. You [kept] your mouth shut and you had a job. Also, we were working fairly steady at Glen Lyon, and other collieries weren't. We didn't want to hurt that. So you're looking out for yourself and your family. The union and the bosses worked together. It was the union officers got the better jobs. At that time you were satisfied if you had a job. My roots was here so [I decided] I might as well stay here.

"The men at Glen Lyon were forced to go with the United Mine Workers. Men were for Maloney but you were afraid to say it. If you supported Maloney you would lose your job. The companies supported the union; they cooperated. You could put up timber and they wouldn't even pay you for it if they didn't like you. If they were against you they'd push you out, that's all. If you [spoke] out too much they put a stick-and-powder in your porch. The leaders of the union were always against Maloney for they had good jobs with the union and their local was getting one thousand two hundred dollars [part of the dues] from the district. We got a leader in Glen Lyon: Stanley Kisinski.† When you go for a job in Glen Lyon you have to see him. If you insulted the president of the local union you wouldn't get a job no place—even at another colliery. The companies would stick together. They would ask where you worked last [and] why you [left] your

---

*Thomas Maloney of Wilkes-Barre led a movement in 1934 and 1935 called the United Anthracite Miners, a group that attempted to split from the United Mine Workers, in part because the UMW was thought to be too closely tied to company officials to adequately represent the rank and file, and also because Maloney himself had personal feuds with UMW officials in District 1.

†Name changed at the request of the respondent.

job. They would call and tell you they didn't want you if they got a bad report.

"If you were president of the union local at Glen Lyon it was hard for anyone to run against you. My friend Joe Doris ran for president and they made him leave town. He had to move to Baltimore. That's the kind of union it was in Glen Lyon. Kisinski was [the] biggest guy in the union there. Nobody could beat him in Glen Lyon. One time the votes were counted and Kisinski lost; they [went] in the other room and [counted] the votes again and Kisinski [won]. I knew that good. At some of the elections at the union local they had ballots numbered and a list of numbers so that they could usually tell how you voted."

Sudol: "You had to attend the majority of union meetings if you wanted to run for office. If you never went to the meetings you never [knew] what [was] going on. They passed a ruling. You had to attend so many meetings to run. If there was a good man, they would go along with him, but the men were scared. If somebody would say a little too much, the first thing you know he would lose his job. John [Sarnoski] would know; he lost his job. Kisinski gave the foremen orders: 'We don't want that man.' "

Sarnoski: "So I had to go to another mine to work, and they wouldn't hire me. They blackballed me. Kisinski was president and if anyone ran against him he was out. They were like a bunch of 'Gestapos' in Glen Lyon."

Stewart: "In those days the president of the local union and the men on the grievance committee had the best jobs in the colliery. You would see them in the morning always talking with the mine foremen in the offices. That was true all over. If you wanted to get one of these committeemen on your side, all you had to do was 'sugar him up,' give him one of the better jobs in the mines, and he was your baby. If you were a union official and you were supposed to work seven or eight hours a day it would 'rain' several days a month. But you couldn't find them sometimes. The laborers they had working for them covered up; they wouldn't tell you where they were. If he didn't cover up he wouldn't have a job. That official might be gone home by 10:30 in the morning. His laborer stayed there until 2:30. You take the section foreman's book to the mine foreman and when it came back these union officials would have seven hours. So you'd raise hell about it. I was told more than once, 'You're lucky you got a job.' "

Sarnoski: "You know when they had the miner's convention and Kisinski was president, who would go? President, secretary, and other officials would go for two weeks. But then laborers would still load their cars and [the officials] would still be paid for loading so many cars a day even when they weren't there. And they got the best places in the mines, where the coal was easiest to load. So [Kisinski] was getting money from the local for the convention and when he came back he [was] gonna get paid just like he was working. Figure this out!"

Sudol: "At one time Glen Lyon had two locals [and] things were better. When you put in a grievance things were solved. They had one local for the outside men and one for the men in the mines. I remember good grievance men like Sam Somone. He was good. He'd say right to the boss, 'Buddy, you pay this man what he's got coming or this colliery doesn't work.' "

Sarnoski: "My buddy Joe Doris was running against Kisinski in the 1930s for president of our local. I could hear them counting the votes and I bet Doris was ahead three to one. Then you know what Kisinski done? He said [there] was too much noise in the hall and with a cop he took them over to the jail to count again. The next day he took the ballots to the district office and a week later they announced Kisinski had won. Figure this out! They wanted to count the votes at the district office. They didn't want the miners to see them. Doris had to move to Baltimore. He could have gotten a job here, but it would be in a hole with water where you couldn't stand it very long."

Sudol: "At Glen Lyon in the gangway sometimes you would have to load rock before you could get at coal or put timber up. The gangway was the main road going in. But the union limited you as to how many cars you could load. You could load only so much coal, so much rock, or put up so much timber. But the company complained that they wanted the limit broke so the miners could load more coal. The limit started to break [after World War II] when machinery came in. Other collieries didn't have a limit.

"The reason Glen Lyon had a limit on production is so the jobs would last longer because if you worked in a gangway you would only load four; if you worked in a breast you would load five and go home."

Sarnoski: "The company wanted to break the limit. Before that I would load only five cars, get eight dollars, and go home. If I loaded another five cars the company would pay me less so they [would] make more money on all the extra cars I would load. That's how they wanted to break the limit.

"Every colliery had its own rate sheet. At the Susquehanna Coal Company [in Glen Lyon] they paid more than they paid in Wanamie. The local union at the colliery determined the rates. In the contract they would specify what you got paid for each car loaded and for props. But if you didn't get it in the contract you wouldn't get paid."

Stewart: "During the Maloney strike [1934–1935] there was a lot of people that went to work and many were afraid to go to work. You brought insurgents in here. And the state police came in and they were just as bad as the ones that were called out on strike. The state police treated the people even worse than the ones that were trying to break the union. At Wanamie there was a lot of support for the Maloney union because the people got tired of United Mine Workers and what they were doing. The

United Mine Workers and the bosses were hand in glove. They were work-ing together. Maloney came in and tried to break that. Men were also mad that some collieries—like Glen Lyon—were working and others were not. They felt here was favoritisms and collusion between union and companies. I remember one Christmas I had two children and only two days' pay in my check.

"The insurgents never shut down the Wanamie Colliery, but they tried to shut it down. The thing was that those men who supported Maloney and those who supported the United Mine Workers, they were born and raised together. They were good friends. They [the insurgents] didn't want to stop you if you had the guts to go to work; they left you go, but they give you a good kick in the ass when you were going.

"I was fifty-fifty on Maloney. Some days I went to work and some days I didn't. If I could get away with it, I went to work. When you came home at night they'd be calling you 'bluebird' all the way up the street. You didn't know what to do. You would be called 'bluebird' or 'seal.' Like I

Author's personal collection

A MINER AFTER WORK, WANAMIE, C. 1937

say, I just turned my head the other way and went to work. The next day you'd go outside and you'd feel bad. There'd be one guy standing at the bottom of your steps and another standing down the road. Rather than run through them you would join them. A couple days after, if you wanted to go to work, the door was always open to go."

STANLEY SALVA

Born in 1905 to parents who had immigrated from Galicia, Stanley Salva first worked in the coal mines of Glen Lyon, Pennsylvania, at the age of thirteen and eventually played an influential role in the affairs of the United Mine Workers of America local there. In this account he relates how communities protected their jobs and he describes the intricate system of relationships that grew up between workers and local union officials. In Glen Lyon the effort to gain control over the workplace was not a simple struggle between labor and capital but involved union officials as well.

"I started working at the coal breaker at thirteen years of age. In those days if you weren't fourteen yet and started working you had to go to continuation school one day a week. You started picking slate. But when I was seventeen I drove mules in the mines. Sometimes I would put sprigs of wood under coal cars to slow them down. That was called 'nipping.' Eventually I started laboring at the Susquehanna Coal Company in Glen Lyon. The company was really owned by the M. A. Hanna Company in Cleveland. They owned soft-coal mines too. Around here they owned mines in Glen Lyon, Shamokin, and Nanticoke.

"You had to work hard but you didn't mind it because you were young and able. [For young men] it was a practice that as soon as you were old enough and strong enough you went into the mines and made money. That's what I wanted. Not many were concerned about leaving the community and going elsewhere. The only time people left was when they closed the breaker down for repairs in 1936 for six months. They put new equipment in the breaker in 1936. That's a time when lots of people left. Some went to Detroit to automobile factories. Some never came back.

"I labored for a long time with my father. You had to get mining papers to be a miner and you couldn't get them until you worked in the mines at least two years. Eventually my father got older and said to the boss, 'I will labor for my son now if you make him the miner.' I actually worked inside the mines for thirty years, and another twenty-five years outside the mines. My parents wanted me to stay in school longer than I

Pennsylvania Historical and Museum Commission

PICKING SLATE IN AN ANTHRACITE BREAKER

did. But you knew that they would be unable to afford your going to school and not working. You had to make your own money.

"In 1925 we were on strike. A few of us guys decided to go to New Jersey to get jobs for a while. I worked in a freight station in Patterson, where my aunt lived. But I came back [after the strike] because my mother and father were here. Even the company expected you would come back and work for them again.

"Once we started to work after 1925 it was steady. During the Depression, in fact, Glen Lyon kept on working. We worked so steady we were mentioned in Ripley's *Believe It or Not*. Yet in Nanticoke the same company didn't work a full week. They had a lot of slack time. Every once in a while we might have a day or two off. And the mines would never work on Polish holidays: Three Kings' Day, Christmas Day, and St. Joseph's Day.

The company never had no objection, although as time went on they didn't like it because they wanted to sell more coal. In other words people were pretty religious.

"In Glen Lyon the union local had put a limit on production. In order to distribute the cars evenly they kept it for a long time. For instance, if you had a good place to work [where coal was easily accessible], the company used to allow you to fill more cars because you could load faster. But that wasn't fair. So what we decided was you couldn't load more than was required for a normal day's pay. In most of the places it was five cars a day. In some gangways it was four. In easier places maybe you only had three as a limit. If you were over the limit you would pay a fine. We wanted everyone to have an equal load and pay. We had to watch that the boss might not let a 'pet' of his load more cars than the other guy and make the coal last longer.

"Hell, some bosses played favorites. They could give you better places to work, easier jobs. Every place in the mines is not alike. In some places you would have to work harder than in others to produce coal. A boss could get money if he did you a favor. It was hard to prove, but the men knew about it. You met a boss at the bar and made sure he got his free drinks. Lots of them did that.

"I belonged to the union right after I started working. I held offices like auditor, and later president, of the local. We used to have three locals in Glen Lyon. They were all under the United Mine Workers. At that time [1920-1930] they figured they had to have one for the miners, one for the company hands, and one for the outside employees. I joined the local for the outside employees at first when I worked in the breaker. After 1930 the national office wanted us to do away with our three groups and have one local. But the locals for the miners and company hands wouldn't surrender and they remained separate. But we had joint meetings by 1935 and I became president of both. One reason was because I could speak Polish good and most of the men were Polish or Slavish [Slovak].

"If the company didn't treat us right we went out on strike. The company had a rate sheet or schedule of wages which differed from colliery to colliery. When I was on the grievance committee of our local I had to put pressure on the company to get copies of the rate sheet. I would also get mad when companies would try to hire some of their friends from out of town or [when] some boss would hire his friends in. A union leader could stop a man from getting a job. In the 1930s we made sure that the people in Glen Lyon got jobs first. If you lived elsewhere you couldn't get a job in Glen Lyon while I was president. We would just tell the foreman he wasn't allowed to hire [such a person] and he would listen. [The companies] were afraid of shutdowns.

"We also had a problem when the company would dock the pay of men who they said were loading too much refuse in the cars. We had to reach an agreement that a man would be allowed at least five hundred pounds of refuse in a car. He wouldn't be penalized for that. Maybe a miner would have sixty cars of coal loaded during a period, but they would pay him for fifty and dock him ten cars for rock and refuse. I fought that.

"Sometimes a miner would try to pay me for a better spot to mine, [a place] where he could get better production. One man and his buddy were working an area and tried to offer me money so he would be permitted to load coal from two places, taking away part of the coal from the man working next to him. He had thought we would favor him because he had given me ten dollars once when I was running for school director. But we [the grievance committee] wouldn't take no money off him, and we ruled that two men would continue to work in the same place with the tonnage evenly split.

"As a union official you could help a man get a job or a different job once in a while. You could see the [section] foreman or fire boss or even the general foreman. He mostly had all the authority, so you kind of talked to him. He usually didn't want to see no trouble and he wanted to be on the right side of the union. At Glen Lyon, I talked to Bill Harvey, the general mine foreman. They were all Welsh—never any Poles. In fact, after the First World War, when no one could get a job in the mines, the Welsh could come over and have a job while still on the boat. Our people couldn't get a job, [but] the Welsh came right in and settled heavily in Nanticoke and this valley. And when we forced only the hiring of men from Glen Lyon [Poles and Slovaks] we stopped the Welsh from coming from Nanticoke.

"Most of the bosses had been brought in from Shamokin, where the Susquehanna Coal Company had their first mines. They brought their experienced men here, and some would bring their relations from Wales."

STEVE KIKA

Long before the 1930s, steelworkers found it difficult to influence matters both in the workplace and in the communities where they lived. Steve Kika recalls the powerlessness of workers in McKeesport, Pennsylvania.

"My father worked in the steel mill in Pottstown and he worked on the railroad too. He got me a job on the railroad carrying water for men when I was thirteen years old, for ten hours a day. We used to ride the train between Reading and Philadelphia. We used to carry water to the men and walk a mile to get water for them. They used to have the men picking up thirty-to-forty-foot-long rails in between the tracks by hand and throwing them up on the cars. That was real work.

"I worked there for a couple years, and I used to help the conductor measure the rails. Then I was running around with different groups who worked near Reading at the bridgeworks. We had to travel by train. If somebody had a horse and wagon, we would travel that way. Finally I got into the foundry there, where they make all kinds of sanitary equipment, like faucets and things like that. And that is where I worked until about 1916, when I was fifteen.

"We had to struggle the best we could. In the meantime, this relative of ours here [McKeesport] wrote my dad saying, 'Come out here and bring your son and we'll get work.' At that time I was the only one working. I had three brothers.

"But they laid my dad off the railroad when things got dull. We then came to McKeesport. Just my dad and me came. The rest of the family stayed back there until we got a place to stay.

"My dad got work in the tin-plate mill. They had plenty of work; this

Pennsylvania Historical and Museum Commission

SEPARATING TIN PLATES

was during the war. He was employed first, then I was. He was a laborer in the old finishing department. It was hard work in the finishing department. They called it the black-plates department. We worked for a dollar forty-four cents in there, twelve cents an hour. When I got home in the evening all I would do is to go to sleep. I couldn't even pick up a piece of bread, my fingers were so racked up from the steel mill. The tin plates were real warm then, but not real hot. I would have to pick those darn things out and put them up so the women would sort them out. If there were any spots or anything on the tin plate, then they would throw that in a separate pile, and that was rough.

"Yes, I worked in the same department my father worked [in]. I was getting along all right, but I'll tell you, it was rough work. I tell my grandson that I don't know how we're here today, 'cause of how we used to work. They had ethnic women working over there. Working by the hot mill, that black plate. After it goes rolling, there would be maybe eight sheets, and they would take bars and separate the sheets. They had to be sure they were geared to certain sizes. They were mostly women—Hungarians, Polish.

"In 1918 I was drafted. I wanted to volunteer, but my mother had a big thing about it because I was the keeper of the whole family. My father still worked. I could've been exempted. The heads of the tin plates [the mill] said, 'You don't have to go; we'll take care of you.' 'No,' I said.

"After the service I went back to the tin plates in McKeesport. Let me tell you something I'll never forget. [Some] of the boys was coming back over from the service, and they couldn't even get their own jobs back. Bill Green was the head of the AF of L, and there was an organizer around the Pittsburgh area here, I'll never forget his name; it was Hall. He was a tall fellow like me, and he only came here to organize semiskilled workers. Let me tell you something, he wasn't here very long. We had the old mayor Lyle here in those days. He was a 'bugger,' and we had to meet secretly. We did have a place there on Market and Fifth on the fifth floor. We would meet in small groups, and we tried to organize. This was right after World War I. There were quite a few people that wanted the union, but we didn't even get to first base. As soon as we tried to do anything, they would have the state police around here on horses. I'll never forget. The work was down in some places, and we decided to have a big, mass rally. All at once all these state police come. We called them 'Cossacks'; those horses were trained to fight. They would go in and grab you just like a mad dog.

"This was all company stuff. Jesus Christ wouldn't be able to come down here and let you have a meeting. [Then the workers] got after [the police]. Some of the men started to go up that way and the state policemen were scattered. [The men] just picked up rocks and started to throw them at the state policemen. After the war, conditions should've been better.

But they had the police and their control. The men couldn't organize, and when that organizer came here we talked it over and decided, 'Well it looks like we aren't going to make it.'

"I stayed out for a while in 1919. I didn't like to go back because I was kind of afraid. I thought that we should have some kind of organization because doctors have some kind of organization. Others have them. Why shouldn't the poor man have them?

"They had their stooges keeping their eyes on us. Sometimes we would even know, but we kept our eyes open. We kind of figured we'd have to think about who's going to be watching us now. They would offer them [the stooges] some money. We didn't care. They didn't have nothing on us outside of we were trying to do the right thing, to help one another and to get along and have a chance to say something. When payday rolled around, some of those ethnics had to pay their supervisors maybe ten dollars, and they didn't have too many five dollars coming [in in] those days. And some of the ethnic groups had a few extra dollars that they would buy something for the boss to keep on working. That's why we wanted a union.

"Interest in organizing disappeared until the NRA came. During the Depression, before we started to organize, I had a good standing because I was a good worker, and I knew how to do everything. I didn't like the supervisor. He was a rat, and he called us together. He says, 'Boys, some of you are single, and we got some boys here that have a few children. Would you be willing to˜split the time up with them?' I was married then, but we didn't have any children. So we agreed to split the time.

"In 1932, I joined an unemployment council. I tried to do anything we could; we contacted our representatives. We even went to Washington and contacted them. 'What are you going to do with these people?' [we asked]. 'We have no work. We have nothing. We need some help. What are you going to do about it?'

"I hardly ever slept then, running around and staying out late at night, having get-togethers. They were evicting people out of their homes, and we tried to do something about that too. They got some help because we got some food and things like that, and some of these real estate agents let them stay in their homes. This fellow, 'Buck,' evicted people out of their homes. That burned me up; I seen all that stuff. He gave some ground here for Penn State campus [in the 1960s], but when the people were starving and everything like that, he got the deputy sheriff to come and evict them out of their homes.

"We got nothing from the mill. We had to go, like a grocer or something like that, and give them food, and credit for a couple of months. And they would give them so much till they would get back to work. You would go around finding little jobs. That was the kind of thing I didn't like."

JOHN CZELEN

Monessen, Pennsylvania, was another mill town in which workers'
early movements toward organization were turned back. John
Czelen tells of this movement and the steel strike of 1919.

"I remember I was just a lad in 1919, four or five years old; this I remember vividly. We had in Monessen a main street called Ninth that took
workers into the working areas on top of the hill. To travel to work and
return from work, you had to go by Ninth Street. I do remember the 'Cossacks'; I remember the strikebreakers wearing guns; I remember the
grouping of strikebreakers with their arms traversing the streets. And I
remember quite vividly the brutality on the part of the coal and iron
police. It must have been in either the latter part of September of 1919 or
the first part of October. The kids would congregate by the streetlight and
play, and we had this coal and iron police descend on us and rear up with
the horse, and terrify the children.

"I know that the wages and the upkeep of these coal and iron police
was carried by the companies and approved by city council. Council records
show that [contributions to their] payments would be made by the company
as to their wage and other incidentals. Now records show the company made
the appeal and agreed to pay for this kind of service. This service was intended to discourage unions and to deny rights that people might have
wanted to undertake during these organizing drives. The Monessen council
decided to continue its mounted police force for another year at a meeting
of the borough council in 1919.

"In this area, there were a number of miners who were very much interested in seeing steelworkers organized in 1919. They felt that their lot
was tied to the steelworkers, and in turn the steelworkers to the miners. So
naturally the miners encouraged them. And you had some mine leaders
who encouraged that kind of activity. Then you had a man by the name of
Finney who came into the valley or lived in the valley. And he was instru-
mental in forming committees throughout the valley. The miners felt that
their lot was tied in with the steelworkers. I'm talking about the rank and
file. Those who occupied the most dangerous, the most underpaid jobs.
The ranks involved miners and steelworkers. You'll note that they were
agitating about that time. They had walkouts here and there. But the
membership board of the United Mine Workers was very much interested
in what the steelworkers were attempting to do. So there was a common
endeavor, mostly made up of poor East European immigrants, some Irish
miners, Welsh miners. They were the poorest, both in the steelworkers
and among the coal diggers.

"My father owned a store [in 1919] and would give the steelworkers

Pennsylvania Historical and Museum Commission

STEELWORKERS IN DUQUESNE

credit. Those people would sign power of attorney and buy merchandise and in turn sell it to other people at a lower price in order to get some cash. That's how hard hit the people were. That is why they were striking. They actually got nothing for the work. Of course it was better than Europe, but when you were over here you needed this and you needed that and you couldn't get it. I know in many cases the colored people would go in a Jewish clothing store. The owner had a big stack of 'power of attorneys.' They bought anything in there and in turn the store owner's wife would take it over to the paymaster at the mill and take it out of one's pay. And if you walked with another person, the coal and iron police would club you. They didn't tell you to break it up. They would hit you. We gave credit. We had something like forty thousand dollars on the books.

"Many steelworkers left during the strike. First some left because of the pressures when seeking work elsewhere [in Monessen]. Another [reason] was that they were blackmailed. They either went back to Europe or to the state of New York. Some went to Ohio. I would say at least fifteen or twenty percent of the people on completion of the strike scattered. Lists were exchanged [among companies] to give you a good picture of the situation. My father was involved in this.

"My father's name was Casimir Czelen. He was a worker and as a worker he felt that the workers would have a union. His group was blackballed; it was the Polish Falcons. I say some of them. Many of them didn't understand the trade union movement. But of those who did understand, they felt that the organization would bring some relief. After the strike was broken, they could not get back into the mills. Fortunately the superintendent of Pittsburgh Steel Company in Monessen was a strong Catholic. In our church, which was Roman Catholic, we had a priest who was a close friend of the superintendent, and [the strikers] had to render an apology for their activity in order to get their jobs back. That was the only way to get it back, through the influence of religion.

"I remember the discussions my dad and the others had with the organizer who came into the valley. They liked it that they could be a member, not for other reasons, but for being a worker. And this was one of the things that sold them. [They were] miserable, [and] telling them that they were going to be treated with some equality, this is what they bought. Because up to that point they were looked upon as 'Hunkies,' as 'Polacks,' as 'Dagos,' as foreigners. The boss would say something to you and he'd say, 'Hey Polack,' or 'Hey Dago, come here.' Naturally they resented that. They might not have shown any open resentment, but inwardly they felt hurt that they were treated as secondary citizens. And incidentally, some of them had their first papers [citizenship]. [The company] would always try to create some doubt in the minds of the workers as the strike progressed. The company became a little more persuasive, suggesting that [the strikers'] leaders were Bolsheviks.

"My dad wasn't swayed by charges of bolshevism, or [the] threat of losing his job. And I know a number of other Poles who weren't swayed. But the economic situation had brought them to their knees. They couldn't just go on. It was a question of leaving this part of the country or giving up what little equity he had—his house. Some of them had a couple of hundred dollars in their home. They had mortages. It was a question of continuing under the conditions that existed or going elsewhere and loosing whatever equity you had. So the decision by the majority was to remain."

TOM LUKETICH

Tom Luketich was the son of Croatian-German parents and was raised in a coal-mining family in Cokeburg in southwestern

Eleutherian Mills Historical Library

LINCOLN STREET, COKEBURG, 1943

Pennsylvania. He remembers well the miners' struggles in the region during the 1920s and his own effort to secure steady work.

"In the twenties there were big coal strikes here. They had a strike here in 1921, I remember. They were having a lot of trouble then. That's when they had the National Guard down here and everything. They camped out across the highway over there. That lasted for a long time, but then in 1927, that's when they were breaking the union.

"They were always fighting. Between them and the 'yellow dogs' they brought in, the company coal and iron police, they would ride around town on them horses, and they had them clubs; they would chase everybody off the street and everything else. They used to call the young men 'rednecks' and they would run their rear end right off the road. They didn't allow anyone around town.

"They brought 'yellow dogs' in when they were breaking the union. About 1925, they brought them 'yellow dogs' in. That's when the company put up fences around mine property. They had them little shanties for the 'yellow dogs' to stay in. At every gate they put them spotlights up on the slate.

"We moved out. We didn't stay here. Our people moved out. All the Croatians moved out because they were union men. They wouldn't scab. Some of them had jobs in commercial mines. They worked there. I don't think there was one Croatian family that stayed in town. The only ones that lived here were the ones that were scabbing. The ones they brought in from West Virginia, the colored people, and all them hillbillies they were bringing in, some from Kentucky, they moved to the Italian section. They stayed here and scabbed.

"We stayed away until after the union was broke. It seemed that everything was lost already. That was back in '31. Then they started moving back in, some of them, the ones that could get their jobs back, [but a] lot of these people were blackballed. The company didn't hire them after that.

"In 1927 the company brought more strikebreakers, even Italians. When they brought them in, them Dagos would fight. That Serbian up there, Lepsivich, was getting ten dollars from the company for every family that they were moving in here. This I know. They were largely Italians. Every one of them stayed right here. The Croatian people moved out. There wasn't one Croatian that stayed in Cokeburg during the strike.

"At that particular time they had a commercial mine agreement. The 'captive mines' wouldn't belong with the union and the companys were bringing all these strikebreakers in. Some of those fellows had jobs in commercial mines like up at Mathers, some at Vespers, up at Frederickstown, in Clyde and them places. Our guys had to move out because the company chased them out because they wouldn't work here. A lot of these people, if they didn't have jobs, the union built barracks for them. A lot of them moved into these barracks and lived along the highway in board shanties. They were bringing all these 'yo-yos' in here to break the strike at that time. That's what I was telling you. These men were riding to work like cattle in a truck. As high as thirty to forty men in a truck.

"People from West Virginia, Kentucky, and the niggers they brought in. We never had a colored family in until the strike. Then after '31, when the mines shut down, the colored families went back of here. We don't have a colored family in town here now.*

"My dad was always a strong union man. There used to be differences in the unions. At that particular time, they used to have what they called 'captive mining.' They used to have separate agreements. Some of the mines happened to be on strike, and ours happened to be one here in Cokeburg because this was a 'captive' company. So my dad and most of the people who were here, good Yugoslavians and a lot of 'Polacks' and Slovaks, moved out of this town. They went elsewhere because they were bringing scabs into Cokeburg to break the union. The people they were bringing in were from Kentucky, West Virginia, and places like that. So my dad was working at one of the Clyde mines up here around Frederickstown at that particular time. We had moved to Bentleyville for a short period of time. I think we lived down there a year or so. That was while this strike was going on.

"There was a family up there, Lepsivich. They had big trucks. They used to haul milk in. Pick up milk cans on the farm and deliver them. But they were hauling these miners to work. My dad was in a bad accident at one time. This guy, Paul Lepsivish, was driving this truck. And up here at Bellsville he hit a concrete abutment and turned this truck over and there were three men killed in this wreck. My dad was one of the ones that was hurt pretty bad. A fellow was killed by the name of Boyer. He was an old Croatian. Then there was Smolar. That's a local resident here. He lived on the corner down here. I can't remember his name though. His family lived here. They went to Detroit after that. Then we stayed out of Cokeburg until that strike was over. They broke the union and everything, and just about the time they were ready to shut this mine down my dad came back. That was in '31. This mine didn't work then for several years.

"The mine was shut down. So then this place didn't work again until December 1936. In December, around the first, they opened the mine back up. I had already worked in the mine with my dad. We were working while the mine was down [1933]. We were traveling around because jobs were hard to get [in] those days. You went where they would give you five days' work. A lot of mines were only working two or three days a week.

"We still lived in Cokeburg, but we were traveling to work. We worked down at Gibson. We worked for Pittsburgh Coal Company. Then we ended up at Burgham until 1935, when we came back to Cokeburg when they opened this up. I have been in this mine since. My dad worked from 1936 until he passed away in 1952. He contracted that miner's silicosis. He had that real bad. He finally died in 1952.

"I started to work when I was sixteen years old. When I got into high

---

*It should be pointed out that blacks and other strikebreakers frequently did not know they were being brought into strike situations.

school I went through the first year. When I got in the sophomore year I quit and went right into the coal mine. I lied about my age and went into the mine, and I have been in the mine ever since—since 1932. That's a long time.

"Before I was sixteen I worked on the farms. I worked on the highway. I worked on a highway for forty cents an hour, ten hours a day. They would only allow you to work three days a week. That was in the thirties. Forty cents an hour, ten hours a day, and they give you three days a week. If you start on a Wednesday, you worked Wednesday, Thursday, and Friday, then Monday, Tuesday, and Wednesday the following week.

"Like I told you, my dad never went to school. He never had any education. My mother went to school in Germany just like you go [in] this country, up until the eighth grade. She didn't go to school in this country. Not one day. But they did want us to go to school; my dad got awful mad

Eleutherian Mills Historical Library

LINCOLN STREET, COKEBURG, 1943

at me when I quit high school. I got a set of tools, and I got a job at Ontario Mine. Did he raise hell!

"My mother wanted me to go to school too, so after I started working in the mine I did go to night school. In fact, I went to vocational school. It was a machine school on tool dye and operating lathes and that. I worked in a tool-and-dye shop for a couple months. Then I enlisted in the navy during the Second World War. I did go to night school. I took courses from Penn State Extension in mining, three years of night school in mining, and that's how I got all my mining certificates.

"I had a lot of respect for my father. I worked in the mine, and I never smoked a cigarette in front of my dad. We had an old outside toilet when I worked in Marianna mine. My dad was good to me, though, because he knew I worked hard. When I was seventeen years old I worked in the mine and I worked like a man who was forty-five years old. And I brought the same pay home [that] they were making. When I brought my pay home I used to lay the envelope on the table, and I would get five dollars on payday. You know what I used to do? We used to come home and I used to hurry up and wash and sneak outside and I would go in the old outside toilet to smoke a cigarette. That's how much respect I had for my dad because I was ashamed to smoke in front of him or my mother. I would sneak a smoke in that toilet. Who in the heck was I kidding? That smoke could be coming out through the top like a smokehouse.

"We were working at Marianna mine, steady night shift. Boy, we would clean up there and we would walk out. Me and them young guys would hurry up and walk out. Joe Rados, Fred Zack, Mike Nicholas, was riding with me. I would hurry up and go outside and get a smoke before the old man would come out. Then, when he come home, Mother used to heat the water on top of that stove, a couple of pots of water. [She would get] that big washtub and put it on the little floor and you took a bath. I would hurry up and get washed, then go outside for a smoke. Smoke would be coming out the roof. So one day Dad came home. He said, 'What's the matter? All the time [I see] smoke down there by the smoke house.' He said, 'If you want to smoke, you work like a man.' He said, 'You go ahead and smoke your cigarette.' I never forgot that. My brother Joe was the same way after he started working in the mine. He would go to the outside toilet to get a smoke. Think we was kidding anybody? The old man was too smart for us. He knew what we was doing.

"Of course, during the Depression, jobs were hard to get. Men worked in mines long hours. My dad, I remember, used to work at Lincoln Hill then because this mine wasn't working. He used to travel in a truck. These guys would haul these miners in a truck like cattle. They used to leave before daylight and they never got home until it was dark. They had what they called a clean-up system in the mines. You had to clean that pile of coal up before you went home. Biggest part of those people that did work in mines at that time, they dealt with the company stores, and on payday they got four big zeros on the scrip. They didn't have no pay coming because they took that whole pay out on scrip for groceries. Biggest part of people at that time were living on welfare. I remember how they used to give down there; they had people distributing this welfare. It was controlled by the company too; the company 'yellow dog,' we used to call him here. So-called people working for the American Red Cross would give you twenty-five pounds of flour a week and jean cloth. They used to make shirts from [that cloth] or a pair of overalls. Once in a while they would give you a pair of shoes. I didn't forget that.

"Twenty-five pounds of flour you used to get through the welfare. I remember there was an Italian family living next to us. They used to get the flour, [but] they didn't have the nickel to buy the yeast with. I remember we used to give them the five cents so they could make bread.

"But during the Depression and when the work was slack everybody dealt in the company store because they used scrip. Tear those pieces off of that scrip instead of money. You would go to the company store and first thing—the company store boss was employed by the same company where the men worked (like Bethlehem Steel had their own store down here)—that guy would get on the phone. He would check with the clerk in the office how much money you made that day, and if you didn't have the money made you didn't get the scrip to buy with. This guy was hand-loading coal. You had to pay for the powder to be used to shoot the coal. He had to pay for caps. He had to pay for a headlight. He had to pay the blacksmith and doctor.

"They extended your credit to the extent of what you had made. The store boss called the mine office clerk and found out how much money you had made, and that's how much credit you got because if you didn't have no pay made you didn't get no scrip. That's how they operated.

"The New Deal was a blessing. You can say what you want, but you better be a Democrat if you are a laborer working for a living. You better vote Democrat. You better work for the Democratic Party and the people because when Roosevelt got in office his first program was that NRA. He came out with the National [Labor] Relations Board or whatever they call it. Whatever it was, he gave the people the right to work. That's when they started to reorganize the United Mine Workers. I think I had a dues book because there was no such thing as a checkoff system then. Because now automatically if you work in the mine they start taking your checkoff dues right off the bat. Then they started taking [an] initiation fee, fifty dollars. At that time it used to be ten dollars to join the union. They didn't have what they called a 'closed shop.' The people had to sign up to belong to the union, and we had cases here in '37, yet, where women had to chase several people around town with brooms to [get them to] join the union. You used to pay your union dues at the union hall. We had red dues books. But then they got the automatic checkoff system. The closed shop, that was a little bit better because that got hired automatically; they had to pay union dues to work. Now it is strictly all union. Anybody that works in the mines today belongs to UMW. Prior to that time when they broke the unions they did have a union come in. They were trying to organize what they called the National Miners Union.

"They were a group of people strictly for labor. Any time you fight for labor and if you are from Yugoslavia, right off the bat they are going to call you a 'Communist' because you are fighting for a living. This is the God's truth. They always pegged anybody that fought for labor, working class of people, 'Communists.' Right away you are a goddamn 'Commie.' You are a Red because you are a radical. You are fighting for something good.

"As far as I am concerned, I have to give those boys [the NMU] a lot of credit. They were fighting for better working conditions, for more pay, because they were down in the dirt for so long working for nothing and starvation wages. My God, they had to do something, and you have to give those people credit. So what appeared after they give them the right to organize, they come out for the United Mine Workers. Everybody joined the UMW.

"I started to work in the mine in 1932, hand-loading coal, pick and shovel. I worked for Ontario Gas & Coal Company. Then I worked for Hillman Coal at Gibson. I was hand-loading coal there. In 1935, at Marianna, I was hand-loading coal, pick and shovel. In those days if you made fifty dollars pay, that was a big pay in two weeks. If you drew fifty dollars, you had to be a hard worker and a good coal loader to make that clear after your expenses and things.

"We were working at Marianna five days a week. I left Gibson because they were working two days. You got about five-dollars-a-day pay in two weeks. Every day we would go look for a job elsewhere. They were working every day, so I got a job at Marianna. They were working five days a week up there. Then I worked there until December 1936. They opened this mine up here, and I have been here ever since.

"I tell you, from hand-loading I worked on the track a little bit. Then I run motor for a good many years. I would say about fifteen years on the mine locomotive. I used to shuttle cars, coal loaders, and pick them up and haul them to sites back and forth. Then I worked as a mine electrician for several years. Then machine shop mechanic. Then I went on in 1952 to fire boss. I fire bossed off and on. That is when I got my fire boss papers. In 1950 I got fire boss papers. In 1951, that's when I was taking Penn State courses in mining, extension courses. Also, I went three years [to] night school [to study] mining. Then I was working in the shop as assistant foreman extra until I went on steady as assistant mine foreman.

"There has been a lot of improvements. I think when the people got the right to organize, that helped them considerably in work conditions, wages, the health and welfare of miners, and also mine safety. It improved considerably since that time. Prior to that time they didn't have any picking up. I think this helped.

"Everybody wants production because when you start paying increases in wages and salaries of employees, you got to come up with production. You got to have production because if there is no production you just can't pay people. Our biggest problem in mining today is a lot of these people today, they are not from the [old] school. They are not like the old-timers used to be. When the old foreman went inside he worked his heart and soul out because he was on what we call piecework; he had to produce to make [money]. [Or] if he didn't load that car carefully, he didn't get paid. Today they are paying everybody a certain scale wage, like these guys getting forty-seven dollars and forty-eight dollars to start with. A lot of these people have that 'I don't care' attitude. They come to work and they act like the company owes them a living, and they let the poor old 'Hunky' work his head off. They know how to brick gold. They will walk circles around the boss in the mine. Believe me, they will. I know this from experience; I worked as a miner when we had to work for five dollars a day back in 1932 and 1933. That is what the miners were getting for labor when the union first came in. They were reliable people because they took pride in their work.

"During the thirties, I had to work on the highway. To get a job on the highway at that time, you went through the Pennsylvania Unemployment Office. They gave preference to the people who were on welfare. You got a card from the unemployment office and then you had to go up on the road and see the boss in order to get a job. You had to have that card from the unemployment office.

"I got a job up here for J. I. Dick in Scenery Hill. This fellow was working for Vesta Coal Company; his name was John Stayshock. Poor soul's dead now. Him and I were buddies, and we run around together. He got a card to go to work on this road. I couldn't get a job because I wasn't on relief. My dad was working in the mine. So he was going to send this card back to the unemployment office. I said, 'Don't send that card back. Give me that card.' I got a job here. I went up and got a job on the highway. I worked under Stayshock. Every time the timekeeper used to come around and ask for your name I would try to avoid him. I worked on that job all summer before anyone found out. Finally someone saw Stayshock's name and knew he was really working at Vesta. They asked me what my name was but never did turn me in. But that's how desperate we were to get work. Now, with social security and everything, you can't do this any more.

"My parents were strict, especially about religion. My dad was a little backward himself because he never went to school. He didn't know how to read or write. But he used to make us go to church. We used to walk from Cokeburg to Bentleyville to St. Luke's Church and go to catechism classes.

"In coal-mining towns like Cokeburg each street was different. One street was strictly for 'Johnny Bulls.' And the 'Johnny Bulls' were all the bosses. It used to be in our town that the street that was going by the church was called 'D Row.' There wasn't a Croatian, Slovak, or Italian living on that street. It was all foremen and superintendents in the mines. Today at our mine we have one 'American,' but not many 'Johnny Bulls.' The rest of us is all good 'Hunkies.' Years ago we weren't educated. The average coal miner did not have enough money to send his kids to school.'

"These guys who were foremen educated their kids and they ran the town. They were the bosses in the mine; they were on the council. The company run the town. The foremen were the only guys with any type of education. They were the 'Johnny Bulls' and they run the town. They were the bosses in the mine, they were on the council, they were on the police force, they were the mayor. They were everything in town. Then as the union come in and people started making a little more money, these 'Hunkies' got a little smarter. They started to educate their kids. They started sending their children to college. Then what happens. Now our school teachers around here are all [of] foreign extraction. Two of our bosses are Croatian. In fact, we have a Croatian mine inspector. He changed his name. I guess it is for political reasons. That's an appointment job. You take most of our foremen at our mine, [they] are Croatians, 'Polacks.' The superintendent is of Lithuanian origin. His dad was at my mine. He was a foreman. Our mine foreman is a Lithuanian. Most of our assistant foremen are Croatian or Italian, Slovak, 'Polack,' all mixed up.

"It seems to me that it seemed to change more or less around the fifties. More around the fifties because prior to that time there wasn't that many job openings. When they started to mechanize mining, it came to the point where they needed more foremen. That's about the time our people started educating themselves a little bit more. Our boys would go out to high school and then they would start taking night courses in mining. Slowly they moved in there and took everything over. Today our engineers and everybody at our mine are all of foreign extraction.

"Most of the people that lived here bought the houses they were in because, what the heck, the company sold their real estate cheap here. A double house like where I lived sold for one thousand eight hundred dollars. That was pretty cheap. Where could you buy a one-thousand-eight-hundred-dollar house or even start to build a house for [that amount]? The only homes in this town that had bathrooms and stuff like that in [them], little bit better houses, were the houses in 'D Row,' where the bosses lived; the company installed bathrooms in those houses. In [the] rest of these the company installed electric[ity], and I remember when I went to grade school we still had kerosene lamps. I think in the late thirties sometime, about '34 or '35, that's when they put the electric[ity] in. Then, as the people bought the homes, they remodeled them. Everybody today has got bathrooms in them; we got good roads, and we got all the conveniences here that you have anywhere.

"I did leave the mines once. There was a fellow by the name of George Stogers who I went up to Detroit with. He had some kind of relation of his that we went to visit. He worked in a tool-and-dye shop. That's one of the reasons I went up there because the war broke out and there was work. But I came back home as quick as I could.

"I never wanted a bigger job in the mines. It was too big a headache and not much difference in pay [from] what I am making now. I got my sight on the outside right now. I got forty-three years in the mines and I got miner's pneumocosis right now and arthritis real bad. I was in the hospital seven or eight days. I haven't worked for two months. I have been off for two months. And that's strictly off the pace, and that's when I got from mining.

"Heck, I never wanted to leave Cokeburg. You kow what we used to do? We were always looking for polka dances and Croatian music. We used to go way up the Craft Street from here on Saturdays and Sundays.

"I guess I had to sacrifice my own interest for my family. I didn't get married until late. I didn't get married until I was over thirty years old because my dad was sick and he couldn't work. He was an old coal cutter in the mines and contracted that miners' asthma, pneumocosis. So he had to quit work and I had to support my family. Rather than them going on relief or something, I felt it was my obligation. I did that until my brother was out of school and able to work. Then I didn't marry until I was thirty-two years old."

JOHN PARRACCINI

John Parraccini came from a farming village in the Italian province of Umbria. He recalled very little industry existing in his native region except a mill that made bricks and tile. Certainly he had never experienced anything like the coal mines around Scranton, Pennsylvania. Arriving in the United States in 1911, he found a new community of friends, but the work routines of the mine were burdensome and frequently more dangerous than those in his homeland.

"My brother-in-law was here, and he [went] back to Italy and married my sister. Then he served in the [Italian] Army for two years, and [after that] he came back over here. He asked my father if he could let me come over with him. He said he would get me a job and felt that I would like to come over. You know, many people used to leave Italy then and come over here with the idea to work a couple of years and then come back. So I told him I'd be glad to come. So my brother-in-law was my sponsor because I was under age. I had to have somebody to take care of me until I was over there. So I come over with him in 1911.

"But you know what happens when you're in a place so long. I got up into my twenties and I got a notice of going to register for the service. That was usually what you'd do. You'd go to register, pass a physical test. If you were in physical condition they'd take you for the army, two, three, four years. That was World War I. When my brother talked me into [joining] the Italian Army, I had an idea to go back. So I went to the Italian consul here in Scranton, because they used to say if you don't go back and serve your country, you'll never be able to go back again. So I went down to the consul with intentions to go back, but other friends of mine had gone back, and they were really sorry they had, so I didn't. And then I wrote to my mother. I got married and never went back until 1968, with my wife.

"I wasn't taken into the American Army, because I was a miner. The miners in the First World War were considered like they were in the service. I guess they needed a call and that's the only thing that they had here. You were to fill out what they called 'questionnaires' and then bring that to the superintendent of the colliery. Well, if you were a good producer, a good worker, the superintendent would sign it and say, 'I need this man.' And naturally you'll find someone that's not always in good humor, whether miner or laborer, and naturally the superintendent won't sign the questionnaire. And they used to take them in the service.

"Before I came to America the only thing I know about was this mine-working. And nothing else [did] I know then. I knew a little bit about America from the people who were working in the mines. They were going down in the mines in the elevator. My poor mother, when she heard that from a friend of hers, she don't want me to come over here, because you know how the old-timers used to be when they were over here. This fella [who] used to be here, [he went to America] and he came back, and my mother asked him, 'How was it in America. How was the work?' He said that they send you down with ropes into the mines and if your light goes out you'd be in the dark. So she don't want me to come.

"I pay for the trip, forty-three dollars. But in them days that was a lot of money. My brother-in-law came with me all the way through. He slept on the top, I slept on the bottom. And then he was working on the ship. When we got into New York, we got off and stayed with these men. So then we went through the checkers, where they check you. I was kinda afraid because I didn't know the other guys so well, and I was afraid I'd miss my brother-in-law. So after we got on the steamboat, then he came, and we came across. But nine days on the boat I couldn't eat nothing. I was sick as anything; all I could do was drink a little beer. And then when I got here I was here for a week and I was [still] sick from the ocean.

"I came right to Scranton. My brother-in-law had a job when he first came, and then I got a job too. We came to Peckville because I had some relatives there. My brother-in-law, he went up to Eynon. That's where he used to be here before. So he was going to take me up there. But my cousin told me, 'You stay here and I'll get you a job. And I'll take you to the mines for a couple of days and you'll see the mines.' And then a friend of my family found out that I was here, and he said, 'Come to work with me.' He said, 'If your father know that you come to the same town that I am, and I not take you to work with me, your father would be mad at me.' They were great friends. So I went to work with him in Jessup. I became his laborer. I board with my cousin and several other boarders. There was all kinds of people there. There was Italian, Polish, English, and Irish. I was on the low part of Jessup; then we move up on the top part of Jessup. There was mostly Italian and Irish.

"Well, it wasn't a bad home, but it wasn't what we have today. There was no carpets. There was no rocking chair. There was no couch. Just common wooden chairs. I remember there was a great big table, and benches on each side of the table, and a great big kitchen. It wasn't what you'd call a regular boardinghouse. A man and a wife, they used to take boarders in. Imagine, we were about twelve boarders and there was this man and his father and his mother. They were old. And [besides] himself, there were two children and his wife, in a six-room house. It was really crowded, of course. When you were young you didn't mind it. And in a six-room house the boarders used to keep the upstairs and the family the downstairs. And we used to throw *boccie* balls. Not the regular big one, but a smaller one. That was our main game, like on Sunday, after work during the summertime.

"There were a lot of picnics. The mines used to hold picnics every year. And then for about a week there was a picnic around. There used to be all kinds of games on those picnics. Many times we used to have big rocks, and fellas would try to see who [could] drill the hole through first. Everything along the lines of the [work in the] mines. And it really was enjoyment, because the people used to be together. It wasn't like today; there was no cars to go anywhere. There was no radio to listen to.

"In those days each gang would have its own place to go. Either because you were friends with the saloon keeper or you just started to go there. And you'd go there after work and play a little game of cards and have a beer. And a lot of the time they'd have pool rooms and you'd go play a game of pool, have yourself a drink. Most of the time I was never much of a drinker. And that was enjoyment. Because after work there was nothing else to do. You don't go riding, because you don't have no automobile. And you just sit around among friends and tell them stories and play different games...cards, *boccie*...

"I got married in 1922. For a while we stayed with her sister, but then we went on our own in Jessup. And later on we moved to Peckville, and then back to Jessup for a while. Then in, well I forget the year, we moved back to Peckville to stay.

"I started as a laborer in 1911 and I quit in 1959. Forty-eight years in the mines. I worked for my father's friend about a couple of years. And then I got my own job mining. I became my own miner. I worked with different companies; of course, not with too many companies. I worked with the Temple Coal Company, in Surey Creek Colliery. Then in 1929 I worked with Underwood Colliery, owned by the Pennsylvania Coal Company. And I was there until the company closed down. And after the company closed down, a new company came in and they used to call it the Reality Coal Company. I worked with them for about seven years, until I retired as a miner.

"In the mines you got to do everything. The miners, they used to cut the coal, drill their own holes, charge and blast them. [They] cut off the coal for the laborers, and some of the miners, when they had enough coal, they would go home. They'd leave the laborer alone with the coal. And [the] laborer's job was to load the coal and clean the rock that was around the coal. But that [wasn't] it, of course; you had to timber your place if you needed it. Years ago they didn't use no fire line to blast out the coal. You used what they call 'squibs.' See, we used to drill with a hand machine and load our coal and put our 'squibs' in and light [them] with a lamp or a piece of paper. But then later on, when new law came, we had to use batteries to fire our holes, and we had to have a line of electric wire to do that. And we had to take care of everything that way. When the engine broke down—not all the time but most of the time—we had to do the repair. Of course, they had a regular guy to do that. But you'd lose so much time, and you'd have to go do it yourself. But it wasn't only that you had to blast the coal but there was a lot of other things you had to do too. You had to help build the platform that bring the coal in on the cars. There was a lot of work to it. It was dangerous, but once you get used to it, you don't think about that. Of course, there is always danger. Especially if you have a bad roof, you got to be careful. A lot of times that's when the accident happens. Some were careless, but I was lucky.

"I was injured once, not too much. Otherwise, I was lucky. I was hurt. A small rock on the roof hit me, but it wasn't much. You know, when a rock hits you it hurts.

Eleutherian Mills Historical Library

UNDERGROUND IN AN ANTHRACITE COLLIERY, C. 1935

"When I first started it was ten hours, and then it came down to eight hours a day. But even when it was eight hours, in 1912, you had fifty-four days' strike. And I had just come here in 1911. And that's when eight hours started. But work was kind of slow. And men wouldn't come out until they get the hours. So they used to put in nine, sometimes ten hours up until it was late in the evening.

"We had kids in the mines. The kids used to come in there as a 'nipper,' or door tender. We used to have a door in different spots to circulate the air. So they used to have those boys, and they were supposed to be thirteen years old, but some of them were eight, nine, ten years old. And they stay there when the mine cars come out. They were supposed to open the door and when cars go by they were supposed to close the door. And when they learned that, they used to get a job of driving the mules. And them they used to call a 'runner.' They used to have 'sprags,' or pieces of wood. And when this car came out, they used to sprag them, putting wood under the wheels. They used to sprag the car according to how fast it was going. If they know the car would make it they wouldn't put no sprags in it. But if they know that the car would go by there, then they would sprag it, put the wood, so it would stop. Later on, the motor came out, and there wasn't much of this spragging, running business.

"A lot of times when I worked in the Jessup Colliery it used to be a lot of gas in there. I happened to be there, but I wasn't hurt. But other men were hurt, and some were careless when the motor came on the spark and lit the gas. I remember three or four different explosions, and the guys at work were hurt bad. Once even the fire boss was killed in an explosion. And I remember once there was a cave-in, and five men were caught in there. There were two miners and two laborers and the foreman. The roof started to shake so bad, [and] the foreman knew that he had four men inside. He said that he was going inside and that he was afraid that this might come down anytime. So he run in there to get the men out and when they were coming out the whole thing come down. And in fact I work there for three weeks with the other gang to get them out. It took about three weeks to get them out. There were five of them; all five of them were killed. They were lying on the road. The boss was the first one [we found]. In fact my shift, my gang, found the first one. And then we discovered the last one, but we didn't take him out; the following gang took him out. They were telling me that the last one wasn't killed in the fire, but that he died later on. He was covered with the timbers. That's the only time I see a cave-in that trapped a man in like that."

LEE ROY HORLACHER

Lee Roy Horlacher was born into a family of proud, skilled workers in Hazleton, Pennsylvania, in August 1894. Growing up in a working-class family, he became concerned about the status of working people and he began reading socialist literature. Before his eighteenth birthday he was leading a strike of textile workers in his hometown. Although he became more involved in the socialist movement than most of the other workers whose thoughts are recorded here, he was not alone in his general protest against the powerlessness of laborers and the marginality of the workingman's status.

"My grandfather was born in Hazleton of Scotch descent and was a mechanic. He built collieries and laid out timbers, but [he] was also a gambler. At that time the collieries were built with heavy twelve-by-twelve timbers. My father was a carpenter and a mechanic just like his father. He worked for a piano company at one time. And then he worked at the Hazleton Manufacturing Company. They made cabinets and items for stores. They were known as a coffin factory.

Wyoming Historical and Geological Society

MINERS DESCENDING, KINGSTON

"I went as far as the fifth grade but didn't finish it. My father wanted me to work since we had a big family, and children growing up at that time were expected to work. While I was fourteen when I quit school, I had already worked before that.

"While I was still in school I worked with my father. He taught me how to make wagons and various things. One day he gave me a saw and told me that from now on it would be my saw. He said that I would have to learn to file it and learn to take care of it. I handed it back to him, but he said, 'No sir, file it yourself.' He had me run it down with a file, and he had me do it over again about five or six times. Then he had me cut a board in half. He looked at it and said, 'Well, it's a hell of a way from right.' That was my father.

"At that time my mother realized that the family was getting larger. It was common to put boys to work at that time. Even before I was fourteen I had made a trip to Lansford, Pennsylvania, to my grandfather's place. I told my uncle down there that I wanted to go to work. In those days you could go to work at the age of ten. I had gone down there on vacation, but I was tired of hanging around with old people and I wanted to go to work. My uncle managed to get me a job at the No. 7 mine of the Lehigh Coal & Navigation Company. I was only ten or eleven, but I started picking slate. I did it until my father came down and found out that I was working in the collieries. And he put a stop to it right there. He didn't want me to go into the mines. My grandfather was killed in the mine from the fall of a piece of coal about the size of a stove. My one uncle had his back broken and he lay in the hospital, and the other had his foot crushed. When my grand-father was [killed], he was brought home in a mule-drawn ambulance.

"When I was in Lansford my uncle took me down to No. 7. I think it was on a Sunday morning, before I went to work. And he was a socialist. When he saw the steam coming up from the boiler shop and going through, he said that it represented the man down below with a shovel, shoveling coal on the heater. He said it represented his perspiration. What he meant to say was that coal would not be created unless there was human labor at-tached to it.

"I only went to the mines on the advice of my uncle. He told me that the first time a breaker boss hit me with a stick, I should pick up a piece of coal next to him and knock him down. So the first man was Bobby Gil-more, who had lost one of his arms. Like all kids, I would let slate go by in the chute once in a while. And once when I did, he hit me on the shoulder with a stick. So I walked over to the broken coal and told him to come over. I picked up a big piece of broken coal and told him that I was going to knock him down with it. I said, 'If you want my attention, just tap me on the shoulder; don't hit me with a stick.' And he never hit me after that.

"Then my father took me back to the Hazleton Manufacturing Com-pany to teach me the wood-carving trade. That's where he was working making coffins. I worked there for five cents an hour. I cleaned wood shavings, and my father had to bring a little bench for me to stand on in order to teach me the carving. He picked out a group of things. They used to slap the corners on coffins. He carved one and cut it and showed me how to use the chisels on it. The wood carver's chisels are sharpened dif-ferent from those of the ordinary mechanic. After he was done he asked me if I could carve one like that. He said, 'You can spoil one if you want to, but get it in your head, get it in your head.'

"I don't know how long exactly I worked with my father, but working for your father was more or less a handicap. I had some trouble in the mill. They had hired some Italian boys, and we used to like to get away from the bench whenever we could and play. But my father was a first-class mechanic and he ran a machine right opposite me. When he would go away anywhere, I was always fooling around. We would put wood blocks in an air-suction bag and listen to them hit the fan.

"I can't tell you the exact date that I left there, but finally I turned around and decided I would go work for a man by the name of Bill Slusher, who was a pipe fitter. So I worked for him for a while and learned how to fit pipes for hot-water systems. He later asked me if I would like to stay with him and take an apprenticeship. I said, 'Why, I'm getting more wages right now.'

"I had left that coffin factory because I was tired of being under the pin of my father all the time. After I left there and worked for the pipe fitter, I went into the silk mill in Hazleton and learned weaving broadcloth silk. It was in the DuPlant Silk Company, a French concern. And they were looking for learners. You learned how to thread the shuttles and how to pick back any mistakes and start all over again. I don't know just how long I did that, but it was at least until 1913. I worked a while and planned to leave a shuttle in there to cause a smash. I wanted to get fired because when you got fired they had to pay you cash to get rid of you. I wanted to get my wages all at once when I left since I was running away from home.

"In 1913, before I could get fired, a strike broke out at that mill. When the workers walked out I went to the miners' headquarters on Alder Street about two or three blocks from where I lived. I talked to a man by the name of Lewis J. Gergotz, who was influential with the miners. He was a miner by trade and a Hungarian. I had remembered Gergotz because he used to throw socialist magazines on our porch. He threw them because he thought my father was interested in socialism, but I was reading them instead. Lewis Gergotz met me in a picture house one time and asked me about the magazines. I told him that I had been reading them. I told him I thought it [socialism] was a good idea. I didn't see why we had to make millionaires of some men and paupers of others. This was my first exposure to these ideas. I was still at the silk mill, but Gergotz was inclined toward the Industrial Workers of the World [IWW]. I was inclined to believe him when he talked of direct action instead of political action.

"When the silk-mill strike broke out I immediately went to Gergotz. I told him the situation. He excused himself and came right down to talk to the strikers. They were mostly girls and quite a few boys. They were mostly twisters who twisted the ends together instead of tying them and pulled them through a reel. I had been working with them on the Jacquard looms and had learned to weave broadcloth with pictures in it. The company was cheating the weavers. They were actually cheating most of the workers out of the yardage they would complete when they took it off the looms to measure it. They figured how many 'picks' across the cloth.

Some would have one hundred and some would have ninety. And you were paid by the picks, but they were cheating on the number of picks.

"We started the strike on a St. Patrick's Day morning. The miners were out of work celebrating St. Patrick's Day. I was standing with the strikers in the street when the police chief came by and said, 'Get the hell out of here. You're raising a lot of hell.' I told him, 'Nobody is raising hell around here except you and your scabs like you.' My father had told me that the chief and his brothers had secretly worked in the mines when the miners were on strike. So I was quickly hauled down to the mayor's office in the police wagon. The mayor told me I had insulted a police officer and said that I should apologize. I said that I'd never forget that. They said that I would have to pay a five-dollar fine and eat bread and water for five days. I still wouldn't apologize. So I served the five days.

"After I got out of jail we were forced to leave Hazleton. Lewis Gergotz and I went down and got a freight train. I had to leave to get work because nobody would hire me. I was blacklisted. We had also been reported to the mayor's office by a detective by the name of Van for holding meetings of the IWW in Hazleton. So Gergotz and I left for Philadelphia.

"We didn't spend any time looking around for work but went directly to Philadelphia in 1913. My mother wrote to an aunt in the city who looked me up where I found a place to live and told me that she was already part of the IWW. She told me to come with her and she would introduce me to the other Wobblies in the city. So I got a room in the same building as my aunt and we went to IWW meetings together. We also went to socialist meetings, anarchist meetings, and any meetings we could. I spent all of my time mostly running to different meetings.

"During the day, we found work in Philadelphia weaving velour bedspreads. When we started working there we didn't know the place was on strike. We were strangers. But that night they let us out the back door instead of the front gate. They said there might be pickets in the front. Then we realized that the place that hired us was on strike.

"I don't know much about Gergotz's background outside of the fact that he was from a Catholic family. But he wasn't religious. He was more or less an evolutionist. His parents came from Hungary and he worked in the mines.

"I worked around for a while and then finally the Industrial Workers of the World sent a fella down to Philadelphia by the name of Bill Levy. And he had been in prison somewhere in the West. He was pardoned by Woodrow Wilson, I think. And he came down to Philadelphia, and he was then considered an organizer in charge of organization of the Industrial Workers of the World, which was located in Chicago. So he took an interest in me and insisted that I go up to New Bedford, Massachusetts. There was a small organization there, mostly Portuguese. I was in New Bedford—how long afterwards I don't know—but I was there about six or seven months. And under the fear that I had been picked for the draft, I registered. I was working for the IWW. I was paid by the IWW. I stayed in New Bedford, Massachusetts, and later on they told me to move [to Philadelphia].

"In New Bedford, I didn't get too much [work]. In other words, [the IWW had a] very small group [there]. Then in Fall River, there was a group there, and they met in a little place not much bigger than this room. And I went in there. Of course, I couldn't talk Portuguese with them, but I made myself understood. So I worked with them hard for a while, mostly in cotton mills. So one day it was a hundred and seven degrees and the police were on our neck all the time; they would just walk in there. So I ordered them the hell out of there one night, [told them] they had [no] right to come in there. And everybody in the group agreed that I was right. So then the police officers in the town wanted me to appear at the city hall, and I appeared, and they wanted me to give them the list of all the members of the IWW. And I told them that was out of the question, I would not give them the list of the men. So then [one of the policemen] went on about the hall. Now, we're trying to rent a bigger hall, and there was a woman who had a hall two or three blocks below us, and every once in a while when we would send somebody over to talk about lending the hall, then they would always send somebody from the police over to warn her that she was looking for trouble. And we would never get a direct answer from her. So finally we turned around and we found another buy that was close to the City Hall in New Bedford on Main Street. So we went down and we rented that. And we had it inspected because in those days there was a limit of how many men were going to be in it. So then I was asked to appear at the mayor's office. So I appeared there at the mayor's office and he talked about the inspection. 'Oh,' I said, 'We've already had the hall rented.' He says, 'You have to have an inspection.' I says, 'It's already been inspected.' Well, it was shortly after that I got my call to go to the army. So I moved back to Philadelphia.

"I came back to Philadelphia with the idea of telling the draft board I wouldn't serve, forcing the issue. So [Levy] says, 'Well, we don't know whether they'll lock you up right now or what to do.' I resisted because I was opposed to the capitalistic system. To begin with, I was opposed to war, to go out to war and kill off a man that may be my best friend. And it was a capitalistic war to begin with. I even spoke on street corners in Philadelphia, on Marshall Street. And I spoke against war. 'The only way,' I says, 'to prevent wars, is not to fight them.'

"And they took me and other resisters to Camp Meade, Maryland. All the fellas in there—some of them I don't know their names or anything else—were put into a barracks. There were Mennonites and socialists from Reading. A lot of them were scared and I don't know what all. But they

Pennsylvania Historical and Museum Commission

LEE ROY HORLACHER (*far right*) AND FELLOW CONSCIENTIOUS OBJECTORS

didn't have the knowledge that I had. They told me I would get in trouble. I said, 'It don't make a damn bit of difference.' "

LOUIS HEIM

Louis Heim was born in 1895, the son of a German-Lutheran blacksmith. His father took a job with a foundry in Lebanon, Pennsylvania, in 1900, when Heim was five years old, but his father died several years later and Louis was forced to leave home to earn a living. He roamed from one job to another and finally returned to the Bethlehem Steel plant in Lebanon, where he attempted to support a family of his own.

"I left home at age twelve and got a job through our church at a sanitarium in Philadelphia. I was a bell boy and would deliver ice water to the patients and whatever else they needed. I even gave them medicine. At a dollar and a half a week and room and board I certainly didn't send any money back to my mother. I was lonely at first, but the nurses took to me and made it real pleasant after a while. After two years the sanitarium closed and I went to a South Lancaster, Massachusetts, hospital run by the Seventh-Day Adventist Church. I tried to attend classes there, but it was difficult because I worked in a bookbindery for ten cents an hour as well. Later I went with a friend to work in another sanitarium in Maryland for three years until I was seventeen.

"Every once [in] a while I would get a letter from my mother or brother, but not too often. I might see them once in a year.

"I left Maryland when my friend sent me the money to come down to Florida where he had moved. Then we roamed around to North Carolina where I had an uncle who was running a pine-logging camp. There were mostly colored fellows there. The uncle asked us to run the camp for a while, but I didn't want to because I was only eighteen years old and didn't know anything about it. I finally agreed to be an overseer for a while. But I relied on these big colored fellows, who knew what to do. And I found out they were getting rotten meat to eat because the old overseer was getting a kickback. I said, 'My God, that stuff is rotten.' I found a good butcher and got them good meat. And I didn't carry a gun and a bull whip. Well, these colored fellows would do anything for me. I guess I was there for about a year.

"At eighteen I had no goals. I just roamed. I went to New Orleans and worked in a cotton warehouse after the camp. But I finally got tired of that and came back to Lebanon. I was about twenty years old and had lost a good deal of my Pennsylvania Dutch accent.

"When I returned to Lebanon I got a job working for Montgomery

Ward as a salesman. I would go out to these farmers and sell them anything, especially because I could understand Pennsylvania Dutch. Then Montgomery Ward closed up and I became an automobile salesman until the Depression hit in 1930. I sold the Star car; it was good one and had a Liberty engine. But the boss was one of these fellows that spent money on things other than the business. He finally got in an accident and the business folded up.

"So by 1932 I had a wife, two children, and no job. I was renting in Lebanon [and] it was rough. My brother-in-law was boarding with us, but when he lost his job he could no longer pay board and had to leave. We surely couldn't keep him.

"The darkest day of my life was one January morning. It was raining, snowing, and sleeting. I had one-half of a raw potato and my youngsters shared a bottle of milk and some bread. About 9:30 my little girl came to me and said, "Daddy, I'm hungry.' Well, I made up my mind that I was going to get something for those kids to eat if I had to shoot somebody. I started down the street and ran into a friend whom I knew employed men and said, 'Listen, can you give me a couple hours work so I can get something for the kids to eat?' [He] couldn't, but [he] told me to go to Associated Charities in Lebanon. And I went down there and walked around the block three times before I got [up] nerve enough to go in. I told them my name and things began to happen. They gave me a slip for [goods] at the American store and then [they] gave me a quarter-ton of coal. But when I got home there was much more than a quarter-ton of coal. I checked with the dealer, and he told me an anonymous friend contributed the coal.

"Then this Public Works Program came along. At that time this country was ready for anything. You get a bunch of hungry people and they would do anything. I think Roosevelt's program saved the self-respect and the sanity of a lot of men. It did mine. It bothered me that I had no work; that I had nothing. [I] had too much idle time trying to get money to feed my family. This WPA program paid me for my work. We built the old sewage disposal plant, repaved the streets, and we built a school over on State Street; I was a night watchman on the construction site.

"Then I heard they were hiring over at the steel foundry and I got a job over there. They put me on chipping. But after two weeks the dust was so bad that my lungs were polluted. When I coughed, black dirt would come out. I had been grinding and chipping off the rough edges when the casting would come in, with an automatic hammer and a grinder which produced all the dust.

"Then I went over to the Bethlehem Steel mill. This was around 1937. I had actually worked there once before in the 1920s as a young man. But I left; something didn't suit me so I walked out. I didn't like to be pushed around where I was working in the blacksmith shop. The foremen had their 'pets,' who could get away with anything, and I didn't like it. Some men would give the boss money; some farmers would bring in potatoes, chickens, eggs. I never did that. I wasn't going to pay for the job. And this was common practice until the union came in for the job.

"In 1937 they sent me to work in the heat-treating department. When I started they were making track bolts for the railroad. I would have to feed the bolts into slots which would thread them. They called it 'playing the piano.' If one wasn't trimmed right you had to throw it out so it wouldn't jam up the machine.

"Then I went up to the soaking-rod furnace where they heat-treated the rods. You shoved the rods in the furnace, then pulled them out and loaded them on a bed. Then you would get up on the beds and straighten them. Finally, the furnace operator I worked for contracted tuberculosis and died and I got his job and then I had four helpers. I remained at that job until I retired at age sixty-five.

"The boss at the heat-treating plant, Tom Kirshner, was a fair man and never pushed us. See, you really couldn't push the men here because it took a certain amount of time to treat the rods, and if you pushed too hard you would have failures. I had some time to relax; you had two fifteen-minute breaks each day. When I ran the furnace I mainly had to see that my heat was right, and I believe if things are working right to leave them alone. You had some operators who would start messing around and soon their machinery would give them trouble."

JACOB LIGHT

Jacob Light was born in 1898. Eventually he bought his father's farm near Lebanon, Pennsylvania, but he discovered that maintaining his family required that he work both in the fields and in the nearby Bethlehem Steel mill. At one point his weekly work schedule prevented him from sleeping from Sunday until Tuesday evening. Inside the mill, moreover, foremen exerted pressures of their own.

"I first started working at Lebanon Valley Iron & Steel when I was fifteen years old, as a call boy. A call boy would go out and call or get extra men if work crews were short of men on a given day. I kept some of my wages and gave my father some. When Lebanon Valley went bankrupt I went to work for a tinsmith who put roofs on. He put tin and slate roofs [on] and I worked there for a few years. At that time there were six children and my dad said, 'If you would go and hire out you would keep one-half of your money.' Well, I was after the money. For a while I was even a 'maid' [servant] in the farmhouse of Dr. Bamberger. I would help out in the house.

"Then after my job with the roofer I went over to a new forge at Bethlehem Steel. I was sent to the warehouse, but they had a pusher boss over there who was no good. He was supposed to check up on you. Of course, he was no good because he was about as dirty as you could get. If he didn't like [you] he would try to prove things against you so you would lose your job. See, I was shipping this galvanized material out of the warehouse and I had four slips. I always signed my name on each slip. I always put JHL on them. One day I got a lot of stuff out. But the main checker in there was a good guy. And I had big boxes to get out. We had to weigh the boxes [and] put the sizes and address on them. So I got the head checker to weigh the boxes. And this day when I came out of the afternoon shop I was called to the office. The boss told me, 'You know, you made a big bull [mistake].' We knew he was going to take me over the coals. The boss said, 'You get paid to do this job right.' I said, 'What else am I doing?' That job I done right. I have proof because when I put bolts in those boxes I put extra ones in so that in case a few were lost the customer would still get what he ordered. And I got the head checker in there and he said that's what we were supposed to do and he told them everything I said was true. The pusher boss had said that we put six thousand less bolts in the order. But do you know who took the bolts out of there? The pusher boss. I said, 'Get him down here in the office.' You see, a fellow in the electric furnace had told me about this pusher boss. He told me that this pusher boss would steal bolts and make it look bad for men he didn't like. And the pusher boss got one week off [without pay]. Their general manager then came down and told him, 'From now on you don't bother Jake Light any more. He does his job right but you don't do your job right.' I guess that pusher boss didn't like me because I wasn't one of his friends.

"When I worked at Lebanon Valley it was so hot on the beds that I wore thick, steel hinges on my shoes and woollen underwear on my legs year-around on account of the sparks. It really kept my legs cool. I stood on plates that were cherry-red [so] I had to have them heavy shoes. If the sparks went through my underwear they would burn my skin. I never really thought of quitting, because I was used to that place. And when Lebanon Valley went on strike, me and some guys just went to a quarry and worked."

Part III
ORGANIZING IN THE THIRTIES: DEFENDING THE WORKERS' WORLD

*At that time J & L already had
started their espionage system, their
beatings. People who were out trying
to organize, to get people to sign up
to join the union, were beaten.*

Domenic Del Turco, Aliquippa

*I'll tell you, I just wanted to get a
job and take care of my family.*

Wayne Hendrickson, Elkland

It is clear that by the onset of the Great Depression in America, several generations of industrial workers had created a complex world that subtly shaped their expectations and loyalties. Memories of past labor battles, struggling but generally caring parents, family needs, neighborly assistance, routinized work, and limited power and inequalities on the job all intermingled in their consciousness. Collectively, this mélange of experience and feeling effectively shaped the foundation upon which they built their lives. As nebulous as this consciousness was, the historical drama from which it emerged and the people who moved under its influence were inescapably real as hard times worsened after 1930.

The Great Depression created an unprecedented reaction on the part of America's industrial workers, for it posed an overwhelming threat to the family- and community-based worker enclaves scattered throughout the nation. Workers organized on a national basis, thereby transcending their family and community base, but they did not abandon the values of

119

Library of Congress

SWOC Headquarters, Aliquippa, 1937

the workers' world. Larger organizations and strike situations often raised workers' consciousness to new levels, to new perceptions of power and social change, to be sure. But the intellectual and emotional foundation of the working-class thrust of the 1930s remained the family and community. The men interviewed here often expressed concern over power and inequality in explaining their movement toward unionization, but they were essentially the products of a family-community system that expected their support, a system that had provided for their needs for several decades. These workers had learned early in their lives that they could not change society; the experiences of their parents were still fresh in their minds. But employment security as a basis for family stability was important enough to be defended at all costs.

Some have argued that the thrust of labor reform at this time came primarily from labor leaders like John L. Lewis or liberal Democrats in the federal government. As long as historical inquiry is confined to the activities of such men, this will be the inescapable conclusion. But our probes inside the workers' world suggest that labor and governmental leaders may have been reacting to a larger ground swell of popular support for workers' rights and security. The workers' initial attempts at reform were unfocused, but the recollections presented here clearly indicate that these workingmen took matters into their own hands.

The major stimulus toward a grass-roots labor movement at the local level was unemployment. Orville Rice and others were out of work frequently before 1937. Moreover, some men clung so tenaciously to their jobs that they would never think of taking a vacation. Even more revealing is the fact that these men were reluctant to stray from their enclaves if they could help it. Louis Smolinski and Stanley Brozek returned to the mills where relatives had initially gotten them jobs and worked with them, even though periods of idleness there had forced them to look for work elsewhere in the past. Of course, unemployment weakened family stability considerably. As Brozek affirmed, there were no unemployment or pension benefits. "In 1937," he explained, "with a wife and a couple of kids, when I got my last pay check I was done."

Indeed, the strong community and workplace ties of the enclave actually facilitated the unionization and organization drives when they emerged full-blown. Any reluctance on the part of an individual worker toward organization was usually overcome by the irresistible pressure brought to bear by friends and peers working in the same department.

Throughout working-class enclaves in the early 1930s, men acted on their own to reverse the rising tide of insecurity and, as long as they were at it, to correct existing inequities. Before John L. Lewis formed the Steel Workers Organizing Committee (SWOC), Stanley Brozek tells us, steelworkers in Braddock broke from the old Amalgamated Association of

Iron and Tin Workers and formed their own "Emergency Council." In Aliquippa, according to Michael Zahorsky, men began talking about organizing before SWOC arrived, despite the company's attempts to instill loyalty by providing the workers with picnics and other kinds of entertainment. In fact, Domenic Del Turco reveals that Aliquippa sent a delegation to Lewis as early as 1934 urging him to organize a steelworkers union.

Once this tide of organization generated by massive insecurity reached significant proportions, men began to expand their objectives and seek redress for the years of unfair treatment that gnawed at their sense of justice. The list was long. In Aliquippa there was bitterness over work schedules and kickbacks to foremen for preferential treatment. Everywhere suspicion had been generated among workers over uneven pay rates; "fair-haired" company boys were thought to receive more. In fact, secrecy over wages was so prevalent that in Braddock no one would reveal the contents of his pay envelope. Sometimes, according to Tom Brown, a person could be laid off simply for smoking. Essentially, however, workers challenged company and community structures with organization drives primarily to preserve the integrity of their family-, community-, and work-based enclaves. They had been powerless and treated unfairly for years, but they did not choose to move against this system until the economic dislocations of the early thirties threatened their community base. Workers were now willing to mount challenges to company power and risk injury and violence. Louis Smolinski, for example, ignored the urgings of his parish priest to stop his activities. Furthermore, the strong legacy of the enclave served workers well as an integrating mechanism that facilitated unionization and collective activity. By 1937, then, at least in the towns studied here, the movement toward unionization was not only a strike for social change but both an extension of the enclave and a determined attempt to preserve it.

DOMENIC DEL TURCO

Domenic Del Turco was the son of an immigrant from the Italian province of Abruzzi, the birthplace of many immigrants to the Pittsburgh area. His father worked at the Jones & Laughlin plant in Aliquippa. In 1924 Domenic joined his father in the welded-tube department of J & L and eventually became active in the steelworkers union.

"There wasn't much work in Sharpsburg so my father heard J & L had opened up here in Aliquippa. In 1908 he came down there and put an application in and got a job. And he stayed here. He worked in the welded-tube section. That's where they make pipes. They need to make welded pipe. They'd weld them and make all kind of pipe, for welding with couplings, to screw on. That's all he made there. He worked on the skalp end of the furnace. They used to feed skalp into this furnace. It would come out a pipe. See, they are welded together.

"Skalp is a piece of steel that is cut to a certain dimension. And then, when they weld this pipe, that pipe comes whatever size you want it, whether it's half-inch, three-quarters, or an inch. My father was the man that pushed the skalp into the furnace. He did that until he had to retire. He became disabled around fifty years of age.

"There were a lot of Italians in the butt mill. 'But mill' means simply you weld the pipe together; it becomes fused together like that and it's called a butt. So that's what they call the butt mill. And it's a welded pipe; that's why they call it the welded-tube department.

"He never talked about the company or unions. He just went to work and minded his own business. There was no such thing as unions discussed there at that time. Because if they would have discussed about unions then, you wouldn't have been there. The company had absolute control of the town. The name of the company was the Jones & Laughlin Corporation.

"I was born in Sharpsburg in 1906 and came to Aliquippa when my mother came down with the family. I was two years old then. My mother had a daughter. My oldest sister and brother were born in Italy. They were left behind with an aunt until such time that things looked better here. My oldest brother, he was the oldest one, and my sister, and I'm next. I was the first one born here. And all the rest of them, the next four, were born in this country. There were five of us born in this country, two born in Italy.

"I was only able to go to school until the eighth grade, after I graduated from the eighth grade. And the reason for that was we had problems with some people in this country which weren't exactly the type of people to know. They demanded money and things like that. It was the 'black hand.' And the result was that they bombed our house. They were extorting my dad; they were getting money till my dad finally decided to call it quits, because it was breaking him. And we had a little store to supplement our income, and they would come in the store and ask my mother for two hundred, three hundred, five hundred dollars. They were Italian Americans. No doubt about it. They knew their own people.

"And that's how we went back to Italy, because my mother was scared. They had young kids and was afraid something might happen to the family after they bombed our house. So my dad asked them if they'd like to go back to Italy for a while, till this thing blowed over. And that's what happened. We went to Italy in 1920.

"I returned to Aliquippa in 1924 and went to J & L and applied for a job. I was two, three months from being eighteen. So they hired me. I got hired in the welded-tube, same place my dad worked.

"I was sent to welded-tube because they needed younger people there. It was [a] type of work that the younger man was more adept at. They could learn faster, and when you're young, you get around faster too. The reason for that was because you had to be fast in doing this work, because when the pipe came out of the mill, then it came down on the floor, and you had to sort it out. So you was under continuous operation, all the time.

"No, we didn't have any union at all then. But they brought Negroes from the South to put them against whites and keep us from organizing. They could get them for cheap labor. Of course, even the whites were getting cheap labor. There's no secret about that. We got no vacations. I was hired in 1924, and from 1924 to '29, five consecutive years, I worked six, seven days a week, ten hours in the day, ten and a half at night, no vacations. Nobody got the same rate. They had what they called the 'fair-haired boys'; they paid them a certain rate. And the rest got a lesser rate. One would be getting a higher rate and one would be getting a lower rate. Well, that's because that was a company policy. They figured it all depends whether you were sympathetic toward the company.

"In one case, they fired a foreman after it was exposed that this guy was making a lot of his employees kick back. When they finally started protesting, they got rid of him. I don't know where they sent him, but I think they might have sent him somewhere else.

"They didn't have no company union then either. The company union came in J & L in 1934. As a matter of fact, it became prevalent in all the steel industries in 1934.

"If accidentally [a] guy shot his mouth off and said, 'How much you making on your job, boy?' that's how we used to find out. We got to checking and found out that some of the boys who were considered company people—when I say company people, that [means] they were leaning towards management more than they were towards the people that worked in there—were making more. And there was no secret that a lot of people were getting higher rates than other people who did the same type of work.

"They spied on you. Sure, that's the idea of giving them a higher rate. Certainly there was nothing new about that.

"Let me give you another illustration. When we first started working on organizing the union, we had a man named Mike Keller. I don't mind mentioning his name because he died for the cause. He was a Serbian man from Aliquippa. A 'fair-haired boy' for the company—I don't want to mention his name because his people are still living there—attacked him. When we were first organizing the union in Aliquippa, the police department was against us, the fire department, every governmental group was against us. That's why they call Aliquippa the 'Little Siberia.' You couldn't even breathe in there without somebody stooging on you. While we was just out organizing the union, Mike Keller was one of these aggressive little Serbian men. In 1935 Keller was standing right in front of the police, in the middle of the street. I was not too far from him. Now this guy was a little fella; Mike Keller was little fella. He was about five feet, two inches. And this guy walked up to him [and] without any reason at all started beating him up. Now this man was big, he was about six one or two, weighed about two hundred thirty or forty pounds. And he beat this man up so bad, five or six years later he dies from the effects of the beatings. He busted his ear drums, kicked him in the head, kicked him in the stomach so bad; he was beat up so bad. And the police were standing right there and they wouldn't move, because they had orders not to interfere. That's how J & L was trying to control the people. But it didn't work, because guys were so incensed about this thing that we were more determined to organize the union.

"You had to be a 'fair-haired boy.' Everything in town was controlled. You could not get a loan unless it was O.K.'d. You couldn't do anything in that town unless it was O.K.'d by higher powers to be. The banks were controlled by the corporation.

"To show you how this area was under control, even when Roosevelt came into office the Republicans still had the town under control over the county. And we were put on WPA. There was one prominent citizen here that had a big place, farmland, a lot of land. I'm not going to mention his name either, because that's water over the dam. But we used to go up there, clean, cut his trees down, oil the roads and everything. We used to do all that. We used to get a scrip, a one-dollar scrip every week, no cash! We used to work a ten-hour day on WPA. We got a dollar-a-week scrip. For a dollar a week you could get some beans, porkchops.

"Since they had orders from all local governments, county governments was in charge of putting these people to work. So naturally this guy figured that here was a good chance to take care of his property. He was in with the corporations. He was a local businessman.

"In the 1930s, before the union, we would work a few days a week. They tried to enlist me in the Communist Party, and I told them that communism and unionism doesn't mix. 'I'm a union man [Amalgamated Association of Iron and Tin Workers at this time], and I'm going to stay a union man. I don't want no part of communism.'

"An organizer came down, and I was going to work. I heard him call my name. I turned around and he gave me a false name. He told me his name was Ben Gold. But I found out later on it wasn't. And he says, 'I came down purposely to see you. You're a very aggressive young man. You're an educated boy and you have a good vocabulary, and you are a forceful speaker.' And he said, 'We can use people like you.' And I said, 'Are you representing a union?' He says, 'No.' 'Well,' I says, 'you're talking to the wrong man, because I am already committed to the union. And I am organizing the union [Amalgamated] in this community and this valley.' "This was 1934. And he says to me, 'Well, we still could use you.' I said, 'If you're talking about any party, you're talking about the Communist Party.' Of course, I was aware that there was a couple of organizers sent down talking to the people. He said, 'Yes.' That's when I told him. I said, 'The Communist Party and unionism doesn't mix. I'm a labor man and I'll stay that way. And I'm a Christian. I don't believe in communism.'

"Because at that time, according to the federal government, the Communist Party in this country was behind the eight ball. It just wasn't accepted in this country at that time. And to illustrate the point, we had a few of our good union people that were interviewed by the FBI several years later about their leanings towards the Communist Party. What happened was they foolishly signed a petition one time without reading it, and here it was a petition that the Communist Party was circulating around. So when he came to me and asked me to sign a petition, I said, 'I don't sign anything until I read it.' So I read it; I gave it back to him. I said, 'I will not sign this petition. I am not a member of the Communist Party, and I don't intend to be.' 'Well,' he says, 'you do that. We're trying to establish democracy.' I said, 'Your kind of democracy, not mine.' The results was that this poor guy—I don't want to mention his name for he became a union official later on and he's dead now—had to go through a grilling for about several hours by the FBI in this country. They asked him why he signed that petition, and was he a member of the Communist Party. We were able at that time to convince the federal government, the FBI, that he foolishly signed it without even paying attention. At that time the union was coming in; everybody was signing everything, you know, not knowing what they were signing.

"We heard about this organizing over in Ambridge, and we decided to go over and listen to the organizer, because he couldn't come into Aliquippa. As I said before, this man, P. J. Call, who was then burgess of Ambridge, was a union man himself. He told the people that any time they want to they could meet in Ambridge to talk about union. They would get police protection. When I heard about this organizing in Ambridge, of this plant, we went over and listened to him. His name was John Tepowsky. And boy, he was really a good one!

"He was from the Amalgamated. He was the organizer for the Amalgamated. And they started the speaking, and we went over to listen. Well, that's when we first found out that the union was coming in. In the meantime, we had a man who later became financial secretary of our organization. This man knew these organizers because they originally came from the coal mines, some of them. And some of them were with the Amalgamated for years, you know. And he made contact with Tepowsky about coming to Aliquippa to organize. This was about the fall of '33. Well after that speech over there and all that, a lot of people in this plant over here in Ambridge decided they wanted to join the union and started organizing. And the upshot was that the company, of course, wouldn't recognize [it and] there was a strike. And of course we heard 'bout the strike, so we went over. In this day, the deputies and coal and iron police and everybody else were there, and then a riot started. They started shooting [in Ambridge], antigas pellets. And there was homes there. This one guy was standing on his porch watching all these things go on, and a stray bullet killed him. It was J & L who deputized over in Aliquippa, and sent them to Ambridge to break the strike.

"Then, after that, we started [organizing] in 1934. We talked to Tepowsky and a man named Martin Gestner. He was an ex–coal miner one time at West Virginia, the man I said that contacted him. And Tepowsky asked Gestner to get us a charter. We wanted to become members of the Amalgamated. And so we paid at that time thirty dollars for the charter.

"And then we started really organizing. We had quite a few people then. We already had a large group, about forty or fifty, somewhere around there. Then we went up to as high as six thousand members, which is a heck of [a] lot of members, considering that the people we were affiliated with wasn't doing anything for us. We found that out later.

"Jones & Laughlin Steel Corporation hired Pinkertons, and the Burnses, believe it or not. And one of the Burnses or Pinkertons, whatever he was, became vice-president of our union when he came down here. He joined the union. The company asked him to join our union just to spy on us. And this guy was trained for this. He was an ex-boxer. He was a lightweight, but boy was he good!

"Now don't get me wrong, I'm not trying to minimize what these other people did. But the two plants that really were strong [for the union] was the welded-tube and the seamless. The strongest group of people that were for the union [Amalgamated] and really held to it was, like I told you, Mike Keller and the Serbians, the Croats, the Ukrainians, the Italians, and the Irish. Of course, the Irish wasn't as large a group as the rest of them. But those five groups were very aggressive groups.

"The organizing part of it, I like [that] the best. The strength that we would have. It was emphasized by one man. He said if we organize, we have strength. You got the power to fight power.

"During the Amalgamated days, the organization didn't have any power to convince the company that we wanted recognition. And I recognized that, and I knew that if we didn't have a powerful body behind us, we would never get nowhere, because at that time J & L already had started their espionage system, their beatings. People who were out trying to organize, to get people to sign up to join the union, were beaten. I escaped a beating one night while I was out signing cards.

"Later on, there was division in the local union itself. We were dissatisfied with what the Amalgamated was doing, and so a more aggressive group—you can call us radical if you want to as far as the union is concerned—decided things didn't look so good. So we decided that we wanted to send somebody down to see John L. Lewis in Washington and see what he could do about it.

"Finally, even though we had taken opposition, the majority agreed. So we held the dues back. Well, what happened was that the Amalgamated Association wanted to know why we weren't sending dues in. And we told them that we were not satisfied with what they were doing, and we expected them to get recognition for us from the company so we could become a bona fide union organization. And they told us, 'If you [don't] send in the money, we expel you people.' I said, 'I don't give a doggone if you expel me or not. Go ahead and expel me. So what?' Well, the upshot was they held a convention in the West End of Pittsburgh with men from another town. And so the upshot of the whole thing is we had our own convention and we made plans. And so when we came back, we in Aliquippa sent a car over to people [in] Washington, D.C., with a letter. And there was six people going down, and these six people was in a Buick touring car. And they had this letter to give to John L. Lewis. So they went down. We couldn't do it because the officers left; good Lord knows what the company would do to the members. Lewis talked to them and all. He says, 'I promise you that we will organize the steelworkes in the very near future.' And Philip Murray, who was then with Lewis for the miners, was appointed by Lewis to organize the steelworkers. And then when we were successful we had a three-day strike down in J & L to convince J & L we meant business. That was 1936, when the SWOC came in.

"Eventually Philip Murray met with these corporations and told them, "We want you to recognize the union.' They wouldn't, so there was a strike called in the steel mills in 1937.

"In the meantime, a committee was set up to negotiate with the Jones & Laughlin Steel Corporation. I was one of the members of the committee. After three days J & L agreed to recognize us as the bargaining unit for the employees. And that's how it began. Then we had an election on the premise that they would hold the election and the union would lose the election, that they wouldn't recognize them. So what happened is we took it and got 7,000 for and 1,000 against.

"What happened was we had an awful time trying to convince the black brothers to join. It wasn't a matter of trust. It was a matter that the company had put the fear of God in these people.

"Just like I said, one day the company brought forty nonunion Negroes to work in the plant. They came off this bus, about forty of them. They started marching in just like a group, already prepared. We tried to stop them. The first thing you know, they started swinging. We doggone near got murdered down here. I had a blackjack, and I started swinging my blackjack. I broke the doggone thing. But those guys didn't know that I had broken it. They weren't getting near me. They were afraid they were going to get hit with it.

"These guys went in. They [had] to come out. 'Tonight and tomorrow we'll be waiting for them,' I said. 'We're going to get these guys.' [Then] our union people down in the mill brought out these pieces of pipe about three feet long, about three-quarter-inch pipe; that's what they call the scrap end of the pipe, they chop it off. 'We're going to wrap it up in the doggone newspapers and we'll wait for them,' [I said]. Well, they must have got wind of it, because them guys stayed in that doggone plant and didn't come out. And all the time we had the dues inspection they didn't come out. Then I was talking to James, a black union member, and I told him what happened. He says, 'I know, I'm ashamed of my own people. But, I'm going to talk with these guys, and I'm going to tell them, "You're going to get killed if you don't quit messing around. They're going to beat your brains in for you. We're not playing Ping-Pong here, my friends, we're fighting for our bread and butter here. We're fighting for our life." ' So after that incident we didn't have trouble with Negroes because then they started joining the union.

"It wasn't because they were reluctant; the company told them [it] wanted them to come to work and didn't want them to belong to the union. If [it] did, they wouldn't be around."

MICHAEL ZAHORSKY

Michael Zahorsky, a second-generation Slovak American, worked most of his life at the Jones & Laughlin plant in Aliquippa, Pennsylvania. Here he describes the measures the company took to keep the union out of town and relates the details of local organizing.

"I was a sticker puller at first; I worked at a coke works, then I was a millwright helper in the rectangular coke ovens. I worked there several months, and then I went into the tube mill. I was a gauger in a tube mill. It wasn't like a continuous run in the mill. They made pipe out of a slab, maybe a piece of skalp, twenty, twenty-five feet long. And I had to write because there was a lot of people that were illiterate that worked in the mill at that time. And [being] a young kid, I was pretty sharp. They made me a gauger. And I had this job as a gauger for a while, and then there was a young kid who was fifteen years old who got killed, and then they got all the young kids out of there. They checked on us, and they figured it was too risky for us, climbing in big piles of skalp. It just fell over on him, actually squeezed the guy to death. Then I was in a blow-engine room of the blooming mill, and this is some of the biggest engines that they have in the industry; [it's] where they roll the great big ingots and blooms. And I was doing all right. The foreman was a friend of my father's, and they used to drink together, and I got this job as an oiler. I had to go among these various cranks and the various revolving wheels and all that. And one day the foreman came up to me and said, 'Hey, Mike, how old are you?' I says, 'Sixteen.' He says, 'You're too damn young to be among this stuff. You better go someplace else.' So then they run me out of there, and I got a job in the office in a chemical lab. And I would run errands around there, and I would write out little reports. Then I left J & L and went down to a steel mill called Colonial Steel, in a little neighboring town about five miles down the river. I worked there as a laborer for a while. I worked around the steam hammers. I kind of liked the forging hammers. And then I got a job in a glasshouse. I worked in a glasshouse. I used to work twelve hours a night.

"I finally came back to J & L in the blacksmith shop. I never lost any time. I went from one job to another because I worked like hell all the time. I never had to have anybody with a finger up my butt to keep working. So it seemed that they laughed about it—how could I leave one job and go to another job and keep going? Because if you do it today, they'd probably blacklist you. They wouldn't want you in their employ; but I was very fortunate in that respect.

"I was a blacksmith at J & L for almost thirty years. And that was very hard work. In addition to that, now I took pride in the place where I worked. This sounds stupid to say. You wonder how the hell you correlate a beautiful blacksmith shop with a shop in a mill. But our shop was always maintained neat and clean, good production. We conducted safety meetings and things of that nature.

"In the steel plant we do everything, even make horseshoes. Of course, the horseshoes, we call them government jobs. You know what a government job is? In any industry where you do work, it's paid for by the company, but you're doing it for someone else on the side. Even some of the supervision would come in, and I made horseshoes for them, or I made rings for foremen. They needed chains. They had farms or something, and they needed chains. I welded chains for them. They needed tongs; I'd make a million tongs. But I did everything from small forgings—I made tongs, all kinds of hand tools, masonry tools, and tools they needed around the mill, all kinds of wrenches or forgings from which they turned gears or shafts. You know, we done all that stuff.

"This is one area where you had all ethnic groups. You had all nationalities. You had Scotch; you had Irish; you had Italian; you had Croatians; you had Slovaks; Serbians. You had a mixture of everything. The blacksmith shop was not dominated by any specific group like you do find in some industries.

"In the blacksmith shop it's almost impossible to work by yourself. You must have a helper, and if you're doing some very small job, like welding small chains, you can do it yourself. But if you've got something where you've got to have striking with a sledge or operating with a steam hammer, you must have a helper. And if it's a very large forging, you're going to have people that's assisting you with a hammer. You might have five, six men on a team, just like in a regular forge shop on a flat die. In a blacksmith shop, you use a flat die. We use a lot of various forging dies, but it's not like a drop-forge shop, where you stud a blanket to a mold and you slap it down with one punch of a hammer and then you have the piece, just like a molding, a casting and all. In a blacksmith shop you've got to do a lot of hand specialty work. It's really a wonderful craft.

"While there was a mixture, it was only natural for an old-timer to favor his own kind. If he was a Croatian and he saw a nice strong young Croatian boy that he kind of liked, he would try to get him there to be his helper. An Italian would do the same thing, just like the Slovak. But it's a natural thing. Maybe he even had a daughter and wanted him to marry his daughter.

"In the blacksmith shop you could start out as a helper, but you had to learn to drive the hammer. I learned to strike a sledge and learned the various movements. You're holding tools in your hand and you rely on the man striking the seldge or steam hammer. To learn to run a steam hammer you got to be extremely careful. It's a hazardous thing, so you didn't operate the hammer immediately. Sometimes they have the presses or they have the steam hammer or they have the bolt header. You had to learn how to operate these machines. But you would come in as a helper and you would work up to be a hammer driver or first helper like that.

"After Roosevelt was elected in 1932, the Democratic Party promised labor that they were going to get them some freedom at their work. One of these freedoms would be the formation of a union. The companies were alerted to all this, so the companies were not going to be caught asleep. So they started organizing what were called the company unions. In Jones & Laughlin, and a great number of the steel companies, they call it the employees' representative plan. They called us together and said, 'We're going to get big-hearted now.' In other words, this is probably what this amounted to: 'You're going to have your own representative now. Instead of going to your foreman with your gripes, you're going to have your own representative in the various departments for your gripes and your grievances; you're going to go to him with this.' And they organized about two years before the steelworkers organized. And the company was very lavish with the money. Oh, they were lavish. They put on some of the most beautiful picnics you ever saw. They spent up to ten thousand dollars. They brought nationally known, prominent bands and comedians here. They gave the kids all the pop and soda and hotdogs they wanted. They brought in all kinds of rides and concessions. They went all out! In other words, they spent unlimited money to keep the union out.

"I remember [how it was] in this mill here in 1936. We talked about it months before John L. Lewis decided that they were going to help the workers get organized. And they called it the SWOC, the Steel Workers Organizing Committee. I'll never forget—[it's] like yesterday. It was in 1936, shortly after the flood. An organizer of the SWOC came into Aliquippa, a man by the name of Joseph Timko. He was a Slovak; he came in from the coal fields. Why he came in to see me I don't know. But I lived down the end of the street here; the house is razed now. I was just getting ready to leave for someplace, and I didn't have too much time to talk to him. I wanted him to come back. But anyhow, we had a pastor at that time by the name of Monsignor Joseph Altany. He's pastor of St. Michael's Church in Munhall now. And he came from the coal fields. He came in from Nemacolin, Pennsylvania. And he was a man's man. He was a humanitarian. He felt that the company owed the people something. And Timko came in and we talked to him. Of course, everybody feared for their jobs; everybody did. Don't let anybody tell you they didn't. I talked to a lot of these fellas after it was over with, and they said, 'Well, I didn't give a damn,' 'To hell with it,' and this and that. They talked like that, but they all had that fear of the job, because the company fired many. I knew personally every one of the men that they fired here at the mill. They framed these men. I know 'em all. Most of them are still living. I think there's only about four living in the community. There were dozens of men who lost their jobs and nobody knew why. It was because of their interest in the organization of the union.

"Timko didn't come in here with any fanfare. He came because the police force was dominated by the company and everything. The county police were also controlled by the company. He came here incognito on a friendly visit. And, of course, he disclosed to us that he was a union man. Manny Woods, another organizer for Phil Murray, came in here around the same time, from Castle Shannon. And this town became fired up very fast. We had some wonderful people.

"They would hold meetings secretly in various homes. They would also meet in some of the neighborhoods' halls. And there was never a meeting held, it seemed, that there wasn't a stooge of the company there. It seemed that the meeting wasn't half over sometimes and someone would walk out, probably to call a raid by the company police. The company could deputize the police then. The deputies were like the old coal and iron police and they had [the] authority of state policemen. And the company used that to the fullest.

"Here in Aliquippa, as I have said, the company started to combat the organization of the union by this employees' representative plan. Then, when they heard there was going to be [a] strong organizational drive here, they set up what they called the Committee of 500. This committee was made up of professional people led by a certain Doctor Gelland. They also had high-school teachers and business people in the community. They thought they were doing the right thing when they said that the union was going to come in here and take all the money out of the community. And this feeling of theirs against the union got to be damn strong

Library of Congress

Steelworkers' Rally in Aliquippa, May 1937

here. You know, they went around the mill and they wanted us to sign papers that we'd join this committee as vigilantes against any outsiders wanting to come in and organize. They would tell us, 'Well, we don't mind you people organizing yourselves but we don't want nobody from the outside coming in here and stirring up trouble in the community. We got a wonderful community here.' And the Committee of 500 was extended to [a] committee of five thousand. That meant that every fourth person in this community was signing up here to be in this committee and oppose the first strike they called around here, in Ambridge, across the river.

"The committee went up to Ambridge. They even took ex-servicemen. I saw men cry. And they said, 'What the hell am I going to do, Mike? I have to go. They're going to take us.' And they put arm bands on them and they gave them clubs and even guns. They took them on trucks from the J & L plant and took them down to the Ambridge bridge. They had a movie camera set up and everything. I was there and I saw that, that afternoon. I would say that ninety-eight percent of them went against their better judgment for fear of losing their jobs.

"So they used tactics like that, but it didn't work. Governor Pinchot's wife—she was a son of a bitch when it came to the rights of people—came to Aliquippa and held a meeting [in 1937]. I thought there was going to be [a] thousand people killed. There were thousands and thousands of people congregated in the center of town. And do you know the company had manual machine guns in the windows in the hotel. If need be, they was prepared to 'mow 'em down.' Hard to believe. Mrs. Pinchot came into town and led the parade of steelworkers. They marched up to the Polish hall in what we call Plan 11; it is the Negro section of town today. And she [gave] a speech there. She spoke for the organization of the steelworkers. That was the first real break."

LOUIS SMOLINSKI
AND STANLEY BROZEK

Stanley Brozek and Louis Smolinski were second-generation Polish Americans. Brozek was born in 1910 in the coal-mining town of Trauger, Pennsylvania; his father had followed friends from Poland to the H. C. Frick coke mines there. Smolinski's father had immigrated first to Rankin, where he labored in a wire mill, and then, in 1913, to Braddock, where he died from a mill injury at the age of forty-three. Brozek and Smolinski offer a glimpse of what it was like getting a union started in Braddock in the thirties.

Brozek: "My dad worked first in Fayette County but had some friends in Trauger and moved there. He worked at the A. C. Frick mines, loading

Pennsylvania Historical and Museum Commission

Steelworkers' Neighborhood in Braddock, c. 1930

slag into the coke ovens. My dad started when he was thirteen. At that time you went to school and you worked. He always used to tell me how he used to fall asleep in school. So he started at Frick and I distinctly recall him telling me that he ran a little dinkey. The dinkey ran lorry cars and dumped the coal onto the side. He stayed there until 1913, when he came to Braddock to work in the Edgar Thomson Works.

"My first real job was in the same mill as my dad. I had odd jobs like working the fruit store and selling newspapers before that. My dad helped me get the job in the mill. At that time usually a father could speak for his son. He spoke to the superintendent. That's the way it was in 1928. I worked in the general labor department at first and transferred into the open hearth in 1929. Then came the big layoffs of 1931, 1932, and 1933. Since I was one of the youngest ones in the open hearth, I was among the first to go. In those years I got a job as a sales-route man for the Grand Union Tea Company. And I stayed there until I got tired of working six days a week on the road and traveling all the time. And then my dad got me back into the mill by talking to a superintendent who was a good friend of his. He said, 'My boy wants to come back.' So he gave me work because I was there before. I got hired back, in 1937."

Smolinski: "I started at Edgar Thomson in 1929. My brother worked there and brought me a letter from the boss saying I could start. I was doing all kind of labor work and gradually worked up to the boiler. When the Depression started there was no work and I got a job myself at Westinghouse. I got laid off up there, though, and I never thought that I would ever come back to the mill. It was a boom in 1937 and I got back to the mill. But 1938 was a bust again and I thought of getting out.

"I thought I'd like to get out into business or politics. I thought I would like to get into something that would serve the people. As a young fella in the mill I worked ten hours a day, sixty hours a week. And I thought to myself, 'What the hell am I going to do here all my life?' Of course, never thinking that things were going to change. So anyway, I thought to myself, cooped up here for ten hours a day, 'Why can't I do something outside and mingle with people all the time?' So actually my aspirations were for something outside, mingling with people. That's the way I felt when I was a young fella.

"Before the mill, I had been in a glassworks. You know, every glass blower had his own boys to take care of—the core boy, the mull boy, the carry-in boy. And I was carrying in and then I was the core boy. Everybody was getting different money. When the mull boy quit, [the glass blower] got another boy. I said, 'No way. I'm not working if I can't be the mull boy. I'm next in line for that job.' He said, 'No, he's going to work.' I said, 'O.K., I quit. I'm on strike.' And he couldn't do no work because he didn't have nobody else to carry the stuff in. So finally after about an hour he came to me and said, 'Come on. You're the mull boy.' Then everything was all right. We went back to work. But I didn't stay there long. That's when I got a call from the mill.

"At the Edgar Thomson mill the maintenance department was mostly Irish people. All the electricians and everything, practically ninety percent, were Irish. The Polish people dominated the foundry. And in the finishing department there was Polish, Slavish, and colored, [but] not too many colored."

Brozek: "The Irish had, when I was a youngster at the open hearth, the first helper, second helpers, and most of the slaggers. We had a few Slovaks. The Irish also predominated in the machine shop, and the Scotch, Irish, and English were roll turners. I know the foundry was Polish because I worked right across from it.

"One of our problems was the differing wages. William Jacko was our president around 1940. He was put on our union's wage and equity committee to standardize wages according to job class and the contents of jobs. Jacko told me that he found over two thousand four hundred different kinds of wage rates at United States Steel. At our boiler shop for years the men were afraid to show their pay envelopes to each other. We got paid by cash, and if you got even two or three cents more an hour it was good money. Nobody would let you see their pay envelopes in the boiler shop, and that's the truth.

"Some got more pay because they brought the 'boss' a drink or a meal. Logan was the boss at the boiler shop. I remember the old Slovak people talking down on Calvert Street: 'Oh, Logan is going to get a chicken dinner or some chicken soup.' "

Smolinski: "In 1934 the company proposed their own union. As soon as section 7A [of the National Industrial Recovery Act] was announced, they proposed the company union. I was standing on a corner one time and a few fellas come down and passed out cards. They said the Amalgamated Association of Iron, Steel, and Tin Workers was going to have a meeting in Homestead. They gave me a lot of these tickets to pass out for all steelworkers to go to the meeting. I said to him to come to Braddock and organize Braddock. He told me he couldn't do it unless he had two hundred signatures. I said that would be easy, and me and a couple of other fellas went out and got three hundred, and they put an organizer in Braddock. The Amalgamated officials said you can't serve two masters. And when Phil Murray took over, he told us to go in and break that company union. So we went into a meeting of the company union and asked for a raise of a dollar a day. We had five company representatives and five workers at the meeting. One of the superintendents of the engineering department even voted for us; he said he could use the raise. A week later he wasn't a representative anymore."

Brozek: "I became aware of the whole thing at the time Louis was active in the Amalgamated Association of Iron, Steel, and Tin Workers with a fella named John Chorey. Now Chorey used to come to my dad's house quite often. And they would talk union. And Louis had quite a number of meetings in the old hall in Braddock. And even though I worked for Grand Union at that time, I had so many union people come to my dad's house, I got interested in it. And so I learned just by hearing these fellas talk about their problems. They complained mostly about shortened work or hours and working conditions. My father also complained about the strike in 1919 and the way the 'Cossacks' came around with their horses and just beat you up. I recall a bunch of kids sitting on our porch, and they came down and told them to get the hell out of there and stay in the house. That's the way it was.

"It was this way when we were organizing in Braddock. Some of the union officers couldn't walk the streets. If my brother-in-law would see me

Author's personal collection

Louis Smolinski (*right*) and John Chorey

coming, he would cross over [to] the other side of the street so as not to be
seen with me. When I went in different taverns it was the same thing. We
found two members in our organization who were spies for the company.

"The company never offered you a vacation. My dad started working
in 1899 and never got one until 1936. What was the purpose of giving him
one [in 1936]? It was to discourage him from joining the union."

Smolinski: "A lot of guys would never take a vacation because they thought they were doing the company a favor.

"In 1934 we first tried to organize the Amalgamated in Braddock. I was a delegate to the convention in the West End of Pittsburgh. We were supposed to go on strike and voted for it. But at another convention about two weeks after that the Amalgamated wouldn't give us credentials. They told us that we weren't a recognized organization and they didn't want rabble-rousers and everything. So we had a meeting; we had to rent a hall about two blocks away from the Amalgamated place. State troopers were there on horses and everything; they made sure there was no trouble.

"The Amalgamated had put organizers in these different towns and tried to organize a union. They had some old puddlers and people like that. But it was an old organization by these old fellows. And they wouldn't let everybody join. After that first convention they disqualified most of us. We were unhappy with the Amalgamated when they threw us out of that hall. They didn't want no part of us, I think. So from there we started an emergency council. We had our council when the Steel Workers Organizing Committee came in.

"You take our finishing department. Well, that's where the organization came from. Mostly Polish and Slavish worked there and we all got together. There were rail straighteners, rail drillers, rail chippers, pilers. Some of those rails weighed almost a ton. You know, it was a 'Hunky' union. Well a lot of them Irish and every damn thing called it that. Some of the bosses and other damn things called it a 'Hunky' union. Everybody from the finishing department was in it. And there [were] many Negroes there too, and some could even speak Slovak. But when we first started our council we had a couple of Irish guys like Benny Dolwide from the storage department and Tom Connally from the maintenance department. But everybody was afraid, and nobody would want to be seen with you. I went to one meeting in Ambridge and couldn't get a drink because no clubs could sell anything. So I went to my uncle's house with five other guys and knock on the door. He let us in but told us to hurry up and have a drink because he didn't want anybody to know that we had been there.

"See, the Republican party controlled Braddock at that time. Let me tell you a story. We had a burgess named Callahan. In 1938 he tried to make a comeback. He was defeated because when the Depression set in the people started swinging away from the Republican party to the Democrats. So Callahan and his group were slowly being eliminated politically, losing office by office. In 1938 Callahan wanted to make a comeback in one way or another. I forgot what he ran for in Braddock. And I'm working at the polls down in the First Ward. So Callahan and I had a pretty good talk. He loved to take a drink. And he started telling me stories about what happened years ago. And he said, 'I wish I had only a dollar for every ballot that I sent floating down the river. I'd be in Florida living it up.' And then another thing—this is all coming back to me now—when I moved into my house in Braddock in 1935 I was fixing the coal stove. I took the coverplate off the stove and out falls ballots, a whole bunch of them. I'm thinking, 'I'll be goddamned.'

"We even brought Mrs. Pinchot to Braddock. We had her down here twice. And that's when my parish priest called me up and said, 'What you got this chick in here for?' I said, 'What do you mean?' He told me that I couldn't let her speak here. He started raising hell with me. 'You have to leave her go,' he said, 'and cancel that meeting.' I told him that she was a good organizer and [I said,] 'I ain't canceling nothing.' I guess the company got after him or some damn thing. I don't know why he opposed her. He was a Polish priest."

Brozek: "I'll tell you some incident that happened to me in the late twenties. In '28 I graduated from North Braddock High School and started working in the open hearth at Edgar Thomson. When I was first there I saw this colored kid get out of the pits and sit down. Then old Pete Quin, a boss, come by and thought he was looking [away from his work] and said, 'That's it. You're fired.' From that day on I figured, boy, this system ain't for me. And my uncle, Al Marsh, he was active in the union field with the coal mining, with Phil Murray up in District 5. He moved to Ambridge and got a job with the American Bridge Company. So I says, 'Uncle Al, I like to play a saxophone.' Now, in them days we had no high-school band. Otherwise, I'd been there with one of their instruments. So he got me a saxophone in 1928, [and] I played with a musical group for a number of years after that. But anyway, this had to be around 1930, because I had to have been off half the time. And I remember him callin' me up on Saturday. He says, 'What are you doin', Stanley?' I says, 'Tomorrow, I have nothing for tomorrow.' [He says,] 'I want you to come down to Ambridge. Bring your gang down, or else bring a few down, as many as you can scrape up.' So anyway, I got my brother and I got another fella that played banjo. My brother played a trumpet and a banjo. I had my saxophone. So we go down into Ambridge. And I never asked him what the hell it was all about. I figured, well, he's gonna have a little shindig or something. So Sunday we go over to—now this was in—we go over to Aliquippa. He takes us up to Aliquippa. Now Aliquippa was a hotbed for unionism. So we go to Aliquippa; there was about ten trucks lined up in front of this Croatian house. And so we come along and we get into one of these trucks. At that time you were allowed to take gangs in trucks. If you remember goin' back all them years. They'd take them to picnics, you know, in trucks. Today they prohibit that. But anyway, so we—my uncle and us fellas—went in one truck and we start goin'. And I said, 'Where we goin'?' He said, 'We're goin' to a picnic ground.' You would be surprised to know how long we rode to go to that picnic ground. And whatever bumpy roads we got to go [on to get] to that picnic ground. So I says to my uncle Al, 'What's cookin'? Boy, we must have passed fifteen picnic grounds before we got here.' He said, 'Stanley, this is a union meeting.' I thought, 'What the hell are we?' He said, 'We have to hide. We have to go so damn far away from town.' And that's the kind of, that's the fear, you understand, that was in these groups of people. And they were all mostly Croatian at that time. That was from [the] Ambridge and Aliquippa group, because I never forgot their lamb. You know how the Croatians cook lamb. It's salty as hell. And I'll never forget eating that salty lamb over there. Now that, that's my early experience, the fear that people had within them. Because if the company found out—if, say, it was close to Ambridge (there was a lot of picnic ground right around Ambridge), say they had [the union meeting] right over there—why the company agents would be right over there or the company bosses. And the first thing you know there would be arrests.

"We wanted that union in 1937. What benefits did we have? When you were laid off, what benefit could you get from an insurance policy that you paid one dollar a month into? You had nothing else. Whenever a group would band together they would say, 'We've got to have something better than this. We have nothing to take care of our family [with] when we [are] sick.' Today we have something. In 1937, with a wife and a couple of kids, when I got my last pay check I was done. There was no unemployment compensation. There was no organized relief. So we had a goal."

Smolinski: "The older men were primarily interested in a pension plan. The company already had a plan, but the most the fellas ever got was thirty dollars a month."

Brozek: "We weren't Communists either. Now in 1937 when the union first organized and we got our first contract, we had no publications. We had what I call a "half-moon' printing machine. We made leaflets with a stencil and ink. Then we felt we had better get some kind of regular publication if we are going to keep our people informed. So a fella named Orville Rice and me were named to start some kind of a local paper to pass out every month to the men. We didn't know anything about printing. We made our first one with a typewriter and a mimeograph machine. It was so crude, I tell you, I was ashamed to pass it out. But then along comes a fella [Teddy Bartman] into the local and asks me if I want to learn something about printing. I said, 'My God, I need somebody to help!' I never questioned who he was. All I knew was his name. I didn't even ask him where he works. I assumed he was a steelworker. So what do you think? He taught me everything about stencils and putting out a paper. And we found out he was a Communist. They were overenthusiastic. But we only had a few—you could count them on your fingers—that would really claim to be a Communist. I'll tell exactly what happened. That's right, it had to be before '41 or '40. That's [when] I believe the connection come. When this Teddy Bartman left, I started getting a call from a fella named Myers in East Pittsburgh. And Myers wanted me to subscribe to the *Daily Worker*. I said, 'No, I'm not interested in the *Daily Worker*.' So what do you think, Myers would pay me a visit every Sunday with the Sunday *Daily Worker* and [give] it to me for free. So I accepted the paper, and Myers would have a little bit to say. And then, finally, I got a visit from a fella named Burkhart. If you remember that Burkhart, he was a 'Commie' organizer in Local 601 in East Pittsburgh. Burkhart made a personal visit. I still remember it. How he came into my [home]—we sat in the kitchen on the couch and my wife was at the other side. And Burkhart gave me the spiel about signin' the 'Commie' card. He was with another fella. Lord knows I forgot his name, but I never forgot Burkhart. Because he come along and gave me his spiel and, actually, practically begged me to sign a 'Commie' card. Now that's the one experience that I never forgot.

"Now, the last one—I never told this to anybody. This is the first time. About 1944, '45, I was the recording secretary for Local 1219. And one of our girls quit. One of our office girls quit. And I'm in the office in the evening. And this girl comes in and she introduces herself. And she actually introduces herself as a member of the Communist Party. And she asks me what could I do to get her in our office as the office worker. Now you saw how that works. First there's Teddy Bartman with the newspaper. There is this fella Myers with the copy of the *Daily Worker*. There's this fella Burkhart chasing me, understand, to sign a 'Commie' card. And then in '45 or '44—it was in that period—they hadn't forgotten me. Here come this— and it was a Jewish girl too! She came there and she come along askin' me to give her some [work as] a secretary. She wanted to see what I could do to get her a place in our office as a clerk. Now that's the way that outfit works. I wasn't interested in their setup. I just felt that they have a program where the end justifies the means, you understand. And they will lie and cheat. And they don't give a damn what happens to you as long as their aims are satisfied. Their ideals are satisfied. No religion at all; that thought never entered me. It is just the idea that they'll do anything. And they'll even betray ya to further their aims. One time the *Pittsburgh Press* accused me of signing a 'Commie' petition. Oh yeah. They had me listed as signin' down there. My name got on that petition. And it was fake, like a number of other things. So I went down to the *Pittsburgh Press* to argue it out with them, you understand? Now the newspapers at that time had the upper hand and they laughed at me. I remember. The guy practically stared at me when I was down in Pittsburgh. And I never forgot that either.

"One way we signed up a lot of men was through 'dues inspection.' The 'dues inspection' really helped where we picketed the gates at different plants. We would form groups from Braddock, Duquesne, Clairton, and all of a sudden we would surround a mill like Homestead. Nobody went in unless he showed a union card. That's what we call a dues picket line. And that's what used to bring them in line. One month I collected nine thousand six hundred dollars. We always had a dues problem until we got the check-off system. Yeah. Say you was makin' four, five, six dollars a day. So you say your dues are ten dollars a month. Suppose you had to pay it by cash and come up to the office and pay it. We found out that so many would just pass that office. We had cash payday. So many would pass and they'd say, 'I'll see ya next month. I'll see ya next month.' Well, if you wait three months now, and you have thirty dollars to shell out, do you know what happens? You just let it drag and say to hell with it. And that's the same thing that happened at that time to quite an extent. They would just neglect. I would say a good percentage of that was pure neglect. And then when you try to hit 'em on the head to get the four, five, or six dollars, you have a hell of a time. How many times was it thrown up to you, 'Hey, you S.O.B. sucker, you're payin' and I'm not. I'm gettin' the same as you.' So I was laid off in '37 and started to act as recording secretary for my local. I think in '38 or '39. So then there was—something happened amongst the grievance committee. And I was told to write a letter to Harry Brittle, the superintendent. Well, you know, we all had a militant nature. We weren't gonna write no 'please' letter, you understand. And I wrote a letter to Mr. Brittle. And I guess it had a little warlike attitude to it. And he got mad as hell! And I forgot who told me; whenever they went up to discuss things and old Harry Brittle was there. At that time the superintendent used to step in, like Slick. He said, 'That Stanley Brozek will never get hired in this mill again.' So they started takin' 'em back, in '39 I think. Yeah. So I started goin'. Nothin' doin'. And I remember Graham was taken from the foundry and was made chief of personnel. And I went up to see 'im. I forget how many times. And do you know, I would sit in his office sometimes for fifteen minutes. And he wouldn't say a word to me. He wouldn't even talk to me. I'd be waitin' for him to say somethin'. So anyway, that lasted about nine months. So Chorey was the grievance man in the rolling department and Charlie Boyle was in maintenance. So then I says, 'We are going to file a case of discrimination due to my union activities.' At that time you could pick your grievance man. So I picked John Chorey, who was chairman. So John Chorey, he's arguin' my case. And what happened [was], on that basis—that I was discriminated against for my union activities—I got rehired."

ORVILLE RICE

Orville Rice was born in East Pittsburgh. His father was an Irish migrant who worked on the railroad in Ohio and then found a job

*in a coal mine near Turtle Creek, Pennsylvania. Whenever work
was slack in the mines, he would return to railroad work in
Pittsburgh. Orville was born in 1908, the youngest of seven
children. Because older brothers and sisters helped support the
family, he was allowed to finish high school before entering the
Edgar Thomson Steel Works at Braddock in 1929. Getting a job at
Edgar Thomson was not too difficult because one of Orville's older
brothers was already working there in the loading department.*

"My mother died at an early age. I was only twelve when she died. My
father raised me, and my sister kept house. It was one of these fine things.
The grandmother comes in and picks up where there was distress, pain,
and when you're having problems and so forth, and the youngest sister,
she kept house for us with her family. The only thing I wanted to do was
something of [a] necessity, and that was to go to work and earn some
money. I went to a brother-in-law who was an inspector at Edgar Thomson. He got me a job as a laborer in the Edgar Thomson plant of U.S.
Steel with the laborers at the converting mill. At the converting mill they
made steel. That was the first steel-making process in the industry. We
have a conventional converter. Originally it was Andrew Carnegie's. It was
one of his plants. And they had the old Bessemer converters. And we
worked there. I did everything. We cleaned up and watched the vessels as
they were preparing to blow in steel. Whatever had to be done, you did it.

"I was on a labor gang. Everyone was mixed. There was no [segrega-
tion]. Everybody worked together and shared together. There was no seg-
regation or ethnic jealousy as has been told about or rumored in today's
society. You see, the blacks, the Slovaks, the Irish, everybody is together.
Now this was in '29. And after that I was there for some time and my
brother-in-law got me transferred to the electric department where I got a
job as a craneman. And a craneman was more money. You'd make more
money. And the work was less physical for one thing. Much more attrac-
tive as a work room. You learned from the operator. They had no training
program at that time. You went up and you learned from the operator. He
taught you. And as you, reasonably, was able to control the cranes, why
then you were on your own. You had to learn, as you went along, other,
more sophisticated things necessary to do such [work] as changing rolls
and such.

"The electrical and mechanical merged and it became the mechanical
department, I mean the maintenance department. From there we moved
around to various mills. We had five mills. We had No. 1, No. 2, No. 3,
and No. 4 rolling mills, and a building mill. So you moved to the various
mills as you were needed. And you learned the operations. And then eventually our mill, we had...You're coming into the Depression now. So

Pennsylvania Historical and Museum Commission

A DUQUESNE MILL

after the Depression—you know, from about late 1930 until 1936, probably—the NRA come in, which reduced the number of hours per week [we were] allowed to work. When the NRA came in, that meant more people were hired, because the hours were reduced. At one time I was makin' seventy-five cents an hour workin' on the crane, workin' ten hours a day. And then, when the Depression come in, they reduced our wages without tellin' us any reason why. No negotiation at all; they just knocked us down to thirty-five cents an hour. But in the meantime, whenever work would be slack, and in the Depression, there was a lot of workers laid off. Those that went on welfare—this was before they had public welfare—the plant, that is the corporation, issued welfare vouchers to the employees that were laid off. And they would go every week and get a basket. And then, when it was all over, the company demanded that they pay back in dollars and cents the value of all the items that they had received in their baskets during the time that they were laid off. The company was paying for them, apparently. The total cost approached two thousand dollars, depending on the size of the family and the size of the basket you received. And then when [you] started back at work the company took out so much from your pay. It was on the basis of the company store.

"We were laid off, off and on from 1930 until 1936. At one time we were unemployed for as long as six months without getting a day's work. You might report for work every day of the week for seven days and not get a day's work. Then you might get a day, a day and a half, or two days. This was going on through the years [till] it come down to the point where you didn't have anything and most everybody was living on welfare flour. Things were so rough. You didn't have money to buy coal and so forth. In our town we organized the older men to help. One of them organized the group that went out and mined coal in these abandoned mines. This was in Monroeville. We lived in East Pittsburgh. The people from East Pittsburgh, the committee, banded together and had the younger fellas [go] out and dig the coal. The operation was supervised by the old coal miners such as my dad, and so forth. They used to be coal miners but now were unemployed. They used to haul the coal in with a truck after their work was finished during the day. That would be from about four o'clock in the afternoon until it got dark. But all the widows got a load of coal first and then everybody who helped, or everybody who worked in the group, got their coal in alphabetical order. It was communism in its truest sense. And it was how the people stuck together. They had no welfare at that time—that was before welfare was organized. But you got flour from the government, what they called Depression flour. And the truck again hauled the flour, and everybody who carried the flour into the various houses who were to receive it worked for nothin'. This was all gratis. It was very cooperative. It kept the people together.

"Sometimes you'd look for other work. You'd answer an ad in the paper, and every ad that you answered was a sales job. Picking up a vacuum cleaner and going door to door. You didn't even have any money to take a streetcar ride to the agency in which you were applying for the job. There was no jobs available for a nonprofessional. And very little work was available for the professional. It is hard to realize in this day and age how severe unemployment really was. Even in a plant like ours, at Edgar Thomson. [It was] not a little plant; at that time they employed in the neighborhood of about five thousand. Even the engineers were laid off, the plant guards were laid off. There was no work. They were down completely. And the plant guards' positions were taken over by the supervision. There was no security, absolutely none! And if you were the friend of a boss, or if you had a friend who was the friend of a boss, then you had a possibility of getting priority when a job would be opened. For instance, you reported and maybe twenty would be standing in line, and there may be only five jobs available. And the boss would pick out the five men who were going to work and the rest of them would go home. The [ones picked] would be favored [men]. And just before my time, yes, payoffs were very open and widespread. The favored men would bring the boss whiskey and—I have no proof—but [it] even [got] to the point (that was pretty well rumored) that bosses were sleeping with the wives of some of the men that were given preferential treatment. Now this is before my time. This is in the early twenties. During my time the boss said either you work or you don't. When we come back to work after the Depression—[during] one of the long stretches of the Depression we were off about six or eight months— we were lined up in what we called the shanty, the recording room. And the boss said, 'Who can run the crane on No. 2 mill?' All the men, the older, more experienced men, had not come back to work yet, because they had had their I.D. cards lifted by the company at the time they were laid off, and they were still out on the street. I didn't have welfare. As you got your welfare you had your I.D. card. The I.D. card was inside your check; that was your number. But I didn't get any welfare, because I was single. So I still had my I.D. card. Whenever the work resumed, whenever they reopened the plant for work, I still had my I.D. card. We were lined up [looking for work] and there was another fella in the same position as me. He was much older than me and more experienced than me with the position. And the boss picked me because I was a craneman at No. 2 mill. And the next day we lined up the same way and the boss picked me again. Well, being a younger fella and thinking this was unfair, I spoke up and said that I had worked the previous day (more or less being an idealist). [Well,] I was burned by the boss. 'Listen, sonny,' he said, 'you do what I say or you go out the gate.' Ironically, after we got the union—with the same foreman—we had a couple of differences. He was an old 'Johnny Bull' and he was stubborn.

"I was first motivated, more or less, to join a union about 1934, '35. Father Rice* was touring the district advocating that the young people, as well as the older ones, get interested in [the] union. 'Get interested in organizing your union,' [he said]. At that time they were threatened with communism. Communist organizers run for the Steel Workers Organizing Committee [set up] by the United Mine Workers Union [and they] were making great inroads and had a lot of influence. Some of the more alert individuals involved, like Father Rice and so forth, could see what was coming. He advocated, along with Father Joyce, that a number of the

---

*The Reverend Charles Owen Rice, a prominent priest in the Pittsburgh area during the 1930s, was known for his sympathetic views toward labor.

young folks [who were] interested [should] fight the Communist influx. They were more or less afraid, apprehensive that the Communists would take over after the union became organized. And understandably so, because [the Communists] had been trained and they knew what unions were all about. We were young, practically young punks comin' out of school. We didn't know what the hell it was all about. But we knew we had a cause and we knew it [was] right. We knew that it wasn't right the way the companies were treating the men. I was never so shocked in my life. When I come out of school [I] went up on the crane and saw the menial jobs that were performed by the blacks. When I first went into the mill they had them down in the sewers. But it was the most menial thing, cleaning out oil-sludge trenches and everything that was menial. They were never given any effort, any opportunity rather, to rise above the level of laborer. It struck me! I had a sickening feeling whenever I saw this because I went to grade school and high school with blacks, and the valedictorian of our high-school class was a black. Of course, they had a little advantage there, insofar as they were Catholic [schools]. And I had gone to grade school, parochial grade school, and to public high school. And they were very good athletes on top of that, and they were very good families. We considered them on our level.

"I heard Father Rice speak at our parish one Sunday afternoon advocating that we get interested, join the union and get interested and inject our voice in the union. And much to my surprise, all of a sudden I found myself on my feet. He said, 'Yes?' I said, 'I'd like to ask a question.' 'Yes, go ahead,' [he replied]. I told him my name and I told him the question. The question in substance was this: 'What in the hell are you [doing] out here giving us hell for not gettin' interested in the union? When here our parish priests have never, never alerted us to the conditions? Not once have they made any effort to teach us, to give us the facts of life concerning the union.' I said, 'We [are] like stray sheep.' It [was] shortly afterward that Father Rice started a labor school in Central Catholic High School. A friend of mine and I went down and attended every week. And this is the first that we had learned about unions. We had Father O'Hensley, who was a priest in the diocese of Pittsburgh. He was teaching economics. We had a Father Joyce, who taught us public speaking. And we had an Amalgamated member come out who taught us public speaking. And on union tactics, Father Rice—he was the principal teacher on union tactics.

"I went to the labor school in 1936 while I was running a crane in the rail mill. The company had what they call a company union, [but] we didn't know what it was all about. So we voted for our representatives. They were very passive. And when it came down to hard-nose bargaining, why there wasn't any bargaining. A couple of our men from maintenance went and testified against our company. And one was from the pike shop. These two went to Washington to testify at that time against the company. This was when the union was on the brink of breaking through. A lot of antiunion, procompany propaganda had been pushed up to this time. And this is the time before the Wagner Labor Act came into being. See, the Wagner Labor Act came in and guaranteed the rights of the laborer, the worker, to organize. And I couldn't work elsewhere. There were no jobs to be gotten. And as an untrained worker I had nothing to offer. I was a nonprofessional. I had no skill to offer. I'm a laborer. I come out of high school and [went] right into the mills and started labor. After we could— after 1936, '37, and '38—I did go to Edgar Thomson diesel school, diesel engineering. I went two years there.

"In the rail mill there were no representatives from the SWOC. There were volunteer workers such as Stanley Brozek's dad, John Chorey, and Louis Smolinski, and a few of these who had gained experience in the old Amalgamated Association of Iron, Tin, and Steel Workers had some association [with] or knowledge of what they called the 'Hunky Strike.' This [was] a strike that was called about 1919. It was a strike that was participated in [in] greater numbers by the Slovaks and the Poles and so forth. These people were much more active in trying to unionize at that time. And rumor had it, or [so] it was claimed, that the company infiltrated the ranks with their spies, who in turn agitated, 'Strike, strike, strike.' [But] when the strike came off they were not organized well enough. They were too weak, in too weak of a position to be able to fight the company with a strike of any length of time. And they weren't organized with the groups in the more sophisticated operations, such as the open hearth, the rail mills, and so forth. This was in 1919. And as a result of their former experience they realized much greater than us people—the younger employees and even some of the older employees—that the iron was hot. The time was ripe to strike, to 'strike the iron' for organizing the union.

"Mainly [what] I used to see at the meetings was most of the older workers. You didn't have any of the younger fellas. When the SWOC was organized, they would have their meetings. And mostly the older people, it would be the older employees that would be there, the middle-aged and the older. I would say from forty up, forty-five and up in age. At that time I didn't realize the danger involved, because I had no knowledge—I had no understanding of what the 1919 strike was all about. And we would go to the SWOC meeting and they would give you a report and try to give you a pep talk about what is goin' on and how we have to get these cards signed and so forth. I didn't have any knowledge of what the danger was until I was told, 'Either get rid of those damn cards or you won't have a job.' Now, you signed somebody behind a column or down in a scale hole, or wherever. And you had to watch, too, who you were signing up, because if word was carried back to the boss what you were doing, then you were in jeopardy. It got to the point where our general superintendent, by the name of Slick—I remember this plain—he called us, assembled us all over in the motor room of the rolling mill. And he got up there with tears in his eyes, advocating—in fact demanding—that we not sign a union card, because, [he said], 'We are a benevolent company. [We have] always treated you people as sons, practically. [We] are the ones who are providing your livelihood, and these—the union organizers coming in here—are like a bunch of scoundrels, outsiders trying to tell you what to do. And the only thing they are doing is jeopardizing your job.' He put on such a good act that I went out of there with second thoughts. He was saying, 'I'm a good guy and you're our boy. And we take care of each other and we work together and we live together, everything but play together.' And this was quite impressive. I thought there was some legitimate reasons for the union with what I saw. It sounded pretty easy to get a job, but after you were in there you were treated more or less on a friendship basis. You had older men, who had no possible chance to advance. And they were shunted aside. And they were treated on the basis of how the boss felt about them. If the boss felt he liked them, or they knew somebody that knew somebody that knew the boss, that's how they were treated. You wasn't judged on your ability, in the main. For instance, we had motor inspectors' helpers. But they had no chance of advancement to motor inspector unless somebody died or was pensioned. The union in later years come along and advocated a training program. And it would be called an apprentice program where[by] the younger employees given proper training would be judged by examination periodically, and raised in rank and wages to a higher level to compensate for their knowledge and their ability. We never had this in the old days. And this more or less progressed in every avenue or in every job classification. And this is one of the things—I was more or less an idealist. I thought fair play should have been exercised. I was surprised by the lack of fair play when there was no union, when I started workin' there. Because I never knew of anybody who was being honest with the other fella. Even in the union we had some who advocated what they called 'jazzin' the company: 'Tell lies to the company in negotiations because the S.O.B.'s, they lied to us.' Well, we know that. But it was always my feeling that you don't lie to them. You have no crooked roads— no crooked paths to go and straighten out. You conduct your negotiations on an honest, upright basis and you will be more successful in the end.

"Sure, we had people who were afraid to join the union. Do I remember them. And how, I remember them! People on the upper, on the better-paying jobs were the ones who were difficult to organize. When we had our first dues picket you paid a dollar a month. It was supposed to be a two-dollar initiation fee. We would forget about that and just get them to sign a card. They would sign a card and when it come time to pay their dues they wouldn't pay their dues. So, as a result, you had maybe fifteen hundred members, but you weren't getting [all] the dues. We sat around a pot-belly stove getting splinters in our ass passin' the hat tryin' to get coal. These men wouldn't pay the dollar a month. Now, I'm talking about the better-[paid] people. They were passive. Everybody's the rank and file. But the idea is, the [poorer-paid] employee was more willing to pay the dollar a month than the higher-paid employee. In other words, the fella who was gettin' the bigger piece of the pie was the one who did not want to run the risk of being stigmatized in the eyes of the company by [their] knowing that he was a member of the union. Secondly, [if] it would so happen, he [might] be demoted. If the company [found] fault with his work, he [might] be demoted. It was realistic. He was being realistic because he had reached the pinnacle of his class. But laborers, the helpers and so forth, they were more willing to pay their dues. They were willing to pay their dues, and they did pay their dues. Now, we come along to the SWOC—the knowledgeable individual such as John O'Malley and Louis Smolinski and John Josycak and these people. They were not only willing to pay their dues but they were willing to risk their position so see the union be accepted. I remember the first dues picket we had. We had a dues picket. You showed your card as you entered the gate. And if you didn't—if your card was not stamped with having paid your dues for that month—then the pickets would brush you aside and shoulder you, and this, that, and the other. And I could remember one of our heaters, I had been after this guy for a full six months to get [him] to join the union. And he lived in my neighborhood, and I couldn't convince him. And what did he do? He gave another individual five dollars to go down to the union and get him five dollars' worth of stamps to punch on his cards, but he wouldn't tell me about it. I was so strong for him. I was organizing, you know, up on the crane. It didn't matter to some of us. We were brash enough to [do that]. [It was] not that we were courageous; we were just brash enough. We didn't realize the danger involved. But we were so imbued, we were so convinced that the union was the proper thing. And as such, we [had] to band together in order to increase the value of that labor. And then you realize the true value of that labor. I am not an engineer and I wasn't an engineer and I wouldn't be able to sell my service as an engineer or a doctor or a lawyer, and such and such. That is what I thought about. And I saw so many people around, you know, workin' in the mill, workin' in the factory, [and] so forth. They were barely makin' ends meet. You were just makin' enough to keep body and soul speakin' to each other. This does sound a little far-fetched, but that's how it was.

"When we were going to the meetings, someone from the international office would speak, like Dave McDonald. This was the organizing stage.

You'd go to the meetings where the district office would have organizers talk. And what we heard them say, generally we generated that into local enthusiasm. It was surprising; to some extent it was a lot of local motivation. [But] on one occasion there was a socialist come out of Westinghouse. A fellow by the name of—what was his name, Richman or something. He got a job in our plant. And he later introduced himself to me. I was an officer at the time. He introduced himself to me as a socialist. And he had connections. His father-in-law was a high officer in the Socialist party. He tried to advocate to me the proposition that I would be a leader, one of the leaders in the ranks and that I would be compensated by their, uh, central office. And that I could move up in the ranks. He was telling the truth. I inquired from him, and he was telling the truth. But that was the opposite of my [beliefs]—in other words I didn't go along. I knew enough about socialism to realize that it was, first of all, anti-Catholic. It was against my religion. I'm a Catholic. That in itself...And then I realized, too, from what we had read up to this time, that what we had studied [was true], that socialism can't be entirely successful, although we have our doubts about capitalism. At the labor school, we studied all of that.

"Now, you're talkin' about the heaters and the rollers. The heaters and the rollers and the first helpers and so forth, they were passive when it came to runnin' the risk of organizing, of joining, and of advocating the union. They were passive. But as time went on, the company was relentless in keeping the pressure on all groups. And working conditions, they absolutely refused to introduce better working conditions. *Absolutely refused!* And this—now, this teed off the second helper, especially the second helpers and all those below the first helper. They were—they really became teed off, and every shift that come out, of course, somebody would come out cursin' the boss. And the company wouldn't take notice of this; [they] refused to take notice of this. They kept the workingman's back to the wall, refusing to make his conditions any better. Before we organized, you didn't have any vacations. You didn't have any insurance and such and such. You were reportin' for work seven days a week. And you may get one day, if you're fortunate. You may get work two or three days or you're goin' home—times are slow. But the company absolutely refused to recognize the problems of the workers."

THOMAS BROWN

Thomas Brown was the son of a loader of large bolts of paper for the Hammermill Paper Company. Born in Erie, Pennsylvania, he came from a family that was involved in various labor activities.

His father was active in a local "engineers" union at Hammermill,
and his mother had been president of Toymakers Lodge 1520 at
the Marx Toyworks, which employed mostly females.

"My mother went into the toyworks when things were really tough,
around 1929. I was about thirteen years old, so you know someone had to
get out to make a buck. Nearly everyone was unemployed, and she was
glad to work for fifteen or twenty cents an hour for ten hours a day, five
and a half days a week. Around 1936 they started to organize themselves
within the International Association of Machinists. So I saw organizing
going on in my family and community. I got my education early.

"My father was Irish, and he was in the engineer local of the AFL. He
wasn't an officer, but was an active member. He raised me to be a church-
going man—very much so. I was raised that way. 'Give an hour a Sunday
to God,' [he taught us]. Everyone in my family was that way because things
can't be done well unless someone bigger than us is helping us. I believe
that way.

"In the Depression, hamburger was six pounds for a quarter, but nobody had the quarter to buy the meat. We were just glad to be going to
school and never thinking of the future afterwards. In those days anyone
who had any ideas about going out and leaving high school was terrific.
During the Depression I would get out of school and go and load wood.
They were chopping the wood, and I would distribute it to people who had
coal stoves. By doing so I would qualify my family to get groceries once a
week so we could eat. I had a brother and a sister like myself, so I just
could not continue to go to school. We all had the same ambition in those
days: to go out and get yourself a job.

"I did finish high school and then went to work at the Marx Toyworks
for about six months. When things tapered off around Christmas time, I
went to General Electric in December of 1936. I worked there until 1939,
[when I] was laid off for a while. In 1940 I came back and stayed until the
war started.

"When I was at GE in 1937 we didn't have a union. It made things
tough. If you came in to work and they told you on a Friday night that they
wanted you to work on Saturday and you didn't show up, you wouldn't
have a job on Monday. And you couldn't smoke in the place at all. If you
were caught smoking, you got a week off. In those times they had bull
pens in the center of the plant where everybody could see you if you took a
ten-minute break. And on some occasions the boss would have nephews or
sons in from school. They would lay us off for the summer and bring those
kids in to work for a few months. And in those days if you were off two
weeks you lost your service [seniority]. Twice I went out because someone
needed a job for the summer months. I was brought back in after Labor

Day, but I had to start my service over again. That was some of the things that started us on the road to organization.

"At first they had a company union. They didn't ask you to join; you were just given a card which cost a dollar a year. At that time four or five people would meet with the company each month and discuss differences. They called them the grievance committee. If you were a little bit too vocal or the kind of an individual that they just couldn't talk down, they would lay you off. But some of these guys were with the company all day and would have a nice dinner and cigars. Men on the grievance committee always had real nice jobs for themselves. They always had all the overtime they possibly wanted.

"In the AFL in those days nobody seemed interested in us. They were only interested in skilled people: tool and die makers, carpenters, tinsmen, and the like. No one seemed interested in the semiskilled or the unskilled. That's where the CIO came into the picture back in 1936. I mean, what about the common guy in the shop that runs a machine, or a sheetmetal man that runs shears, or a punch-press operator that sets up a press, or a man that repairs tool dies and that kind of stuff?

"I worked in the refrigeration division from 1936 to 1940. It was strictly mass production. The unit came down the line and boom, boom, boom, refrigerators. I was a crib man and moved equipment for them. I was also a shear operator, cutting up steel for [the] outer cases and liner bottoms they put on the refrigerators. I even worked in the paint department for a while, where they painted the cases. It would be considered semiskilled [work]. But a lot of it was common labor. In my job you could wind up doing a dozen different jobs a day. In mass production you could very well be running in four screws a day or sealing the door or welding. You might even run a punch press or shears. In those days we had about sixty percent men and the rest were women. A lot of women worked with the finished product. They were used because of their small hands. Men had a tendency to be clumsy with small parts. If you knocked a small part off it wasn't going to the customer. And a lot of women were used in the paint department downstairs. At that time in our refrigeration unit alone there were maybe eight or nine thousand employees.

"The only thing in those days that played quite a bit of a part in getting jobs was the Masonic Order. If you wore your ring it seemed to be a factor. Today it has changed and the Catholics like us play just as big a part as the 'big wheels' in the plant. Compared to years when it was mostly all Masonic, we got many guys in the plant who are even in the Knights of Columbus. But Erie was dominated by the Masonic Order. Years ago it helped to be a Mason to get skilled work.

"Before the union, if you had a grievance you could go to this committeeman. But you didn't get very far. He'd shuffle you off. Those men leaned toward the company. They'd spend a whole day with the different gripes and complaints in the different divisions. They would come back down and say, 'Well, that's as far as they can go now.' Sometimes they would tell us that we would hear more about a matter later. But you never heard no more. If you continued to holler, they would think you were a trouble-maker and might lay you off. They'd say they thought you were raising a lot of flack. Once you were laid off you just sat home and they wouldn't call you. They got rid of many of us that way, but since the union came in they can't do that no more.

"I joined the union when it first started. We had to meet secretly because they used to watch us all the time. If they caught you, they got rid of you because they didn't want a union. They had the company union, and you paid a dollar a year to belong. If they caught you handing things out, they sent you home for a day or maybe a week. Jim Kennedy, a bricklayer, used to sneak pamphlets into the plant. Everybody was used to a brick-layer bringing in a bag. They would carry their tools in it and all. We had a couple of women who were custodians and used to clean the ladies rest rooms. They would bring material into the plant and pass it around.

"Erie was always noted to a certain extent as having a bad record for labor. GE pretty much had their own way. They kept Henry Ford out of here, and other organizations that wanted to come in forty and fifty years ago, because they had the thing pretty well locked up and didn't want nothing to disturb their setup.* GE played a part in the Chamber of Commerce. They didn't want some outfit coming in that paid a pretty good scale or a better scale. It would upset their cart because they had this thing pretty well locked up. Other family firms like Hammermill Bond all owned the plants here. They had this town to themselves. They didn't want no big firm to come in from the outside that didn't really belong in the clan.

"In the 1940s, when we got so big and powerful, a 'Red-scare' came into the picture. They dragged us through all the mud and slime and everything they could think of. What they did to the electrical workers from the Atlantic to the Pacific you could never replace. Many guys went to their graves condemned. They crucified the guys. Then, later on, the FBI finally came out and said that after all the years of investigation nothing could be established for sure. But it didn't put us back where we were. I went through that Red smear. I know what it was like. Christ, you come out of church on a Sunday morning and the priest would say, 'Hey, you still with the Red union? Why don't you think it over?' It put you in a real fighting mood. But I don't think [people wanted] to go through that, be-

*Similar comments surfaced in our Bethlehem and Nanticoke interviews. Workers told us how Bethlehem Steel guarded against competition for unskilled labor, which might have driven wages upward.

cause [they were] not only fighting the company, [they were] fighting for jobs to be protected. [We] had these people bothering [us]. They were out at the gate handing out literature for this and that. And we were fighting to defend our own principle, what we believed in. You not only had to go in and worry about your job, but you had to fight the company. We caught these finks once outside trying to bust our organization and take us over to another organization. They were never successful, because we were pretty well solid. So this stuff of trying to be Communists was from people who were out of their minds. None of us were Communists."

JOE RUDIAK

Earlier Joe Rudiak discussed life in the industrial town of Lyndora, Pennsylvania, the center of operations of the massive Standard Steel Car Company. Here he indicates some of his reasons for joining the union movement in the 1930s, among them his family background and his disillusionment with religious institutions.

"After Roosevelt came in I was able to get hired. I was able to pick out a department that I wanted to go into. See, there was no unions in the place. I was able to pick out a department through the cooperation of the foreman and some friends in the department. I went into the finishing part of the freight car. The freight car was completely finished, and all we had to do was take out the flaws that the inspector told us had to be corrected. My job in the finishing department was stenciling on the lettering of the freight cars. That's what I did.

"It gave me a chance to move around. I never went for the money part of it, never. Money didn't concern me a bit. I was single. I didn't have a family, and I was still able to make the play on Saturdays and Sundays. And it gave me a lot of opportunities to enjoy myself on the outside. I worked [was paid for] eight hours a day and I was able to finish up in six hours. It was very clean and there was no whistles blowing, no finishing someone else's job. It payed very little.

"At that time they didn't know what others were making. It seemed that it was very seldom that anybody knew what [the others] made. It was a nonunion shop. There was no union at the time. Even with your buddy that you're working with on the same job, doing the same work, you'd go to the paymaster and [he'd] have the check turned upside down and you'd close it, put it in here [in your pocket]. And it was almost an insult, it was a dangerous thing, to ask the other fella, your buddy, 'How much did you get this week?' So the other people in the other departments—where they were making maybe twelve, fourteen dollars a day, and you were making four dollars a day—they would consider that you were making good money. But you would tell 'em, 'Now look, I'm not making any money. You guys are the ones that's making the money.' But very seldom someone would take out and show you his check.

"My uncle spent eighteen months in the Western Penitentiary. He was involved at that time in the 1919 steel strike. He was involved in upsetting the suburban streetcar hauling scabs in from the country. And he was given a stiff sentence of eighteen months because he wouldn't turn stool pigeon. So, you're living in his house and you're listening to the language and they're talking about so-and-so and all that. And you're in the corner and there's company there and different things and you're listening and now it's getting embedded in you. And I happened to just fall into that. And having a little bit of a cultural background, as far as music was concerned, finally you had to go into the union.

"I was eighteen years old when I joined the union, the American Federation of Musicians. So all of us became union men because we were musicians. That came automatically. Well, you don't know, you have no fear. And I got this job, and I was a union man. And I was very proud of it. They needed us. And finally the Depression came along, and everybody was out of work. And I became doubly union conscious, very union conscious. In fact, I went overboard and didn't electioneer for Roosevelt, didn't electioneer for Hoover. I electioneered for Norman Thomas during those days. And finally Roosevelt became president of the United States and the NRA came out. And I joined the Amalgamated Iron and Tin Workers. They sent an organizer down and he spoke of the right to bargain collectively and have union elections. He came down and I got acquainted with him. We formed an unemployment club, before the NRA came out, with the steelworkers and different things. We formed an unemployment club with banners and all that, just a place to meet, play cards, and smoke cigarettes. Because the churches had failed us, there was nothing open and all that. So Johnny Ludern came in from the Amalgamated Iron and Tin Workers and I joined 'em. We signed up cards and we decided we were going to organize the place. We had a lot of confidence that since Roosevelt became president of the United States, [the] Pullman plant was going to open again. So we decided that the best thing to do was sign up the people on the outside that are unemployed. And when they do go back, we'll have enough cards. It didn't work that way. We did get about sixty percent of them. I just don't know; he [Ludern] had all the cards. And here we were sold out. He was working with management. The Amalgamated man was working with the management. He turned all the cards into the management and everything. We found this out through some of the workers that found Johnny Ludern playing golf with 'em at the Butler Country Club, with the manager of the plant. We questioned him and everything. He skipped town on us and took some money—I don't know how much. I guess it wasn't too much. And that sort of broke the camel's back.

"[Then] the plant got an order for a thousand freight cars and I went back to work. I worked there about two hours. That's when the timekeeper came in, and just about an hour later the employment agent, Burt Hill, came along with two company police and marched me out of the place.

"And there's three hundred men out at the gate that never worked in the place. And they were, you know, waiting. The fellas knew me, some of them. And one fella made a remark in front of the entire gang. They pushed me out of the main gate. They pushed me out and I'll never forget it! He said, 'They threw you out for union activities.'

"I decided to go in the next day on my own. So I went to another gate. The police didn't know me. No employment agent was there, and I went to the same department. It was 6:30, quarter to seven in the morning. Bill Stock was the foreman; he was the general foreman. 'Gee,' he said, 'you're back, huh?' I said, 'That's right, everything's squared up.' He put me on the job. Burt Hill came along again with two police to get me out. The timekeeper came in; about an hour later, Dick came in. And the boss didn't know what was happening—I guess he did know—and I pointed out on the bulletin board 'the right to organize.' And I challenged them. I don't know, I just made the statement and they left me and I kept working. And I was there until the place was almost practically organized.

"After what my father went through, blacklisting and everything, I wanted it organized. And I can't do it myself. There's got to be somebody else with me, more and more workers to go in with me. Now, I don't know who to trust. So after signing the card, a week or two weeks, the first person I signed up was a black fella, Andy Walker. I'm not going into his house or anybody's house. And I signed him up and finally we got together with a few others and got sympathy and everything, but still the workers were scared with the experience of the 1919 steel strike.

"One of the faults that I had was my enemy became the church. They were not doing their job, I felt. I sort of isolated myself from the religious people. They thought I was a Bolshevik because I spoke with the socialist leader Norman Thomas. I sort of isolated myself, but anyway, being a musician, they still had to respect me, and they'd see me at the dances, their weddings. They still had to stay on the good side of me, and they knew I had connections of some kind. And I was very cooperative with the immigrants because I'd try to [solve] their problems during the Depression, try to get 'em on relief, go back to the bank, be their interpreter."

LOUIS HEIM

Earlier Louis Heim described his life as that of a transient
worker moving from one job to another, and he noted the difficulties
he and his family had experienced by the early 1930s. In 1937, like
steelworkers in other mill towns, he began to support the union at
Bethlehem Steel in Lebanon, Pennsylvania. In this excerpt he
describes the internal disagreements that faced the rank and file,
among them the cultural predilections of the Pennsylvania Dutch.

"In 1937 they voted to organize a union. For me, there was no company harassment as far as I was concerned. In our meetings I stressed common sense. Here is what I told the men. I said, 'Look, if you go down to that plant and tear things up, its going to make it hard on us and we'll get nothing. Not only that, if you rip things [machinery] up, how long will it be before they make repairs and we can go back to work? The company will become hard-nose.'

"In fact, during the first strike we had we were supposed to walk out after midnight whenever they gave us the word. I had a furnace full of rods at [the] time the word came around to shut down. I said, 'Wait a minute. I have a furnace full of rods and it's going to take me about an hour to empty it. I'm going to empty it.' Then some big goof came over and said, 'I'm going over and pull the switch.' And one of the helpers, he was a big farmer, said, 'Shall I stop him?' I said, 'If he touches that switch, break his arm.' The thing was this. If we had shut down we would have had a hundred rods in that furnace. Now even before those rods hit the furnace, they had already cost the company a lot of dollars. Well I couldn't see losing them. Once those rods cooled in there it would have created a mess and made it awfully hard to ever get the furnace started up again. 'Listen, this strike isn't going to last forever,' I said. 'When we come back we are going to be able to use those rods.' Well, finally I won my point. But later I got 'bawled out' at union headquarters.

"Then someone got the idea that they were going to throw a stick of dynamite in the electric generators. I said, 'You go ahead and do that. You'll knock the whole plant out. But when are you gonna go back to work?' You always had a few fellas who could only think of tearing things up. They don't see any further than that.

"I joined the union to help my family, but also because of abuses by the boss. If you looked at a boss wrong they could let you go. After the union those things changed. Before the union you had no job security at all. You had to be careful what you said, how you looked.

"In the twenties I quit Bethlehem Steel when there were things I didn't like. But by 1937 I was forty-two years old, I needed a job, and I had a family. So I joined the union. As you get older, you learn to swallow a few things once in a while.

"Most of the opposition to the steelworkers union in Lebanon was over the payment of dues, especially among the Amish and Mennonites. They were opposed to dues; they thought it was wrong. At that time you could still gain union benefits without joining. I felt that all should pay this fair share if they were getting the benefits. In fact, dues were good for me. When I returned I got more money in one lump sum than I ever paid in dues. It was very tough to get a union started in Lebanon. You had your Pennsylvania Dutch. They were very stubborn. The trouble is you can lead them, but don't try to drive them. When our local started a political action committee, I was on that committee and many union officials talked about Aliquippa and what they accomplished there. 'Listen,' I said, 'Aliquippa is one thing and Lebanon is another.' I said, 'You have independent minded, Pennsylvania Dutchmen down there. If you can persuade them, fine. But don't go up there and tell them they gotta do this, because that's the time they're not going to do it.' "

WAYNE HENDRICKSON

Wayne Hendrickson was born in 1910 in Westfield, Pennsylvania, where his father worked as a carpenter. He remained in Westfield until he was twenty, although is father died when he was sixteen. After his father died, the family depended on the wages Wayne's older brother brought home from the Westfield tannery. In 1924, after he had finished the eighth grade, Wayne began earning wages by cracking stone for the state highway department. He did not leave his family of origin until he married and moved to Elkland, a nearby town, where he was promised work in a tannery. Wayne fought to form a union in 1937, but when the Elkland facility he worked for finally closed in 1972, he and hundreds of other men who were in the later stages of their careers lost both their jobs and their pensions. It was a blow which inflicted physical as well as financial suffering on many families.

"In 1930 I couldn't get a job at the Westfield tannery. It was hard to get a job anyplace. I was more than lucky to get a job. Joe Kiaski was hiring at Elkland. I told him that I had two slices of bread for breakfast and I came down to see what I could do. He put me to work for about two weeks and I got laid off. I kept on going back. There was a bridge there and about a hundred men would be on that bridge every morning looking for work. It was a waiting line to get work. After a couple of weeks of going there, they put me back and I worked there [till the tannery closed].

"I'll tell you, I just wanted to get a job and take care of my family. I didn't want to [do] anything else. I could have been a carpenter, as good a carpenter as any in the country. But I didn't like it. The fact is I didn't have the nerve to charge a price [high enough] to make a living on it. If you can't do that, then you can't be a carpenter.

"After I was in Elkland for about two years, I built my own house. It was like a chicken coop at first. I saved up some money and went down to the mill and got the two-by-fours I wanted. They trusted me. I would pay them a few dollars a week, and I got just about all I could use up in wood. You could get a lot of lumber for five dollars back then. Oh it was hot in the summertime. I had a coal stove and only tar paper on the outside. On the backside I had epsom salt bags on it.

"In the tannery they put me in the cut shop, where they cut soles out for shoes. I would check the bags out and put them on the truck for taggin'. I also worked for a time in the cement house and as a shipping clerk. In the cut shop you learned to cut the leather. You had two blades and when the leather came down you would have to run your blades over it. It was a hard job. You had to stand on one foot to make the blades run. It was also dangerous. Andy Wyatt lost one finger.

"The cut shop sometimes had over a hundred men in it and was one of the bigger departments in the tannery. But you had to wait your turn. I had to work there a long, long time before I could become a cutter—ten or twelve years. The reason I finally left the cut shop, though, was Andy Wyatt. He would cut about twenty-five rolls of soles a day and I had to cut forty-eight for the same pay. I could never figure it out; only [the owners] did that. So I went down where they hung heads—just a piece of leather from the head of a cow. You'd cut the leather to a certain shape and load them onto a cart with wheels. I made more money doing this in the scrub shop. I just couldn't see staying in the cut shop for the price.

"In the scrub shop they took the hair off the hides and soaked them for nine days to tan them. Then they would put them on wheels, treat them, and then flatten the hides out. Some would be piled in the cement shop and then would be sent to the cut shop. They tied them up into different grades and sent them to shoe factories all over the world.

"I did work on a grading machine for a while. You had to sort the soles into each grade. It wasn't dangerous and I was often goin' to sleep on the job. Many men would go to sleep. I slept in the chair I sat on. I never liked it. And if you don't like a job then you're no good on it. There was a foreman, but they weren't too bad. They acted in a disgusted manner if you fell asleep. But I wasn't fooled. No one was going to do nothing because if you don't like a job you just don't do it.

"When I first worked at Elkland they didn't have any union. Later they did get the Elkland Leatherworkers Association. That was more or less a company outfit. That was the first one they started. I didn't go to their meetings, however, because it was a company outfit. They collected dues, but if there was something they wanted, they would buy four or five cases of beer and at the meeting they would have that beer. There were a bunch of guys who would vote for anything to get that beer.

"Around 1937 there was talk around about the CIO. An organizer [Joe Massida] came in from Boston. Richard Kreisler, a local man, also helped him organize. But Kreisler's father used to come to the [CIO] meetings and tell the company what was happening. We held meetings in a chicken coop. I own it now, but my brother-in-law owned it then. It was about the only place you could meet. You couldn't meet downtown. There would be war. It was pretty dangerous for us fellas. You could get killed. We would probably have about fifty fans up here on the hill when we had a meeting.

"I mean the company had a big hold on the town and the bank. And the bank had a big hold on the people. Does that make sense? They would turn you down for a loan if the "old boy" said so. I mean old man [William] Ellison, the owner. He lived in Boston, but he could still call the shots in Elkland. They were on the borough council too. A big company has a lot to do with a town.

"They did talk union inside the tannery. But only a few guys were with Massida, [and] they had to sign the men up on the outside—on street corners. Organizers like Elmer Backus were rollers, and Al Wright hung leather. I'd say a good part of the men in the cut shop, where I was, favored the CIO. Of course, as time went on, a lot got 'cold feet.'

"Personally I approved of some of it, but a lot of it I didn't like. I believed in the union, but I didn't think you had to fight. I didn't approve of carrying guns around. The company had guns too. They brought [in] this detective outfit from Philadelphia.

"One day [in July 1937] I went down to help my wife's uncle. He was a carpenter at the tannery. I had to help him get a tool box out during the strike. And I helped my foreman, Jake Clark, run the machines. But the guys called me a scab. I told Jake that these guys are bitchin' about me. I told him I didn't care because of the money or because I want to, but to help him keep the machines running. But I was sick of it all and soon went home. The next day the guys apologized to me.

"These detectives were strikebreakers and the ones that stirred up a lot of trouble. One day the union guys began throwing rocks at the detectives [and destroying the cars of 'loyal' employees who were working inside the plant].

"At first all the men had walked out when the CIO called a strike, but they started to drift back to work soon. I stayed out, though, for quite a

Author's personal collection

MEN RETURNING TO WORK DESPITE CIO PICKETS, ELKLAND, 1937

while, nearly a year. I walked out at first, to tell you the truth, because everybody else did. I wasn't unhappy with the company. But when we start throwing rocks at the people who were going back to work I was arrested. Even women were throwing stones just as good as men.

"When I was arrested along with [five] other guys, they took me down to a jail in Elkland, and then to a trial in Wellsboro. And Chet Astin was the [prosecuting] lawyer. I knew him all my life. I met him and said, 'What are you going to do, hang us?' He said, 'Ain't gonna do nothin' to ya.' He said they just wanted to get after you guys. Chet was working for the company. We had CIO lawyers but went to jail for about five days. I don't think the union worried about us that much, though, because a day or two later we had signed our own bail and were on our way.

"I wouldn't say that the men who wanted to go back to work were loyal. After two days on strike I just think that they wanted to go back to work for their own families, not for the companies. The fact is, the company said that the best men were on strike. In other words the 'stool pigeons' were the ones who were bad workers. I really think the guys in the company had more respect for the guy that struck than those who came back. When I worked for Jake Clark in the cut shop, he gave me a hard time. He knew that I was right sometimes and I knew that he was right. But we always had a lot of respect because I always did a day's work. When I finally came back to work he was pretty harsh for a while and started to lay down the law. I told him to go to hell and done my work. Some of them didn't associate with me for a while, but after a while it changed.

"I wanted to go back to work after that, but they wouldn't hire me. The labor board [NLRB] made them take me back. There was no use leaving Elkland. There was no place else to work. Jobs like that weren't around. I did work in the Corning glassworks for a year and on a garbage truck. Elmer Backus went back to the tannery, but he couldn't take the bad feeling from the other men. Some men never went back to the tannery.

"I continued to go to union meetings. It got so that they would have beer and push through things. They wouldn't let a majority of the people have a vote. They'd hang on and keep you there until you had to go home and get up in the morning for work. They'd push through things that most men didn't want. All the men wanted was pensions, but the unions wouldn't give them pensions when the tannery closed [1972]."

CONCLUSION:
CULTURE AND PROTEST

The memories of ordinary workers recorded here have cast light on many of the hidden recesses of life in America's industrial regions before the 1930s, but perhaps the most distinct impression they have left is that the upsurge of unionization among the rank and file during the Great Depression was shaped by the values and predilections of a family-centered, circumscribed world. Labor protest among the lower ranks of the industrial proletariat was a direct response to several factors, including irregular employment, arbitrary use of power, and family deprivation. Its ultimate thrust and direction, however, were firmly molded by workers whose cultural traits and objectives emerged from the meeting of the industrial with the family-based economy.

Most explanations of this protest have acknowledged the limitations of its objectives, but they have attributed labor's conservatism to external forces acting to temper what was perceived to be a potential militancy. The legislation and rhetoric of the New Deal are now thought to be excellent examples of factors which undercut labor's inherent militancy. Historian David Montgomery argues that the New Deal was simultaneously liberating and co-optive, since it eased the burden of managerial control while subjecting powerful unions to tight legal and political controls. Other analysts of the labor upsurge blame the federal government for creating a "businesslike" relationship between labor leaders and management, a relationship which tempered the "explosive creation" of the mid-1930s. Even the recent surge of interest in the workplace as a framework for discovering the nature of working-class behavior continues the theme of workers as victims and rests on the questionable assumption that working-class militancy was rooted solely in the structure of the factory. Nelson Lichtenstein argued this point recently, observing that the workers' preoccupation with workplace objectives inhibited their realization of larger social and political goals. Montgomery echoes this explanation and continues the theme of workers as victims by stating that their attempts to control the production process were destroyed by managerial offensives such as scientific management.[1]

Rarely acknowledged in discussions of workers' thoughts and actions, however, is the fact that deeply conservative tendencies pervaded the American working class well before the labor unrest of the 1930s. These tendencies emanated from a complex world that was grounded not only in the workplace but also in intricate networks of family, communal, and work associations. It was to this larger world—and culture—that the workers' consciousness and behavior were tied.

For the era after that described by E. P. Thompson in *The Making of the English Working Class*, narrow and restrictive definitions of class no longer suffice. If England's working class was defined by men as they lived their history, so, too, the workers of Pennsylvania forged a world of their own from the complex realities around them. This process of building families, associations, and ligaments to workplaces was cumulative, it spanned decades and generations, and it was achieved at a great cost. Much was endured. Parents assisted children, uncles gained jobs for nephews, and friends forged associations within common boundaries. Individuals who had endured hard times and joy, who had shared lives and experiences over a long period of time, were not about to abandon that world—its memories or its reality—all at once. Regardless of what historians may have written, the industrial worker's immediate instinct was to preserve what was familiar. The integrity of the workers' world came first. Only when that was secure would these men push for control of the workplace or worry about larger social objectives. In a very real and ironic sense, community emerged as a prerequisite for protest because it was simultaneously the workers' ultimate objective. This is not to suggest that workplace issues were unimportant. It is merely to note that most of the rank and file shared a culture and a history that were far more extensive than the workplace itself, and that this culture and history have seldom been penetrated by labor historians. Indeed, workplace issues were often more preeminent for the small groups of highly skilled operatives who confronted managerial assaults on their autonomy directly.[2]

Below the ranks of the skilled workers and artisans who captured the attention of labor historians were the masses of rank-and-file toilers who were reared in strong, family-based enclaves. Some scholars have even suggested that kinship units became the basis for the first type of industrial management.[3] To an extent this was true, because families provided access to the industrial order and socialized children in such a way that they accepted and even pursued steady, industrial jobs; families seldom criticized or challenged the industrial system. Since most of the memories recorded in this study are those of second-generation industrial workers, the primacy of family considerations and even of family management is somewhat predictable. In other instances, however, scholars have criticized historians for limiting their definitions of working-class protest to transition periods such as the passage from preindustrial work to the industrial age. These scholars argue that the accumulation of capital continually creates grounds for worker protest; such is the case in the ongoing process of creating new job categories and condemning old ones. Such criticism is itself restrictive, however, in that it describes working-class protest as a reflex reaction to job dislocation or management's abuse of power and overlooks the wider and equally ongoing lure of family and communal stability and the full complexity of the workers' culture.

Of course, the life reviews presented here do not totally discredit alternative explanations of working-class life.[4] Some workers, for instance, pursued middle-class notions of success and entered the business world. John Butrymowicz, a Pittsburgh Pole, left a glasshouse as a boy to work as a teller in a bank, taking banking courses in the evening in order to avoid the fate of thousands of other young Poles who hired on at the local mills. Maria Kresic recalled that her father, a Slovene immigrant, set up several business establishments and insisted that his son enter college, *despite* criticism from fellow Slovenes that the boy should be sent into the mills at Steelton. Italian immigrants like Ray La Marca had learned barbering or other trades in Italy and quickly established these trades in America. One Pittsburgh Pole worked in a factory only long enough to save enough money to open his own tavern. And Louis Smolinski, a steelworker, considered becoming a salesman soon after entering the Edgar Thomson mill in Braddock. As he put it, "What the hell am I to do here all my life?"[5]

These examples of rising expectations were rare, however. Most industrial newcomers diverted their energies away from personal advancement to the realities of sustaining their families. The people we interviewed affirmed the view that working-class life in industrial Pennsylvania allowed little room for risk taking or long-term investments in personal careers. Commonplace was the family whose children left school as soon as possible in order to enter a wage-earning occupation. While children frequently made the decision to leave school themselves, it was just as likely that the push for an early entry into the job market came from parents who were eager to increase the income of their household. Joe Rudiak, a second-generation Pole, explained that in the company town in which he was raised, few adolescents finished high school and most started work after the eighth grade, including a number who left the community to work in the expanding automobile plants of Detroit. Among some Ukrainian Americans in the 1920s and 1930s, working at an early age was "expected." An electrical worker in Erie recalled that if you could leave school and find a job, you were considered fortunate.[6]

Additional probes of personal histories have further weakened the generalization that workers were driving feverishly toward success and the acquisition of goods. The American working class may never have been as impervious to outside ideas as English workers appear to have been in the period 1870–1900,[7] but by and large its members manifested rather limited social aspirations and continually sacrificed individual inclinations to family needs. Studies of automobile workers in America, Italians in Buffalo, and Slovaks in McKeesport have confirmed the preeminence of family objectives over personal goals. Shoemakers in Lynn, Massachusetts, actually exhibited a diminishing belief in individual opportunity with the rise of the factory system. Interviews with Amoskeag textile workers in Manchester, New Hampshire, revealed a similar emphasis on the present and the family. Mary Cunion, a Scottish weaver at Amoskeag, recounted that "we just took what came," while Mary Dancause saw employent at Amoskeag as a means to support her family. In fact, Amoskeag workers found considerable security and contentment in the flexible work routines of the mill and were often unwilling to leave it.[8] Indeed, at the heart of this working-class view was a sense of realism, an ability to remain pragmatic in the face of the prevailing American-bourgeois ideology. Workers recognized all along that the promise of mobility masked the incredible difficulties and risks involved in any attempt to abandon their status as wage laborers. Long before historians discovered the difficulties of achieving middle-class status, most workers recognized that their opportunities were circumscribed and that ways would continually have to be devised to ensure their livelihood from paycheck to paycheck.

In attempting to understand the rise of a family-centered world, it might be instructive to focus closely on the initial contact industrial workers had with the American occupational structure and on their entry into the economic system. The most striking feature of work patterns in early industrial America was the lack of a random distribution of workers, or, to put it another way, the extent to which workers were grouped. In 1850, nearly half of the Philadelphia Irish held unskilled jobs, for instance, while 67 percent of Philadelphia's Germans were artisans. In Buffalo, Germans dominated crafts such as masonry, cooperage, and shoemaking, while the Irish worked largely as unskilled laborers, domestics, ships' carpenters, and teamsters. This early bunching resulted directly from the workers' possession or lack of skills prior to immigrating. After 1880, however, most immigrants generally came with fewer skills than the Germans and thus intensified the pattern of clustering. By 1911, in seven urban areas nearly one-third of all South Italians were categorized as "general laborers," as contrasted to only 9 percent of the Poles and 7 percent of the Germans. Sixty-five percent of the Poles were in manufacturing and mechanical pursuits, compared to only 28.8 percent of the South Italians.

Greeks were highly congregated in personal-service endeavors, while more than half of all Serbs were general laborers. Groups such as the Swedes, Jews, and Germans were considerably underrepresented in "unspecified labor" positions.[9]

Contemporary scholarship has substantiated the earlier descriptions of initial occupational concentrations. In his massive study of Boston workers, Stephan Thernstrom found significant differences in the distribution of immigrants. In 1890, for instance, 65 percent of Boston's Irish labored in low-level manual jobs, while about half the immigrants from Canada and Germany obtained skilled employment. Moreover, Thernstrom found that clustering continued through two generations. By 1950, Jewish and British newcomers were still overrepresented in managerial and professional classes, and the Irish and Italians were still heavily lumped in the unskilled categories. Even more significant was the fact that second-generation Italian and Irish men continued to be overrepresented in unskilled work while Jewish and British males continued in above-normal concentrations in professional and managerial positions.[10] Recent sociological investigations of upwardly mobile individuals have substantiated the fact that ethnic groups generally followed specific paths in gaining "prominence" after the 1920s.[11]

Studies of individual immigration waves in various locations sustain the impression of limited dispersion into the occupational structure. In Indiana oil refineries, Croatians held jobs in only three categories: stillman helper, fireman, and still cleaner. In the ready-made-clothing industry, Jews predominated in small firms where mechanization and the segmentation of labor were minimal, while Italians were concentrated in large factories that tended to require fewer individual skills. Serbs and Croatians in New York City were heavily involved in freight handling. Italians dominated construction gangs and barbershops in Buffalo, Philadelphia, and Pittsburgh. By 1918, 75 percent of the women in the men's and boys' clothing industry and 93 percent of the females doing hand embroidery in New York City, were Italian. By 1900, nearly all of the 3,000 employees in the Peninsular Car Company in Detroit were Polish. By 1909, Polish women in Chicago dominated restaurant and kitchen jobs, which they preferred to domestic employment. By 1920, 69 percent of all Slovak males were coal miners, and about half of all Mexican males were blast-furnace laborers.[12]

Before rushing to the conclusion the clustering was attributable solely to the operation of premigration bonds of kinship or skill, however, we must note the alterations in the skill levels of American workers that occurred between 1880 and 1920. Historian Daniel Nelson has described the factory of the 1880s as a "congeries of craftsmen's shops." While certainly more than skilled work was performed in these factories, a 1906 U.S. Department of Labor study did note an increase in the division of labor, as a result of which more operations were subdivided into minute operations. The report explained that hand trades were rapidly becoming obsolete and labor processes were requiring less overall proficiency. The substitution of unskilled for skilled labor was already widespread in such industries as meat packing, coal mining, and textiles. By 1920, employers had intensified the drive to establish more efficient operations, reduce costs, and avoid the burden of extensive worker training programs by reducing skill requirements for incoming laborers. The expanded hiring of children, females, and unskilled foreign laborers as well as the decline of apprenticeship programs and highly proficient operatives underscored the trend.[13] In the early decades of the twentieth century the number of blacksmiths, machinists, and glass blowers declined substantially. Apprenticeships among brick- and stonemasons and machinists fell from 39,463 in 1920 to 13,606 a decade later. The number of dressmakers and seamstresses dropped by over 300,000 during this period, while the number of ironmolders and -casters was halved by 1930. Simultaneously the number of laborers in blast furnaces and rolling mills, shirt factories, glassworks, electrical manufacturing plants, and the expanding automobile industry increased markedly.[14]

The dilution of crafts and skills accelerated after 1900 and had a negative impact upon the older immigrant stocks from Northern and Western Europe. Germans in nineteenth-century Philadelphia predominated in butchering, tailoring, and shoemaking positions. As these occupations declined, however, Germans were frequently dislocated and found it more difficult to transfer their jobs to their sons. A similar pattern among skilled Germans in Poughkeepsie, New York, resulted in a greater number of second-generation Germans becoming factory operatives or concentrating in low-paying trades such as barbering and coopering. Indeed, in both Philadelphia and Poughkeepsie, fewer than 9 percent of second-generation Germans held skilled jobs; they began to appear in "lower" trades such as cigar making, which, according to Clyde and Sally Griffen, offered "limited futures."[15]

The blurring of skill distinctions among workers and the implementation of new efficiency schemes were further accelerated during the period of the "new immigration." With proletarian protest growing in the late nineteenth century and with larger concentrations of workers emerging in urban areas, industrial managers began to impose a bureaucratic structure upon the work force by establishing hierarchical gradations of unskilled and semiskilled operations.[16] Some theorists have contended that this restructuring of the work itself resulted in something of a segmentation of the labor market, for it created an infinite number of "entry-level" jobs, jobs which only intensified the process of clustering while making it extremely difficult for newcomers to implement any previously acquired skills. The promise of industrial America to incoming workers was not so much that one could rise as that one could gain access at any number of points of entry. Opportunity was not vertical but horizontal, a fact which tended to blunt the rhetoric that social mobility was attained immediately upon an immigrant's arrival.

If skills were no longer needed to obtain work in the expanding sectors of the economy, something else would have to take their place. That "something else" was the random entry of thousands of immigrant workers into the industrial complex. However, the widespread existence of clusters suggests that a sense of order in matching newcomers with occupations was operative. In even the most cursory survey of immigrant and migrant job acquisition, kinship and ethnic ties invariably emerge as the vital link. But the infusion of these ties is not, as Gutman's arguments suggest, the sole explanation of the pattern. To be sure, newcomers carried strong kinship bonds to industrial America, but without the diminution of skills, these associations could not have been implemented on such a vast scale. Those who would explain immigrant and migrant adaptation as a function of premigration culture,[17] or who argue that immigrants entered occupations that allowed them to implement premigration skills,[18] neglect the structural transformations that characterized expanding industries and the extent to which a match was made between previously acquired behavior and available opportunities in America.

It is true, of course, that even in the period of declining skills, some immigrants did implement their premigration skills. For instance, a group of South Slavs from the Dalmatian high country applied their skills in butchering and boning to newly acquired jobs in the meat-packing industry. A number of Slovene soft-coal miners had spent their early years in Austrian mines. Barrel factories in Bayonne, New Jersey, employed Slovak coopers as early as the 1880s. Skilled Czechs were making pearl buttons in America in the 1890s. The matching of Jewish tailoring skills to the expanding garment industry in New York City is well known.[19]

Instances of skill implementation were the exception, however. Immigrants normally relied on ethnic and kinship attachments to establish small beachheads in a given occupation, and these in turn attracted later arrivals. Although its influence varied from city to city and by 1900 had in fact declined, the Italian padrone system is a well-known example of how a cluster could be established. In Philadelphia, padrones channeled Italian immigrants into railroad construction gangs. Once established, these immigrant chains functioned so effectively that middlemen and labor agents were inevitably replaced by an informal network of friends and relatives. Theorists who accept the "split-labor-market theory" and its assumption that ethnic middlemen emerged from migration streams possessing a "sojourning orientation" overlook the fact that intermediaries usually functioned at the very beginning of the immigration process and were eventually superseded by ties of ethnicity and kinship.[20]

In the expanding industrial sectors of Pennsylvania, our interviews revealed, kinship and ethnicity were particularly effective in distributing the mass of incoming workers because this network overshadowed skills, labor recruiters, and middlemen. In Pittsburgh, Poles established occupational beachheads at the Jones & Laughlin and Oliver mills on the South Side, at Hepponstalls and the Pennsylvania Railroad in Lawrenceville, and at the Armstrong Cork Company and the H. J. Heinz plant. According to Stanley Brozek, for instance, fathers spoke to foremen on behalf of their sons to get them jobs at the Edgar Thomson mill in Braddock. This pattern was reported in many of our interviews. Ignacy M. immigrated from Russian Poland in 1912, relying on his brother in America to get him a position piling steel beams. Joseph D. left Prussia for a mill job that was procured by his wife's uncle. A cousin found work for Edward R. in a machine shop. John S. followed friends from Galicia in 1909, but relatives secured for him a job as a machinist. Charles W. relied on a friend to transform him from a shepherd in Russian Poland to a molder at the Crucible Steel Company. And hundreds of Polish women relied on relatives to find them domestic work in the homes of "Americans" or boardinghouse tasks among the Poles.[21]

Every Italian we interviewed in Pittsburgh had relied on kin or friends to persuade foremen or other supervisors to hire them. Where a relative had already established a trade or business, a position was usually waiting.[22] In fact, kinship networks narrowed the job search considerably. Thus, both the father and brother of Nicholas R. relied on friends to find employment for them on the railroads in 1904. When Nicholas himself arrived in America, his father asked the foreman to "give him a break," and Nicholas joined his kin in laying tracks. Antonio S. obtained work on the railroad through cousins who had come to America from the same village. It was not surprising that Leo G. worked for the Pittsburgh Railway Company laying stone foundations for streetcar tracks; his grandfather, father, brother, and uncle all were employed by the company. Similarly, in 1900 Palfilo C. came to the Bloomfield section of Pittsburgh, where his brother-in-law found him a job on a pipe-laying gang.[23]

A striking example of the Italians' ability to use kinship in order to gain entrance into a particular occupational sector is seen in the accomplishment of newcomers who came to Bloomfield from the village of Ateleta in the province of Abruzzi. From the 1890s to the 1930s, these villagers brought "paesani" to the pipe construction department of the Equitable Gas Company. One of the first to gain employment was Anthony B., who had been a farmer in Italy; when he found work with the gas company, he informed several friends in Ateleta about job possibilities. Amico L., who initially arrived in 1890, returned to Ateleta three times. Upon each return he recruited a friend or relative for the Pittsburgh pipe-line "gang." Vincent L. came to the city around 1900 and through an uncle who was already there, obtained his job laying pipe. After two more round trips from Ateleta to Pittsburgh, he returned to Ateleta for good in 1911, but he later sent over one of his sons, who was hired by sewer contractors at the request of friends who were already working with the firm.[24]

Men were not the only ones to follow kinship and ethnic paths into the industrial workplace. Immigrant women also found such ties convenient. A 1930 study of 2,000 foreign-born women revealed that most had secured their first jobs through relatives and friends. All had worked in either cigar or textile factories, but fewer than 10 percent had acquired the relevant skills for these jobs prior to immigrating. Surveys of loopers of full-fashioned hosiery revealed that the majority had obtained their positions through acquaintances. One study of hosiery loopers concluded that during the period 1900–1930, following relatives into the mill was a "general practice" among younger girls. According to a 1924 investigation of Italian girls in New York City, not only had 75 percent of them acquired their first jobs through friends or relatives but these women were "ashamed" to sek employment alone and would quit a task if friends or kin left the workplace. In Buffalo, Italian women assisted each other in obtaining work in the canneries, while in nearly all cities immigrant women shared information on the availability of domestic work.[25]

What was particularly salient about this clustering was the fact that it was not short-lived; it often prevailed in the first generation born into industrial society. The important data compiled by E. P. Hutchinson are provocative evidence both of grouping and of the fact that initial-entry occupations profoundly affected the subsequent careers of workers in most groups. Through special access to 1950 census data, Hutchinson was able to determine the relative concentrations of ethnic groups at mid-century. For most, there were several significant concentrations: Greeks as cooks; Italians as tailors, barbers, and textile workers; the Irish as cleaners and guards; Germans as bakers, managers, and toolmakers; Yugoslavs as dress-factory workers, cooks, and mine laborers.

Even among immigrant children, who by 1950 were well advanced in their careers, this clustering in entry occupations continued. Greeks were still overrepresented in restaurants, Italians in the apparel industry, the Irish as guards, Germans as toolmakers, and Yugoslavs as miners and dressmakers. To be sure, intergenerational mobility had occurred, but the incidence of ethnic grouping still attested to the impact of these initial occupations. In fact, in the metal industry, the relative concentrations of Irish, Polish, and Yugoslav workers actually increased from the first to the second generation.[26]

By entering the occupational world of their kin and friends, second-generation industrial workers could exploit lowered entrance requirements, and this practice was widespread. Studies of mining families in southwestern Pennsylvania and Illinois indicate that sons were drawn into the mines by their fathers.[27] Between 1920 and 1940, heavy concentrations of Yugoslavs and Poles joined their relatives in South Chicago steel plants. A 1946 report from a mill town stressed that "father-son" work relationships existed throughout the local plant; moreover, of the sixty-one workers interviewed, one-third had brothers in the mill. The National Tube Company in McKeesport, Pennsylvania, was reluctant to move its facilities in 1950 because jobs in seamless-type construction had been "handed down from father to son." Among Philadelphia toolmakers in 1951, one in five explained that the influence of family and friends had attracted them to the work. In a New England textile factory, nepotism in securing employment was found to be so widespread that workers with family connections within the plant were actually held in higher esteem than "unattached" employees, who were presumed to be more transient.[28]

Kinship and ethnicity functioned so effectively in distributing workers that industrial managers frequently encouraged the system. Before, and in some cases after, the establishment of centralized personnel offices following World War I, shop foremen, who were usually too busy to recruit workers, generally relied upon informal contacts with various ethnic groups. At the Pittsburgh Steel Company in Monessen, Pennsylvania, foremen frequented the Croatian Club to obatin references for potential workers and twenty-dollar bills conveniently left on the bar.[29] Foremen and managers were also influenced by existing stereotypes, which favored one group over another. Italians were often thought to be better suited for outdoor work, while Poles were preferred for factory and mill employment. Such stereotyping repeatedly favored immigrant over black workers. At the Illinois Steel Company, blacks were overlooked even when the company's own figures showed that their rate of turnover and absenteeism was lower than that of whites. In Milwaukee, German immigrants dominated the work force at the Pabst Brewing Company, Italians moved into the shipping room of International Harvester, and Poles were preferred for unskilled labor gangs.[30] Extensive documentation shows that in New Hampshire, textile mill managers relied heavily on the ability of French Canadians to attract their kin and train them, even after a central employment office was created.[31]

As a consequence of declining skill requirements and emerging kinship-occupational clusters, family concerns were strongly reinforced. Family objectives now superseded the personal goals of individual members, in part because families were now able to perform crucial functions in the process of job procurement. This ability led to a pattern whereby immigrant parents generally dictated the career paths of their children and thereby effectively diverted them away from personal advancement and social idealism and toward objectives that were of immediate concern to the family as a whole. Oral interviews are especially illustrative of this family dominance in working-class life. In preparing their children for adulthood, parents wasted little time imparting skills that seemed unnecessary from the perspective of men and women who labored in mines and mills. Marie S., who was born in a coal town in 1914, aspired to a music career, but at the age of fifteen was asked by her mother to leave school and help at home in the rearing of her brothers and sisters. She was later joined at home by a sister who left school in the ninth grade. Both girls remained at home, assisting in the household chores and earning extra income by sewing, until they married. They were well prepared for such tasks, for their mother had instructed them in canning, cooking, and sewing since they were eight years old. Another young Pole, Anna S., said she had wanted to study music, but her parents thought otherwise. Believing that it was more practical for her to become a dressmaker, Anna's father bought her a sewing machine and asked her to remain at home to sew and care for her small brother. A Slovene girl wept when forced by her father to leave school after the sixth grade because he felt that a girl didn't need schooling "to change diapers."[32]

In general, girls either remained at home to work on domestic tasks or found employment in silk mills and cigar factories. Boys, on the other hand, were usually sent to mills or breakers. They were often told that learning a job skill was preferable to remaining in school. No particular trade or skill seems to have been favored over any other; the point was to acquire some experience that would help them gain steady employment. Usually they received such training on the job in a position that was secured by their immigrant fathers. The first job for one Bethlehem steelworker was learning to operate a crane at the steel mill where his father worked. Interviews with Poles in the Lawrenceville section of Pittsburgh revealed that during the 1920s and the 1930s, boys worked alongside their fathers at Hepponstalls, Armour Meats, and other plants in the area.[33] In cases where fathers did not provide actual jobs, boys were usually urged to attend trade school to learn carpentry, shoemaking, or patternmaking.[34]

Occasionally this continual imposition of parental wishes generated intergenerational friction, despite the fact that parents seemed genuinely concerned about their children's future welfare. Tamara Hareven argued that marriage did not offer women an escape from work outside the home, because a family depended upon the income of more than one member. But in the coal-mining regions of Pennsylvania women viewed the situation differently. A number of Polish and Croatian women in Nanticoke and Monessen confessed that they had eagerly sought a marriage partner in order to escape their families of origin and the employment burdens they had endured as young people. We also learned that in some instances, when a child attempted to defy a parent and remain in school, an older brother or sister would intervene in support of the parent's wishes. Consider the case of Stella K. In 1930 she was offered an opportunity to leave Nanticoke and live with a wealthy family on Long Island. The arrangement was that she would perform domestic service and simultaneously be allowed to complete her high-school education. Her parents abandoned the plan, however, when her brother complained bitterly because he had been forced to leave high school early to enter the mines.[35]

In most cases where tension and discord surfaced, the wishes of parents prevailed. George M. was the second of four children in a Croatian family. His parents wanted him to begin working, but he wanted to finish high school and enter Carnegie-Mellon University to study electrical engineering. As he put it, however, "I was only seventeen; I couldn't do anything about it." Helen M. wanted to study bookkeeping, but her parents insisted that she help at home. John S., a Braddock Slovak, expressed the desire to enter the priesthood, but his mother's response to the idea determined his fate. "Son, why don't you go and work," she implored. "School won't make you any money." In 1939 Mary M. wanted to attend business school in Charleroi, but her father insisted that she help the family instead. Thus, she and an older sister found employment in a glass factory, and at the age of seventeen one of her brothers went to work at the Pittsburgh Steel Company at Monessen. Mary theorized that her parents "just didn't believe in school."[36] Rose Popovich, another of the workers we interviewed, concluded: "In those days children weren't treated the way they are today. . . . It was always work, work of some kind. No matter how young I was they [her parents] always found something for me to do."[37]

Such disagreements over work and school were not representative, however. More typical in Pennsylvania was the working-class youth who not only abided by his parents' wishes but actually initiated the early termination of his education. Moreover, not all parents minimized the potential value of extended schooling. In a small number of homes children were urged to acquire as much education as possible, even if tremendous economic sacrifices were required of their parents. These children in turn were likely to display a deep obligation to ease the financial burden of their parents by leaving school and turning their wages over to their parents in an almost ritualistic manner. Antionette W. was one of five children raised in a Polish family. At the age of fourteen she decided to work in a Wilkes-Barre silk mill. Although her mother opposed the idea, Antionette explained that she was unable to concentrate on school when money was needed so badly at home. Similarly, her older brother began working on a nearby farm at the age of eleven and an older sister entered a textile factory at the age of twelve. A Monessen steelworker left school early and delayed his marriage until he was thirty-one in order to remain at home and assist his parents. Eleanor D. chose to quit high school. As her immigrant mother recalled, "She was sixteen years old and she just wanted to leave and help in our store." Over the objections of his parents, Eleanor's husband left school at the age of fourteen in order to work with an uncle in a butcher shop. Tom Luketich returned to Cokeburg from Detroit in the 1930s because his father had become unemployed and his brother was still too young to work; he said that he felt an obligation to support his family. Virginia V. actually felt ambivalent toward marrying and leaving her mother; she was persuaded to do so only because two sisters remained at home to provide support. Joseph G. quit school at the age of sixteen and began working in a coal mine near Daisytown because he felt it would be too great a financial burden for his father if he remained in school.[38] This attitude was summarized pointedly for us by Lillian N., who as a young girl had thought of becoming a nurse, but decided instead to leave high school after one year and work in a Nanticoke silk mill. Carefully detailing her reasoning to us, she explained: "I figured I would leave school in the first year of high school. I couldn't go away to be a nurse because I was needed at home much more than anything else because I helped with the children and all. We had to bathe the children, dress them, and put them to sleep. My mother had enough to do with just cooking."[39]

Clearly, family obligations dominated working-class predilections and exerted a moderating influence on individual expectations and the formulation of social and economic goals. The assertion of historians William Goode and Edward Shorter that a family member's participation in the industrial labor force led to a growing independence on the part of workers and a diminution in their family ties and responsibilities weakens considerably in the face of the data presented here. Focusing his attention on women, Shorter argued that working away from home led women to be increasingly affected by the mentality of the marketplace and the pursuit of individual interests.[40] More accurate, however, are the assertions of Elizabeth Pleck, who had demonstrated that industrialization did not clearly lead to a separation of work and family interests, and that such a separation was more characteristic of the middle class.[41]

Even more striking than the predominance of family interests over personal ones was the realistic assessment of survival expressed to us by Pennsylvania's laboring families. To be sure, some clamored for ideals. John Czelen related how Slavic steelworkers were persuaded by promises of "equality" in Monessen in return for their support during the 1919 strike effort. Misgivings about an "acquisitive society" also were woven throughout the consciousness of these industrial workers.[42] A few attempted to leave industrial routines behind and initiate business ventures of their own, but the heart of the worker's system of values—his very ethos—was a fundamental sense of realism. Industrial workers in Pennsylvania's coal and steel regions simply confronted the demands and pressures of their world and reacted in ways that were invariably pragmatic. Rose Popovich explained that her family rented rooms to boarders in the mill town of Monessen because "that was the only way you could get yourself on your feet" and pay the gas and food bills and the rent. A Bethlehem steelworker claimed that his motivation for working was simply that his family was big and left him no time to be tired. John C. claimed it was a necessity to leave school at an early age: "You had to help things along." He picketed for the National Miner's Union "not because I was a Bolshevik but because I was hungry."[43] Steve Kika joined an unemployment council in McKeesport in 1932 not to restructure society but because he was looking for ways to find work. The words of one immigrant woman we talked to reflect the essence of this working-class realism: "I was poor. To live in America is work, work, work. I'm sick and my family was sick. And my husband died so fast and leave me with a mortgage. That was a headache. I didn't sell the home. I go to work and pay my mortgage. I raised the kids. That's enough for me."[44]

This preoccupation with survival strategies and family welfare should not, however, lead one to conclude that Perlman's stress on pure and simple economic issues was correct all along. To accept such an argument would be to assume that economic issues were goals in themselves. In fact, they were only part of a larger cultural system that focused individual energies on the maintenance of the family unit. Perlman and many other labor and economic historians failed to realize that the behavior of individuals in the workplace was an extension of their familial world. Immigrants, blacks, and native-born toilers entered the mines and mills of Pennsylvania prior to 1940 not on their own behalf but because of the needs of their kin. It should not surprise us, therefore, that so many willingly relinquished their paychecks. Personal satisfaction, the control of production, equality, and mobility were usually secondary concerns. Admittedly, what Gutman described as a continuation of traditional values in industrial society was not literally a cultural persistence, for changes and adaptations were widespread. Still, during the half-century of industrialization after 1890, a family-oriented culture defined the framework of individual lives.[45] Yet few historians have bothered to link this culture with the nature of worker protest, especially that which occurred during periods of crisis such as the 1930s. If workers agitated for job security more than for social equality, and if they demonstrated a realism that disappointed those who would have preferred a greater ground swell of social idealism in America, it was because equality and even mobility were largely personal goals, while job security was the key to family sustenance. After all other arguments have been heard, one is left with the belief that for the rank and file in the early twentieth century, labor issues were essentially family issues; culture and economics were simply inseparable.

Within the context of working-class families, placement influenced the aspirations and horizons of working people more than prevailing middle-class notions of success and individualism, and the secondary factors of life in America's industrial regions served to accentuate the sense of what exactly was possible. The work experience itself frequently influenced the individual's occupational and social objectives. Industrial routines were not universally monotonous, but in many instances they were severe enough to force job changes and the formulation of alternative occupational goals. Ray La Marca, for example, found the pulling of steel bars with heavy tongs so arduous that he left his job at a tin mill in McKeesport after only three days. At the Union Switch & Signal plant in Pittsburgh he secured a position that was less demanding physically. Similar reactions to specific work tasks shaped the aspirations of men entering the bituminous coal mines of southwestern Pennsylvania. Those who were taken into the mines by their fathers to assist in loading coal soon began to seek the less-arduous job of a blaster or the somewhat shorter hours of a contract miner. Nick Kiak and countless others who started out in general labor jobs in steel mills quickly set their sights on the position of crane operator. Contemporary observers who claimed that immigrant workers simply "endured" hard labor often failed to notice such subtle shifts in employment inside the workplace.

The severity of work responsibilities also shaped the short-term goals of women. Women who had labored at an early age raising younger brothers or sisters and performing other household duties frequently defined marriage as the means to a less-demanding work pace. However erroneous such a view may have been, it was nevertheless real for those who expressed it. Rose Popovich, who assisted her mother in caring for boarders, convinced herself that marriage might lead to a "nicer life."[46]

The objectives of industrial laborers were not limited by work demands alone, however. Anything that tempered individual goals tended to intensify the hold of family units over their members. One such tempering influence was the circumscribed world in which working people found themselves in their communities. Essentially powerless to direct their economic and social well-being, they took refuge in the regularity and predictability of the family and the worker enclave, where they could exercise some power and gain a sense of order. The powerlessness they experienced in their immediate milieu kept them family oriented rather than outward-striving. In interview after interview, the workers' lack of power, especially in local affairs before the 1930s, was continually emphasized. In Chester, to cite a case in point, blacks who had recently arrived from the South were accompanied into polling booths by local Republican workers who helped them vote "properly." In Donora, steelworkers knew that the dreaded coal and iron police were being paid by the local town council with taxpayers' money, but they were unable to do anything about it. Mining families in Scranton were similarly aware that if they did not purchase goods from local company stores, they would be criticized by their superintendents. When coal companies "dumped" dead or injured miners on the front porches of their homes, the workers' sense of helplessness reached a limit, and families were the only source of solace. Numerous interviews revealed that workers were unable to obtain adequate relief from the Works Progress Administration in the 1930s because they lacked the necessary "connections" at local county courthouses.[47]

A final expression of workers' realism surfaced in the information on job turnover and transiency which was related to us. While such movement may have seemed to pose a threat to family associations, it actually nurtured such ties, for geographical mobility inevitably led to dependence on kin for housing and job information. Furthermore, transiency was an alternative to engaging in ideological or economic protest, which seemed quite fruitless in the many instances where resources and power were overwhelmingly in the hands of others. The fact that workers frequently engaged in strikes or protests should not obscure the fact that more often they did not.

Quantitative historians have repeatedly noted the high degree of geographic mobility among urban industrial populations, but they have yet to offer serious explanations of this phenomenon. The intensive life reviews presented here include workers' reflections on the decision making that led to these moves. Although the causes of transiency were numerous, no variable appeared to be more pervasive than the claim that work was slack. Thus, irregular employment was a fundamental cause of turnover, but other factors continually influenced workers as well. Thousands of immigrants and a lesser number of blacks never intended to remain in industrial jobs permanently, and returned to their native countries or their homes elsewhere in the United States whenever they could. Burdensome work routines led some workers to give up their jobs for seemingly less-taxing labor. Some blacks, including the husband of Amelia Brown, quit their jobs when they were asked to teach a white man the skills they had brought from the South. When blacks felt that the transmission of such skills would allow whites to take over their jobs, they simply sought employment elsewhere. Blacklisting was another factor that forced workers to relocate, especially in the wake of labor disturbances. Finally, many workers sought escape from tasks that were boring or routinized.

The early encounter of workers with industrialized America fostered the growth of a family economy, which sensibly sought basic economic benefits and muted individual inclinations and idealism in favor of group survival. Thus, a framework for the labor protest of the 1930s was established before the Great Depression ever began. David Brody has argued that the Depression experience undermined the prevailing system of labor control; that the welfare capitalism of the 1920s raised expectations of economic well-being and security and that these expectations were exploded by the onset of hard times. According to Brody, the labor activity of the 1930s was generated by a feeling among industrial workers that they had been betrayed by paternalistic employers.[48] The recollections presented here, however, indicate that expectations of well-being were not raised substantially prior to the 1930s and that during this period workers were primarily concerned with survival. What was threatened was the sense of security that jobs provided: regular employment for family members and thus the survival of the family economy itself. In Pennsylvania, expectations seemed somewhat modest and realistic throughout the pre-Depression period as the cadence of industrial life exhibited remarkable continuity. Families generally searched for ways to make ends meet, achieved little in the way of savings, sent their children to work early in life, and valued steady employment.

Much of the analysis of the rise of unions during the thirties, moreover, has focused on the workplace, especially the shop-floor experience. Emphasizing the pace and process of production and internal activities such as the grievance system, some historians have suggested that the impetus toward unionization involved, above all, power and its redistribution, with workers seeking to resist further incursions by scientific managers into the workplace and to expand their control over the basic system of production. This view has been supplemented by indications that men in the shop represented a new breed, often second-generation Americans, who were rational, less intimidated by foremen, calculating, aggressive, and "possessed of an impulse for self-improvement." There is no question that individual workmen were angered by management's abuses of power (although resentment of managerial control may have been more characteristic of skilled workers). However, several qualifications must be made when discussing the quest of workers for control of the workplace. First, it was frequently the case that some of the workers' demands were met, a situation which could lead to quiescence. Anthracite miners in Glen Lyon, for instance, were quite proud that they were able to impose a limit on production prior to World War II. When these men did agitate in the 1930s, they did so not to achieve greater power in the workplace but to end perceived abuses by their own union leaders, who were thought to be receiving favorable treatment from company officials. Second, struggles in the workplace, like working-class behavior in general, were often more complex than a simple contest between workers and owners might imply. Workers themselves were sometimes divided in their struggle for internal power and position. Shared work experiences did not inevitably obliterate personal ambitions. The anthracite miners' quarrel with their own union leaders in the 1930s indicates that the desire for power did not ensure unanimity within the working class. Frequently in our interviews statements surfaced to the effect that some men were favored by their foremen and thus were suspected of receiving slightly higher wages. The interviews also offered considerable information concerning resentment of the arbitrary exercise of power outside the workplace in industrial communities, a fact that has generally been overlooked by those who have studied exclusively the shop-floor experience. Little resentment over the pace of production surfaced at all. Montgomery and other historians have described twentieth-century labor movements as "an unprecedented quest" for social power and control in reaction to the growing rationalization and dehumanization of the work itself, but they have tended to overlook the complexity of human aspirations and the powerful need to maintain the family system which emerged from the clash of tradition with modern industrial capitalism and which in the thirties was shaken to its very foundations.

Indeed, this focus on skilled workers as the catalyst of industrial protest, a focus which has dominated much recent labor history, has obscured the role of the less-skilled masses in generating the unionization drives of the thirties. Montgomery saw twentieth-century workers reacting to management's attempt to control the workplace, and Ronald Schatz highlighted the important role of skilled electrical workers in organizing General Electric.[49] But the data from our interviews suggest that less-skilled operatives like Louis Smolinski, Stanley Brozek, and Dominic Del Turco in Braddock and Aliquippa, for instance, were moving toward stronger organizations on their own and were becoming dissatisfied with existing institutions such as the Amalgamated. Stanley Brozek told us that at the Edgar Thomson Steel Works in Braddock the push toward unionization came from the less-skilled rail straighteners, drillers, chippers, and pilers in the finishing department. Dominic Del Turco related that workers in Aliquippa had already asked John L. Lewis to organize steel before Lewis set up the Steel Workers Organizing Committee (SWOC). Additional evidence indicates that aluminum workers at the Alcoa plant in New Kensington, Pennsylvania, organized before 1933, not because they were skilled workers seeking to stem the rush of scientific management, but because their ranks were filled with former United Mine Workers of America members who had fled the coal fields after the violence of the 1920s and were now implementing familiar organizational responses to irregular work opportunities. In the mill town of Donora, John Chorey, later a collaborator of Louis Smolinski's, was intent upon establishing a union in the nail mill as a solution to his family and employment difficulties because he remembered his father's urging that he carry on the task he had started as an unskilled Slovak steelworker in 1919.[50] The point is that the popular ground swell for unionization to meet needs that were important to the rank and file has been overlooked as an ingredient which *combined* with traditional, skilled-worker discontent over declining autonomy to create a rare, temporary alliance that made the upsurge of the thirties so effective.

Some have even discovered in the rank-and-file militancy of the 1930s an embryonic "revolutionary potential." This theory, advanced primarily by Staughton Lynd, also emphasizes the importance of shop-level activism. Interviewing working-class organizers from the 1930s, Lynd was impressed by the recurring theme of social idealism among working-class spokesmen. He argued that these readers were attempting to initiate a movement for social democracy. "They believed," he asserted, "that the human right to a job should take precedence over the property right to manage an enterprise as the employer saw fit." Such idealism was tempered, but not wholly discounted, in the conclusions reached by Sidney Fine in his study of the 1936–37 "sit down" strike in Flint, Michigan. Fine sensed that for a time the strikers saw themselves as part of a collective effort to better not just their own condition but the nation as well; in their eyes the union was a "social and moral force."[51]

On balance, the evidence indicates that while a grass-roots movement toward unionization did surface in the 1930s, it was not ultimately revolutionary in nature. Brief flirtations with larger social visions emerged, but they were seldom sustained among the rank and file. In his examination of the unionization of the converted-paper industry in the 1930s, Robert Zieger concluded that grass-roots militancy played a major role, but that it was far from revolutionary and was, in fact, somewhat unpredictable, with workers frequently neglecting to pay their dues or maintain a sound organization. In a later study, Zieger observed that the "sporadic militancy" of the 1930s had been somewhat exaggerated, given the degree of antiunionism and apathy that existed among workers. Thousands had joined unions, Zieger discovered, only after careful calculation of their economic interests.[52]

Our interviews with Pennsylvania workers do not specifically refute the assertion by Lynd and others that a tradition of working-class democracy aimed at humanizing society at large was operative or that strains of mobility and self-improvement pervaded the industrial working class. It should be emphasized, however, that such conclusions followed from analyses that concentrated largely on articulate, working-class leaders and intellectuals and stopped short of penetrating the temper of rank-and-file objectives. The limits to the ground swell of union activity in the 1930s noted by some observers may have been determined by family priorities, which continued to direct the objectives of most workers. One modern account of the 1930s which attributes the lack of radicalism in America to a basic acceptance of the "American Dream" by both the employed and the unemployed fails to perceive the larger family and community in which men and women went off to work each day.[53]

Interwoven throughout our interviews was discussion of the desire for job security as the primary motive behind efforts to unionize in Pennsylvania. For all the disagreement over rank-and-file goals, even historians like Brody and Peter Friedlander do not seem ready to discount the centrality of this issue. Because job security was threatened by the uncertainty of the 1930s, family unity was endangered. "Sit-down" strikers in Flint were moved to action primarily because of a speed-up in production *and* the irregular employment they experienced after 1929. Indeed, most industrial workers in the early thirties experienced a loss or reduction in work, not a quickening of the pace of production. In order to stabilize their families' existence, they needed to end the unemployment or shortened work schedules brought on by the Depression.

Some of the disagreement over the motives of workers in the thirties may have resulted from a failure to dissect the course of organization efforts over a given period of time. A close reading of our interviews suggests that unemployment and suddenly sporadic work routines provided the initial impulse to organize. Only after workers became immersed in the current of organization did the question of power—both the companies' abuse of it and the rank and file's own lack of it—begin to crystallize. Consequently, men like Dominic D. became enthusiastic when organizers emphasized the potential strength of workers who were united. When workers found the Amalgamated Association of Iron and Tin Workers to be ineffective, they sought, on their own, attachment to more effective organizations. But power was never their ultimate objective. They sought power in greater measure primarily to attain the goal of job stability—which in turn would bring some regularity to their world and that of their kin—and only secondarily to eliminate various inequities from the workplace.[54]

In the life histories analyzed here, two points seem clear. First, Rank-and-file militancy was a grass-roots phenomenon that preceded and hastened the establishment of organizations such as SWOC. Second, the objectives of the rank and file were not particularly revolutionary or ideological. Certainly workers were concerned about production arrangements, but they were more concerned about job security and steady wages. That is why Louis Heim convinced fellow strikers in Lebanon, Pennsylvania, not to destroy equipment at Bethlehem Steel in 1937; repair of the machinery would have delayed the strikers' eventual return to work. Dominic Del Turco and Michael Zahorsky told us that even before the establishment of SWOC, steelworkers in Aliquippa had concluded that the Amalgamated Association of Iron and Tin Workers was powerless. On their own initiative they sent a delegation to John L. Lewis asking him to begin organizing steelworkers. Louis Smolinski recalled that workers at the Thomson Steel Works in Braddock repudiated the Amalgamated in 1934 and formed their own "Emergency Council," which consisted of Slavs in the finishing department. Moreover, most of the rank and file would probably have agreed with Stanley Brozek, another Braddock steelworker, who explained that he sought unionization because after being employed he realized that he wanted some form of security and compensation for unemployed men who were married and had children. Joe Rudiak claimed that unemployment intensified his support for a union, but he and other men also wanted to rectify abuses by foremen and the arbitrary use of power by companies in local communities where a bank loan was unobtainable unless you were "a fair-haired company boy." However, problems caused by management's abuse of power had existed for years and were not exacerbated until the workers' hold on their jobs suddenly became extremely tenuous.[55]

Clearly, then, for most workers and their families the labor discontent of the 1930s represented an affirmation of a pragmatic world view that included the valuation of job security and a steady wage as the means to family stability. Once the movement to unionize was under way, important issues of power and control crystallized as well, but the enclave mentality of the pre-Depression years proved a persistent force, and most rank-and-file workers never lost sight of their primary allegiances. Within the families and communities of the worker enclaves, measures were taken to ensure the cooperation of all potential wage earners. Workers did express concern about power relationships, work routines, occupational advancements, and even, on occasion, social transformations, but such objectives were ancillary and were tied more to their fate as individuals. Regular employment remained the foundation of the enclave itself.

NOTES

1. David Montgomery, *Worker's Control in America: Studies in the History of Work, Technology, and Labor Struggles* (Cambridge: At the University Press, 1979), pp. 164–65; James R. Green, *The World of the Worker: Labor in Twentieth-Century America* (New York: Hill & Wang, 1980), p. 172; Nelson Lichtenstein, "Auto Worker Militancy and the Structure of Factory Life, 1937-1955," *Journal of American History* 65 (September 1980): 352-53.

2. E. P. Thompson, *The Making of the English Working Class* (New York: Vintage Books, 1963), pp. 9-11. The communal base of worker protest is described excellently in

Daniel J. Walkowitz, *Worker City, Company Town* (Urbana: University of Illinois Press, 1978); John T. Cumbler, *Working-Class Community in Industrial America* (Westport, Conn.: Greenwood Press, 1979); and Edward Shorter and Charles Tilly, *Strikes in France, 1830-1969* (Cambridge, Mass.: Harvard University Press, 1974).

3. See David Brody, *Workers in Industrial America: Essays on the Twentieth-Century Struggle* (New York: Oxford University Press, 1980), pp. 138-53; Michelle Perrot, "The Three Ages of Industrial Discipline in Nineteenth-Century France," in *Consciousness and Class Experience in Nineteenth-Century Europe*, ed. John M. Merriman (New York: Holmes & Meier, 1979), pp. 153-54; Hans Medick, "The Proto-Industrial Family Economy: The Structural Function of Household and Family during the Transition from Peasant Society to Industrial Capitalism," *Social History*, October 1976, pp. 291-315; Michael Hanagan and Charles Stephenson, "The Skilled Workers and Working-Class Protest," *Social Science History* 4 (Winter 1980): 5-13.

4. Stanley Aronowitz, *False Promises: The Shaping of American Working-Class Consciousness* (New York: McGraw-Hill, 1973), p. 140.

5. See the interviews with John B., Pittsburgh, March 3, 1976; Ray L., Pittsburgh, July 11, 1977; and Louis S., Braddock, June 20, 1978. All interviews cited, if not included in this text, are on file in the Oral History Collection, Pennsylvania Historical and Museum Commission, Harrisburg. Initials have been used for last names where anonymity was requested.

6. See the interviews with Joe Rudiak, Pittsburgh, July 21, 1974; Steve Kika, McKeesport, July 27, 1974; and Thomas Brown, Erie, June 5, 1976. For a more extensive discussion of the subject, see John Bodnar, "Immigration and Modernization: The Case of Slavic Peasants in Industrial America," *Journal of Social History* 10 (Fall 1976): 48-50.

7. Gareth Steadman-Jones, "Working-Class Culture and Working-Class Politics in London, 1870-1900: Notes on the Remaking of a Working Class," *Journal of Social History* 7 (Summer 1974): 484-85.

8. Eli Chinoy, *Automobile Workers and the American Dream* (Garden City, N.Y.: Doubleday, 1955), pp. 110-26; Virginia Yans-McLaughlin, *Family and Community: Italian Immigrants in Buffalo, 1880-1930* (Ithaca: Cornell University Press, 1977); and Howard Stein, "An Ethno-Historic Study of Slovak-American Identity, McKeesport, Pennsylvania" (Ph.D. diss., University of Pittsburgh, 1972), pp. 417-37. A similar de-emphasis on social and economic mobility was found to have existed among eighteenth-century workers by James T. Lemon, *The Best Poor Man's Country: A Geographical Study of Southeastern Pennsylvania* (Baltimore: Johns Hopkins Press, 1972), pp. 43-85; and Tamara K. Hareven and Randolph Langenbach, *Amoskeag: Life and Work in an American Factory City* (New York: Pantheon Books, 1978), pp. 43-50, 53, 65-66, 113. According to Herman Rebel, family arrangements blunted modernization; see his "Peasant Stem Families in Early Modern Austria," *Social Science History* 2 (Spring 1978): 285.

9. Theodore Hershberg, "A Tale of Three Cities: Blacks and Immigrants in Philadelphia, 1850-1880, 1930, and 1970," *Annals of the American Academy of Political and Social Sciences*, January 1979, p. 68; Clyde Griffen and Sally Griffen, *Natives and Newcomers: The Ordering of Opportunity in Mid-Nineteenth-Century Poughkeepsie* (Cambridge, Mass.: Harvard University Press, 1978), pp. 67-69; Laurence Glasco, "Ethnicity and Occupation in the Mid-Nineteenth Century: Irish, Germans, and Native-Born Whites in Buffalo, New York," in *Immigrants in Industrial America, 1850-1920*, ed. Richard L. Ehrlich (Charlottesville: University Press of Virginia, 1977), pp. 151-53; U.S. Congress, Senate, Immigration Commission, *Reports of the Immigration Commission, Occupations of the First and Second Generation of Immigrants in the United States: Fecundity of Immigrant Women*, 61st Cong., 2d sess., 1911, S. Doc. 282, pp. 19-20; idem, *Reports of the Immigration Commission, Immigrants in Cities*, 61st Cong., 2d sess., 1911, S. Doc. 282, 1: 130-31 and 2: 497 ff.

10. Stephan Thernstrom, *The Other Bostonians: Poverty and Progress in the American Metropolis, 1880-1970* (Cambridge, Mass.: Harvard University Press, 1973), pp. 125, 131, 139, 141.

11. Stanley Liberson and Donna K. Carter, "Making It in America: Differences between Eminent Blacks and New Europeans," unpublished paper in author's possession.

12. Edward A. Zivich, "From Zadruga to Oil Refinery: Croatian Immigrants and Croatian-Americans in Whiting, Indiana, 1890-1950" (Ph.D. diss., State University of New York at Binghamton, 1977), pp. 37-39; Rosara Lucy Passero, "Ethnicity in the Men's Ready-Made Clothing Industry, 1850-1950: The Italian Experience in Philadelphia" (Ph.D. diss., University of Pennsylvania, 1978); Caroline Golab, *Immigrant Destinations* (Philadelphia: Temple University Press, 1978), pp. 62-63; Yans-McLaughlin, *Family and Community*, p. 46; John Bodnar, Michael Weber, and Roger Simon, "Migration, Kinship, and Urban Adjustment: Blacks and Poles in Pittsburgh, 1900-1930," *Journal of American History* 66 (December 1979): 548; Ivan H. Light, *Ethnic Enterprise in American Business and Welfare among Chinese, Japanese, and Blacks* (Berkeley: University of California Press, 1972), pp. 9-10; John Modell, *The Economics and Politics of Racial Accommodation* (Urbana: University of Illinois Press, 1977), p. 9; Harry H. L. Kitano, *Japanese Americans: The Evolution of a Subculture* (Englewood Cliffs, N.J.: Prentice-Hall, 1968), pp. 104-5; Louise C. Odencrantz, *Italian Women in Industry: A Study of Conditions in New York City* (New York: Russell Sage, 1919), pp. 36, 60; Mary Remiga Napolska, "The Polish Immigrant in Detroit in 1914," *Annals of the Polish Roman Catholic Union Archives and Museum* 10 (1945-46): 34-35; Joseph John Parot, "The American Faith and the Persistence of Chicago Polonia, 1870-1920" (Ph.D. diss., Northern Illinois University, 1971), *passim*; Nile Carpenter, *Immigrants and Their Children* (Washington, D.C.: GPO, 1927), p. 297.

13. Walter Weyl and M. Sakolski, "Conditions of Entrance to the Principal Trades," *Bulletin of the Bureau of Labor*, November, 1906, pp. 681-90, 714-19; Paul H. Douglass, *American Apprenticeship and Industrial Education* (New York: Columbia University Press, 1921), pp. 75-81; idem, "Is the New Immigration More Unskilled than the Old?" *Quarterly Publications of the American Statistical Association*, June, 1919, pp. 396-97.

14. Daniel Nelson, *Managers and Workers: Origins of the New Factory System in the United States, 1880-1920* (Madison: University of Wisconsin Press, 1975), p. 4; U.S. Department of Commerce, Bureau of the Census, *Sixteenth Census of the United States. 1940. Population: Comparative Occupational Statistics for the U.S., 1870-1940* (Washington, D.C.: GPO, 1943), pp. 104-6. See also Gertrude Bancroft, The American Labor Force: Its Growth and Changing Composition (New York: Wiley, 1958), pp. 24-35; and Clarence D. Long, *The Labor Force under Changing Income and Employment* (Princeton: Princeton University Press, 1958).

15. Bruce Laurie, Theodore Hershberg, and George Alter, "Immigrants and Industry: The Philadelphia Experience, 1850-1880," *Journal of Social History* (Winter 1975): 241-46; Griffen and Griffen, *Natives and Newcomers*, pp. 183, 281-82. For an account of declining crafts and new demands for unskilled operatives at a particular plant, see Howard M. Gitelman, *Workingmen of Waltham: Mobility in American Urban Industrial Development, 1850-1890* (Baltimore: Johns Hopkins University Press, 1974), pp. 54 ff. See Also Isaac A. Hourwich, *Immigration and Labor* (New York: Huebsch, 1912), pp. 396-413.

16. See David Montgomery, "The New Unionism and the Transformation of Worker's Consciousness in America, 1909-1922," *Journal of Social History* 7 (Summer 1974): 510-24; idem, "Immigrant Workers and Managerial Reform," in *Immigrants in Industrial America*, ed. Ehrlich, p. 98; Richard C. Edwards, Michael Reich, and David M. Gordon, eds., *Labor Market Segmentation* (Lexington, Mass.: D. C. Heath, 1973), pp. xi-xiii. Montgomery has argued that the new stress on efficiency and production at the expense of skills caused twentieth-century rank-and-file workers to forge a "new unionism," and that this

new spirit led to struggles for greater control of production by workers. Montgomery has not, however, mentioned the larger effort to maintain the family system, which was nurtured by the expansion of unskilled labor.

17. See Herbert Gutman, *Work, Culture, and Society in Industrializing America* (New York: Vintage Books, 1977); Josef John Barton, *Peasants and Strangers: Italians, Rumanians, and Slovaks in an American City, 1890-1950* (Cambridge, Mass.: Harvard University Press, 1975); and Yans-McLaughlin, *Family and Community*, p. 36.

18. Golab, *Immigrant Destinations*. Jews may be an exception to this premise, for they frequently were able to implement premigration skills; see Arcadius Kahan, "Economic Opportunity and Some Pilgrims' Progress: Jewish Immigrants from Eastern Europe in the U.S., 1890-1914," *Journal of Economic History* 38 (March 1978): 237-45.

19. Joseph Stipanovich, " 'In Unity Is Strength': Immigrant Workers and Immigrant Intellectuals in Progressive America: A History of the South Slav Social Democratic Movement, 1900-1918" (Ph.D. diss., University of Minnesota, 1978), p. 128; *American Slav* 11 (April 1941): 12-13; Joseph Pauco, *75 Rokov Prvej Katolickej Slovenskej Jednoty* (Cleveland: First Catholic Slovak Union, 1965), pp. 6-9; Vera Laska, *The Czechs in America, 1633-1977* (Dobbs Ferry, N.Y.: Oceana Press, 1978).

20. The split-labor-market theory originated with Edna Bonacich; see her "A Theory of Ethnic Antagonisms: The Split Labor Market," *American Sociological Review* 37 (1972): 574-79, and "A Theory of Middleman Minorities," ibid. 38 (1973): 583-94. See also Modell, *The Economics and Politics of Racial Accommodation*, pp. 94-96; Robert Schoen, "Toward a Theory of the Demographic Implications of Ethnic Stratification," *Social Science Quarterly* 59 (December 1978): 477-78; William Petersen, "Chinese Americans and Japanese Americans," in *American Ethnic Groups*, ed. Thomas Sowell (Washington, D.C.: The Urban Institute, 1978), pp. 65-92.

21. See the Pittsburgh project interviews with Stanley N., September 22, 1976; Joseph B., May 20, 1976; John B., March 3, 1976; Agnes G., June 25, 1974; Peter H., June 26, 1974; Ignacy M., July 2, 1974; Joseph D., September 17, 1976; Edward R., September 10, 1976; John S., September 30, 1976; Charles W., December 10, 1976; and Francis P., January 16, 1976.

22. See, for intance, the Pittsburgh project interviews with Dan C., March 31, 1977; Umberto B., March 14, 1977; Amico L., July 28, 1977; Vincent L., June 21, 1977; Louis G., May 11, 1977; and Frank A., May 16, 1977. See also J. S. MacDonald and L. D. MacDonald, "Urbanization, Ethnic Group, and Social Segmentation," *Social Research* 29 (1962): 433-48.

23. Interviews with Amico L., July 28, 1977; Vincent L., June 21, 1977; Louis G., May 11, 1977; and Frank A., May 16, 1977.

24. Ibid.

25. Caroline Manning, *The Immigrant Woman and Her Job* (New York: Arno Press, 1970), pp. 106-74; Dorothea De Schweintz, *How Workers Find Jobs: A Study of Four Thousand Hosiery Workers in Philadelphia* (Philadelphia: Univerity of Pennsylvania Press, 1932); George Huganir, "The Hosiery Looper in the Twentieth Century: A Study of Family Occupational Processes and Adaptation to Factory and Community Change, 1900-1950" (Ph.D. diss., University of Pennsylvania, 1958), pp. 6-8; William Leiserson, *Adjusting Immigrant and Industry* (New York: Harper & Bros., 1924), p. 31; Louise C. Odencrantz, *Italian Women in Industry: A Study of Conditions in New York City* (New York: Russell Sage, 1919), p. 283; Corrine Azen Krause, "Urbanization without Breakdown: Italian, Jewish, and Slavic Immigrant Women in Pittsburgh, 1900-1945," *Journal of Urban History* 4 (May 1978): 296-97.

26. Edward P. Hutchinson, *Immigrants and Their Children* (New York: Wiley, 1956), pp. 224-38. See also Peter M. Blau and Otis Duncan, *The American Occupational Structure* (New York: Wiley, 1967), pp. 82-89. Additional profiles of immigrant concentrations can be

found in U.S. Department of Commerce and Labor, Bureau of the Census, *Special Reports, Occupations at the Twelfth Census* (Washington, D.C.: GPO, 1904), plates 10–12.

27.   See Walter Weyl and A. M. Sakolski, "Conditions of Entrance to the Principal Trades," *Bulletin of the Bureau of Labor*, November 1906, p. 690; Bodnar, "Immigration and Modernization"; Malcom Brown and John Webb, *Seven Stranded Coal Towns* (New York: Plenum, Da Capo Press, 1971), p. 23; and Herman R. Lantz, *People of Coal Town* (Carbondale: Southern Illinois University Press, 1958), p. 174.

28.   William Kornblum, *Blue Collar Community* (Chicago: University of Chicago Press, 1974), p. 55; Barton, *Peasants and Strangers*, pp. 145–46; Charles R. Walker, *Steeltown: An Industrial Case History of the Conflict between Progress and Security* (New York: Harper & Row, 1950), pp. 109, 111, 128, 263–64; Gladys L. Palmer et al., *The Reluctant Job Changer* (Philadelphia: University of Pennsylvania Press, 1962), p. 106; John Ellsworth, *Factory Folkways* (New Haven: Yale University Press, 1952), pp. 139–40. Classic studies such as Chinoy's *Automobile Workers and the American Dream* suggest that blue-collar workers lacked high aspirations because they lacked knowledge of occupational alternatives, but these studies do not go far enough in depicting the ease with which kinship could serve as a basis for job procurement. See also Kenneth Kessin, "Social and Psychological Consequences of Intergenerational Occupational Mobility," *American Journal of Sociology* 77 (July 1971): 1–17.

29.   Nelson, *Managers and Workers*, pp. 79–80; interview with George Muzar, Monessen, March 22, 1977. The foreman's power is emphasized by David Montgomery in "Immigrant Workers and Managerial Reform," pp. 99–100, and by Russell L. Greenman in *The Worker, the Foreman, and the Wagner Act* (New York: Privately printed, 1939).

30.   Yans-McLaughlin, *Family and Community*, p. 43; Bodnar, Weber, and Simon, "Migration, Kinship, and Urban Adjustment"; Robert Ozanne, *A Century of Labor-Management Relations at McCormick and International Harvester* (Madison: University of Wisconsin Press, 1967), pp. 184–87; Gerd Korman, *Industrialization, Immigrants, and Americanizers: The View from Milwaukee, 1866–1921* (Madison: State Historical Society of Wisconsin, 1967), pp. 66–67; John Bodnar, *Immigration and Industrialization* (Pittsburgh: University of Pittsburgh Press, 1977), pp. 35–41. At the Bethlehem Steel plant in Bethlehem, Pennsylvania, Germans dominated the rolling mill in a similar fashion; see interview with Nick K., July 11, 1974.

31.   Tamara K. Hareven, "Family Time and Industrial Time: Family and Work in a Planned Corporation Town, 1900–1924," *Journal of Urban History* 1 (1975): 365–80; Hareven and Langenbach, *Amoskeag*, p. 118. See also Kornblum, *Blue Collar Community*, p. 12, for evidence that Poles were recruited into South Chicago mills.

32.   See the interviews with Marie S., Nanticoke, January 16, 1978; Anna S., Nanticoke, October 28, 1977; Helen M., Nanticoke, August 20, 1977; and Stella K., Benton Township, August 7, 1977. See also Bodnar, *Immigration and Industrialization*, pp. 129–30.

33.   See the interviews with Joseph S., Dravosburg, July 2, 1974; and Nick K., Bethlehem, July 11, 1974. See also the interviews with Stanley E., Pittsburgh, September 9, 1976; Edward N., Pittsburgh, October 4, 1976; Walter K., Pittsburgh, September 18, 1977; Joseph D., September 17, 1976; Peter L., Pittsburgh, September 17, 1976; and Charles W., Pittsburgh, December 10, 1976.

34.   Bodnar, "Immigration and Modernization," p. 57. See also the interviews with Joseph D., Pittsburgh, April 11, 1977; John B., Monessen, February 22, 1977; and George M., Monessen, March 22, 1977.

35.   Interview with Stella K., Benton Township, August 7, 1977.

36.   See the interviews with George M., Monessen, March 22, 1977; Helen M., Nanticoke, August 20, 1977; John S., Pittsburgh, June 7, 1974; Joseph D., Pittsburgh, April 20, 1977; and Mary M., Monessen, March 31, 1977.

37.   Interview with Rose P., Monessen, March 14, 1977.

38.   See the interviews with Antionette W., Wilkes-Barre, September 12, 1977; Eleanor O., Nanticoke, November 25, 1977; Mike D., Monessen, February 2, 1977; Thomas L., Cokeburg, June 17, 1976; and Virginia V., Nanticoke, December 6, 1977.

39.   Interview with Lillian N., Nanticoke, July 13, 1977.

40.   William Goode, *World Revolution and Family Patterns* (New York: Free Press of Glencoe, 1963), pp. 56-57; Edward Shorter, *The Making of the Modern Family* (New York: Basic Books, 1975). A call for more investigations into kinship roles is made by Tamara K. Hareven in "Postscript: The Latin American Contest of Family History," *Journal of Family History* 3 (Winter 1978): 455.

41.   Elizabeth H. Pleck, "Two Worlds in One: Work and Family," *Journal of Social History* 10 (Winter 1976): 178-83; Hareven, "Family Time and Industrial Time," pp. 366-71; Rosabeth Moss Kanter, *Work and Family in the United States: A Critical Review and Agenda for Research and Policy* (New York: Russell Sage, 1976), pp. 20-23; Yans-McLaughlin, *Family and Community, passim.*

42.   See John Bodnar, "Morality and Materialism: Slavic Americans and Education," *Journal of Ethnic Studies* 3 (Winter 1976): 1-21.

43.   Interview with John C., Daisytown, May 8, 1975.

44.   See the interview with Steve Kika, McKeesport, July 27, 1974; Rose P., Monessen, March 14, 1977; and John C., Daisytown, May 8, 1975.

45.   Bodnar, Weber, and Simon, "Migration, Kinship, and Urban Adjustment."

46.   Hareven, "Family Time and Industrial Time," p. 377. See also the interviews with Arlene G., Nanticoke, December 11, 1977; and Stella K., Benton Township, August 7, 1977. Winifred Bolin ("The Economics of Middle Income Family Life: Working Women during the Great Depression," *Journal of American History* 65 [June 1978]: 72-73) has noted that only 15 percent of all married women worked in 1940 and suggests that this reflected the cultural stigma attached to the working wife. It is possible, however, that domesticity seemed a preferable alternative to the drudgery working-class women experienced as adolescents in silk mills and cigar factories prior to marriage.

47.   Interviews with George M., Monessen, March 22, 1977; and Helen M., Nanticoke, September 17, 1977.

48.   David Brody, "Working-Class History in the Great Depression," *Reviews in American History* 4 (June 1976): 266.

49.   See Montgomery, *Worker's Control in America*, pp. 4-5; Peter Friedlander, *The Emergence of a UAW Local, 1936-1939: A Study in Class and Culture* (Pittsburgh: University of Pittsburgh Press, 1975), p. 101; James A. Henretta, "Social History as Lived and Written," *American Historical Review* 84 (December 1979): 1293-1322. For an analysis of how tradition and industrial structures can blend to influence working-class lives, see John Bodnar, Michael Weber, and Roger Simon, *Lives of Their Own: Blacks, Italians, and Poles in Pittsburgh, 1900-1960* (Urbana: Univesity of Illinois Press, 1982).

50.   Interviews by Alice Hoffman with Nicholas Zonarich (May 1966) and John Chorey (October 1966), on file in the Labor Archives of Pennsylvania State University, University Park.

51.   Staughton Lynd, "The Possibility of Radicalism in the Early 1930's: The Case of Steel," *Radical America* 67 (November-December 1972); idem, "Guerrilla History in Gary," *Liberation* 12 (October 1969): 78; Alice Lynd and Staughton Lynd, eds., *Rank and File: Personal Histories by Working-Class Organizers* (Boston: Beacon Press, 1973), pp. 1-7; Sidney Fine, *Sit Down: The General Motors Strike of 1936-1937* (Ann Arbor: University of Michigan Press, 1969), p. 340. Ronald Schatz ("American Electrical Workers: Work, Struggle, and Aspirations, 1930-1950 [Ph.D. diss., University of Pittsburgh, 1977], pp. 247-49, 279) studied two locals and found that job security was the main objective in Erie, Pennsylvania, while shop issues were more important in East Pittsburgh, which had greater "radical influences."

Conclusion   191

52. Robert H. Zieger, "The Limits of Militancy: Organizing Paper Workers, 1933–1935," *Journal of American History* 63 (December 1976): 640–47; idem, *Madison's Battery Workers, 1934–1952: A History of Federal Labor Union 19587* (Ithaca: New York School of Industrial and Labor Relations, 1977), pp. 2–4.

53. Sidney Verba and Kay L. Scholzman, "Unemployment, Class Consciousness, and Radical Political Politics: What Didn't Happen in the Thirties," *Journal of Politics* 39 (1977): 322.

54. See Alan Dawley, *Class and Community: The Industrial Revolution in Lynn* (Cambridge, Mass.: Harvard University Press, 1976); Gerald N. Grob, *Workers and Utopia: A Study of Ideological Conflict in the American Labor Movement, 1865–1900* (Evanston, Ill.: Northwestern University Press, 1961), pp. 187–89; David Montgomery, *Beyond Equality: Labor and the Radical Republicans, 1862–1872* (New York: Knopf, 1967), pp. 445–47; Melvyn Dubofsky, *Industrialism and the American Worker, 1865–1920* (New York: Crowell, 1975), p. 41; "The Possibility of Radicalism in the Early 1930's"; David Brody, "Labor and the Great Depression: The Interpretive Prospects," *Labor History* 13 (Spring 1972); Aronowitz, *False Promises*, pp. 137 ff. According to Michael J. Cassity, abstract issues such as local power dominated workers in Sedalia, Missouri, in the 1880s; see his "Modernization and Social Crisis: The Knights of Labor and a Midwest Community, 1885–1886," *Journal of American History* 66 (January 1979): 42–43, 61.

55. See the interviews with Louis Heim, Lebanon, May 24, 1980; and Stanley B., Braddock, June 20, 1978. Job security as a fundamental goal among steelworkers in the 1930s is also stressed by Roger Simon in "Looking Backwards at Steel," *Antioch Review* 36 (Fall 1978): 451–52.

A NOTE ON SOURCES

The interview material used here was selected from a collection of more than one thousand recorded interviews with industrial workers and their families. Conducted between 1974 and 1981, the interviews were structured and arranged by the author of this book, who conducted most of the interviews, trained additional interviewers, and conceptualized and supervised the entire effort. All tapes are now stored at the Pennsylvania Historical and Museum Commission in Harrisburg, where they are available to researchers.

The conceptual approach to the interviews is explained in the Introduction, but the method of initiating oral-history projects and obtaining interviews bears amplification if the reader is to understand the entire research process. Generally the interviews were conducted during distinct projects that centered on a particular industrial community or industry. Thus the Braddock interviews with Louis Smolinski and Stanley Brozek emerged from a project involving steelworkers in several towns, including Braddock, McKeesport, and Alequippa. Similarly, the Stanley Salva tape is taken from a study of anthracite coal miners, and the Wayne Hendrickson interview from a program dealing with tannery workers.

In nearly every instance the interviews were secured with the help of local institutions familiar with working-class populations. For instance, the Philadelphia interviews were arranged through neighborhood settlement houses, the Steelton interview was set up by a local church, and the Pittsburgh and Nanticoke respondents were located by means of the pensioner lists at local union halls. Obviously, such an approach does not necessarily produce a statistically representative sample, and it results in interviews only with workers who said "yes" to our requests and were living in the industrial locations studied. The author does not pretend to have solved these problems. It should be stresed, however, that a great deal of comparable data was generated by the interviews and that the selections included here contributed some new perspectives to our understanding of working-class life.

Equally as crucial to a full understanding of the interviews is the fact that all of the respondents were interviewed after the conclusion of their most productive years. Although research on human memory has indicated that a slight decline in memory occurs after the age of thirty, psychologists now acknowledge that the period following retirement or some other traumatic change is a period of "life review," a time when a sudden emergence of memories and a desire to recall the activities of one's life are experienced with particular intensity.* Indeed, it may not be accidental that most of the respondents in this book were interviewed five to eight years following their retirement. Most were markedly willing to remember and thus responded affirmatively to the author's request for an interview. Such a willingness to recall the past is an indispensable factor in obtaining important historical information.

Finally, the basic questionnaire used in this study has not been reproduced here because it was altered and refined so many times. The author's emphasis was always on the familial, communal, and work arrangements of industrial workers, but the specific questions asked and the overall content of the interviews varied as individual respondents and circumstances dictated. For example, a woman who remained at home and never entered a mine or a mill was questioned more intensively on family life, while a steelworker was asked more questions about the workplace. The interested researcher should note, however, that the questionnaires used in this study are on file with the tapes of the interviews at the Pennsylvania Historical and Museum Commission in Harrisburg.

*See Paul Thompson, *The Voice of the Past: Oral History* (Oxford: Oxford University Press, 1978), esp. chap. 4.

INDEX

survival of, 21; and work, the
link between, 64
Family-community system, 121
Family deprivation, 165
Family objectives, preeminence of,
over personal goals, 168
Family system, need to maintain, 182
Favoritism, 65, 86; in pay scales, 124
Fear, for jobs, 132, 134
Federal Bureau of Investigation (FBI),
126, 155
Females, expanded hiring of, 170
Fine, Sidney, 183, 190
Firings, due to unionization, 132
First Pennsylvania Bank, 16
Food, price of, 153
Friedlander, Peter, 3, 10, 184, 190
Frisch, Michael, 2, 9

Gambling, 47
General Electric, 153, 155, 182
General Steel, 35
Geographic mobility: high degree of,
180; reasons for, 180
Ginzberg, Eli, 8
Girl's work, 175
Glen Alden Coal Company, 80
Glen Lyon Colliery, 83
Goode, William, 177, 190
Graft, 51, 147: for foreman, 79; for
union leaders, 80, 81
Grand Union Tea Company, 135
Greek Orthodox church, 68
Green, William, 89
Grele, Ronald, 3, 4, 10
Grievance committee, 154-55
Grievance system, 181
Grob, Gerald N., 5, 10
Grouping of workers. *See* Workers
Gutman, Herbert, 8, 11, 171, 178, 188

Hammermill Paper Company, 152, 155
Hazleton Manufacturing Company,
108, 110
H. C. Frick mines, 134
Health problems, of miners, 103
Hepponstalls, 56, 57, 172, 175

Hillman Coal, 100
H. J. Heinz plant, 172
Holidays, 40-41
Home ownership, 16, 18, 20, 21, 23,
33, 35-36, 47, 50, 55, 102, 161
Hoover, Herbert, 157
Hours, number worked per day, 43,
68, 98, 107
Housing, dependence on kin for, 14
180
Hutchinson, Edward P., 173, 188

Illinois Steel Company, 174
Illness, 61, 71
Industrial management, kinship units
and, 166
Industrial Workers of the World
(IWW), 111, 112
Influenza epidemic, 71
Informers, 90
Intergenerational friction, 175
International Association of
Machinists, 153
International Harvester, 174

Jailing, 112, 157
Jessup Colliery, 108
Job information, dependence on kin
for, 180
Job procurement, family's role in, 14,
17, 19
Job security, 184, 185; lack of, 159
Job sharing, 90
"Johnny Bulls," 102
Jones & Laughlin Steel Corporation,
122, 123, 127, 129, 172

Kinship, 13-62; and ethnic ties, 171
Kinship networks, 172; as sources of
housing and job information, 180
Knights of Columbus, 154
Knights of Labor, 5
Kord, Edmund, 3

Labor movement: major stimulus
toward, 121; in the 1930s, 119-64;
role of church in, 93

THE JOHNS HOPKINS UNIVERSITY PRESS

Workers' World

This book was composed in Times Roman text and display type by Britton Composition Company, Inc., from a design by Cynthia Hotvedt. It was printed on S.D. Warren's 50-lb. Sebago Eggshell paper and bound in Kivar 5 by The Maple Press Company.